JOE CELKO'S DATA & DATABASES: CONCEPTS IN PRACTICE

The Morgan Kaufmann Series in Data Management Systems
Series Editor, Jim Gray

Joe Celko's Data and Databases: Concepts in Practice
Joe Celko

Joe Celko's SQL for Smarties: Advanced SQL Programming, Second Edition
Joe Celko

Developing Time-Oriented Database Applications in SQL
Richard T. Snodgrass

Web Farming for the Data Warehouse
Richard D. Hackathorn

Database Modeling & Design, Third Edition
Toby J. Teorey

Management of Heterogeneous and Autonomous Database Systems
Edited by Ahmed Elmagarmid, Marek Rusinkiewicz, and Amit Sheth

Object-Relational DBMSs: Tracking the Next Great Wave, Second Edition
Michael Stonebraker and Paul Brown with Dorothy Moore

A Complete Guide to DB2 Universal Database
Don Chamberlin

Universal Database Management: A Guide to Object/Relational Technology
Cynthia Maro Saracco

Readings in Database Systems, Third Edition
Edited by Michael Stonebraker and Joseph M. Hellerstein

Understanding SQL's Stored Procedures: A Complete Guide to SQL/PSM
Jim Melton

Principles of Multimedia Database Systems
V. S. Subrahmanian

Principles of Database Query Processing for Advanced Applications
Clement T. Yu and Weiyi Meng

The Object Database Standard: ODMG 2.0
Edited by R. G. G. Cattell and Douglas K. Barry

Advanced Database Systems
Carlo Zaniolo, Stefano Ceri, Christos Faloutsos, Richard T. Snodgrass, V. S. Subrahmanian, and Roberto Zicari

Principles of Transaction Processing
Philip A. Bernstein and Eric Newcomer

Using the New DB2: IBMs Object-Relational Database System
Don Chamberlin

Distributed Algorithms
Nancy A. Lynch

Active Database Systems: Triggers and Rules for Advanced Database Processing
Edited by Jennifer Widom and Stefano Ceri

Joe Celko's SQL for Smarties: Advanced SQL Programming
Joe Celko

Migrating Legacy Systems: Gateways, Interfaces, & the Incremental Approach
Michael L. Brodie and Michael Stonebraker

Database: Principles, Programming, and Performance
Patrick O'Neil

Atomic Transactions
Nancy Lynch, Michael Merritt, William Weihl, and Alan Fekete

Query Processing for Advanced Database Systems
Edited by Johann Christoph Freytag, David Maier, and Gottfried Vossen

Transaction Processing: Concepts and Techniques
Jim Gray and Andreas Reuter

Understanding the New SQL: A Complete Guide
Jim Melton and Alan R. Simon

Building an Object-Oriented Database System: The Story of O_2
Edited by François Bancilhon, Claude Delobel, and Paris Kanellakis

Database Transaction Models for Advanced Applications
Edited by Ahmed K. Elmagarmid

A Guide to Developing Client/Server SQL Applications
Setrag Khoshafian, Arvola Chan, Anna Wong, and Harry K. T. Wong

The Benchmark Handbook for Database and Transaction Processing Systems, Second Edition
Edited by Jim Gray

Camelot and Avalon: A Distributed Transaction Facility
Edited by Jeffrey L. Eppinger, Lily B. Mummert, and Alfred Z. Spector

Readings in Object-Oriented Database Systems
Edited by Stanley B. Zdonik and David Maier

JOE CELKO'S DATA & DATABASES: CONCEPTS IN PRACTICE

Joe Celko

Morgan Kaufmann Publishers
An Imprint of Elsevier
San Francisco, California

Senior Editor	Diane D. Cerra
Director of Production and Manufacturing	Yonie Overton
Production Editor	Cheri Palmer
Editorial Coordinator	Belinda Breyer
Cover and Text Design	Side by Side Studios
Cover and Text Series Design	ThoughtHouse, Inc.
Copyeditor	Ken DellaPenta
Proofreader	Jennifer McClain
Composition	Nancy Logan
Illustration	Cherie Plumlee
Indexer	Ty Koontz
Printer	Courier Corporation

Morgan Kaufmann Publishers
Editorial and Sales Office
340 Pine Street, Sixth Floor
San Francisco, CA 94104-3205
USA

Telephone 415/392-2665
Facsimile 415/982-2665
E-mail mkp@mkp.com
WWW *http://www.mkp.com*
Order toll free 800/745-7323

Transferred to digital printing 2006

08 07 06 05 04 6 5 4 3

Library of Congress Cataloging-in-Publication Data

Celko, Joe.
Joe Celko's data and databases: concepts in practice / Joe Celko.
p. cm.
Includes bibliographical references.
ISBN 1-55860-432-4
1. Data structures (Computer science) 2. Database management.
I. Title. II. Title: Data and databases.
QA76.9.D35C45 1999
005.74—dc21 99-30307
CIP

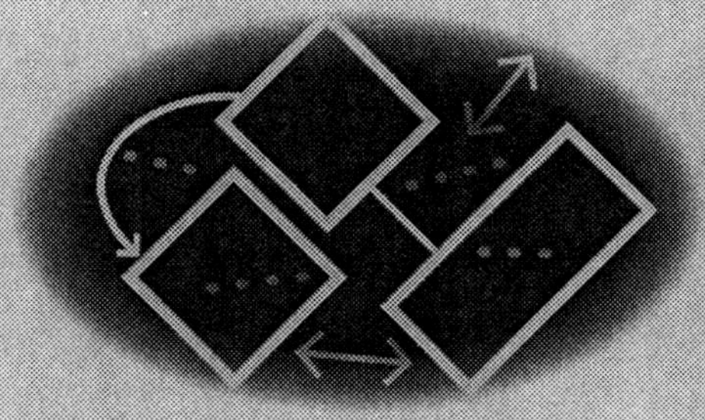

To my father, Joseph Celko Sr.,
and to my daughters,
Takoga Stonerock and
Amanda Pattarozzi

CONTENTS

PREFACE

This book is a collection of ideas about the nature of data and databases. Some of the material has appeared in different forms in my regular columns in the computer trade and academic press, on CompuServe forum groups, on the Internet, and over beers at conferences for several years. Some of it is new to this volume.

This book is not a complete, formal text about any particular database theory and will not be too mathematical to read easily. Its purpose is to provide foundations and philosophy to the working programmer so that they can understand what they do for a living in greater depth. The topic of each chapter could be a book in itself and usually has been.

This book is supposed to make you think and give you things to think about. Hopefully, it succeeds.

Thanks to my magazine columns in *DBMS, Database Programming & Design, Intelligent Enterprise,* and other publications over the years, I have become the apologist for ANSI/ISO standard SQL. However, this is *not* an SQL book per se. It is more oriented toward the philosophy and foundations of data and databases than toward programming tips and techniques. However, I try to use the ANSI/ISO SQL-92 standard language for examples whenever possible, occasionally extending it when I have to invent a notation for some purpose.

If you need a book on the SQL-92 language, you should get a copy of *Understanding the New SQL,* by Jim Melton and Alan Simon (Melton and Simon 1993). Jim's other book, *Understanding SQL's Stored Procedures* (Melton 1998), covers the procedural language that was added to the SQL-92 standard in 1996.

If you want to get SQL tips and techniques, buy a copy of my other book, *SQL for Smarties* (Celko 1995), and then see if you learned to use them with a copy of *SQL Puzzles & Answers* (Celko 1997).

Organization of the Book

The book is organized into nested, numbered sections arranged by topic. If you have a problem and want to look up a possible solution now, you can go to the index or table of contents and thumb to the right section. Feel free to highlight the parts you need and to write notes in the margins.

I hope that the casual conversational style of the book will serve you well. I simply did not have the time or temperament to do a formal text. If you want to explore the more formal side of the issues I raise, I have tried to at least point you toward detailed references.

Corrections and Future Editions

I will be glad to receive corrections, comments, and other suggestions for future editions of this book. Send your ideas to

Joe Celko
235 Carter Avenue
Atlanta, GA 30317-3303
email: 71062.1056@compuserve.com
website: *www.celko.com*

or contact me through the publisher. You could see your name in print!

Acknowledgments

I'd like to thank Diane Cerra of Morgan Kaufmann and the many people from CompuServe forum sessions and personal letters and emails. I'd also like to thank all the members of the ANSI X3H2 Database Standards Committee, past and present.

The Nature of Data

Where is the wisdom?
  Lost in the knowledge.
Where is the knowledge?
  Lost in the information.
—T. S. Eliot

Where is the information?
  Lost in the data.
Where is the data?
  Lost in the #@%&! database!
—Joe Celko

So I am not the poet that T. S. Eliot is, but he probably never wrote a computer program in his life. However, I agree with his point about wisdom and information. And if he knew the distinction between data and information, I like to think that he would have agreed with mine.

I would like to define "data," without becoming too formal yet, as facts that can be represented with measurements using scales or with formal symbol systems within the context of a formal model. The model is supposed to represent something called "the real world" in such a way that changes in the facts of "the real world"

are reflected by changes in the database. I will start referring to "the real world" as "the reality" for a model from now on.

The reason that you have a model is that you simply cannot put the real world into a computer or even into your own head. A model has to reflect the things that you think are important in the real world and the entities and properties that you wish to manipulate and predict.

I will argue that the first databases were the precursors to written language that were found in the Middle East (see Jean 1992). Shepherds keeping community flocks needed a way to manipulate ownership of the animals, so that everyone knew who owned how many rams, ewes, lambs, and whatever else. Rather than branding the individual animals, as Americans did in the West, each member of the tribe had a set of baked clay tokens that represented ownership of one animal, but not of any animal in particular.

When you see the tokens, your first thought is that they are a primitive internal currency system. This is true in part, because the tokens could be traded for other goods and services. But their real function was as a record keeping system, not as a way to measure and store economic value. That is, the trade happened first, then the tokens were changed, and not vice versa.

The tokens had all the basic operations you would expect in a database. The tokens were updated when a lamb grew to become a ram or ewe, deleted when an animal was eaten or died, and new tokens were inserted when the new lambs were born in the spring.

One nice feature of this system is that the mapping from the model to the real world is one to one and could be done by a man who cannot count or read. He had to pass the flock through a gate and match one token to one animal; we would call this a "table scan" in SQL. He would hand the tokens over to someone with more math ability—the CPU for the tribe—who would update everyone's set of tokens. The rules for this sort of updating can be fairly elaborate, based on dowry payments, oral traditions, familial relations, shares owned last year, and so on.

The tokens were stored in soft clay bottles that were pinched shut to ensure that they were not tampered with once accounts were settled; we would call that "record locking" in database management systems.

1.1 Data versus Information

Information is what you get when you distill data. A collection of raw facts does not help anyone to make a decision until it is reduced to a higher-level abstraction. My sheepherders could count their tokens and get simple statistical summaries of their holdings ("Abdul owns 15 ewes, 2 rams, and 13 lambs"), which is immediately useful, but it is very low-level information.

If Abdul collected all his data and reduced it to information for several years, then he could move up one more conceptual level and make more abstract statements like, "In the years when the locusts come, the number of lambs born is less than the following two years," which are of a different nature than a simple count. There is both a long time horizon into the past and an attempt to make predictions for the future. The information is qualitative and not just quantitative.

Please do not think that qualitative information is to be preferred over quantitative information. SQL and the relational database model are based on sets and logic. This makes SQL very good at finding set relations, but very weak at finding statistical and other relations. A set relation might be an answer to the query "Do we have people who smoke, drink, and have high blood pressure?" that gives an existence result. A similar statistical query would be "How are smoking and drinking correlated to high blood pressure?" that gives a numeric result that is more predictive of future events.

1.2 Information versus Wisdom

Wisdom does not come out of the database or out of the information in a mechanical fashion. It is the insight that a person has to make from information to handle totally new situations. I teach data and information processing; I don't teach wisdom. However, I can say a few remarks about the improper use of data that comes from bad reasoning.

1.2.1 Innumeracy

Innumeracy is a term coined by John Allen Paulos in his 1990 bestseller of the same title. It refers to the inability to do simple mathematical reasoning to detect bad data, or bad reasoning. Having data in your database is not the same thing as knowing what to do with it. In an article in *Computerworld,* Roger L. Kay does a very nice job of giving examples of this problem in the computer field (Kay 1994).

1.2.2 Bad Math

Bruce Henstell (1994) stated in the *Los Angeles Times:* "When running a mile, a 132 pound woman will burn between 90 to 95 calories but a 175 pound man will drop 125 calories. The reason seems to be evolution. In the dim pre-history, food was hard to come by and every calorie has to be conserved—particularly if a woman was to conceive and bear a child; a successful pregnancy requires about 80,000 calories. So women should keep exercising, but if they want to lose weight, calorie count is still the way to go."

Calories are a measure of the energy produced by oxidizing food. In the case of a person, calorie consumption depends on the amount of oxygen they breathe and the body material available to be oxidized.

Let's figure out how many calories per pound of human flesh the men and women in this article were burning: (95 calories/ 132 pounds) = .71 calories per pound of woman and (125 calories/ 175 pounds) = .71 calories per pound of man. Gee, there is no difference at all! Based on these figures, human flesh consumes calories at a constant rate when it exercises regardless of gender. This does not support the hypothesis that women have a harder time losing fat through exercise than men, but just the opposite. If anything, this shows that reporters cannot do simple math.

Another example is the work of Professor James P. Allen of Northridge University and Professor David Heer of USC. In late 1991, they independently found out that the 1990 census for Los Angeles was wrong. The census showed a rise in Black Hispanics in South Central Los Angeles from 17,000 in 1980 to almost 60,000 in 1990. But the total number of Black citizens in Los Angeles has been dropping for years as they move out to the suburbs (Stewart 1994).

Furthermore, the overwhelming source of the Latino population is Mexico and then Central America, which have almost no Black population. In short, the apparent growth of Black Hispanics did not match the known facts.

Professor Allen attempted to confirm this growth with field interviews but could not find Black Hispanic children in the schools when he went to the bilingual coordinator for the district's schools.

Professor Heer did it with just the data. The census questionnaire asked for race as White, Black, or Asian, but not Hispanic. Most Latinos would not answer the race question—Hispanic is the root word of "spic," an ethnic slander word in Southern California. He found that the Census Bureau program would assign ethnic groups when it was faced with missing data. The algorithm was to look at the makeup of the neighbors and assume that missing data was the same ethnicity.

If only they had `NULL`s to handle the missing data, they might have been saved.

Speaker's Idea File (published by Ragan Publications, Chicago) lost my business when they sent me a sample issue of their newsletter that said, "On an average day, approximately 140,000 people die in the United States." Let's work that out using 365.2422 days per year times 140,000 deaths for a total of 51,133,908 deaths per year. Since there are a little less than 300 million Americans as of the last census, we are looking at about 17% of the entire population dying every year—one person in every five or six. This seems a bit high. The actual figure is about 250,000 deaths per year.

There have been a series of controversial reports and books using statistics as their basis. *Tainted Truth: The Manipulation of Facts in America,* by Cynthia Crossen, a reporter for the *Wall Street Journal,* is a study of how political pressure groups use "false facts" for their agenda (Crossen 1996). So there are reporters who care about mathematics, after all!

Who Stole Feminism?, by Christina Hoff Sommers, points out that feminist authors were quoting a figure of 150,000 deaths per year from anorexia when the actual figure was no higher than 53. Some of the more prominent feminist writers who used this figure were Gloria Steinem ("In this country alone. . . about 150,000 females die of

anorexia each year," in *Revolution from Within*) and Naomi Wolf ("When confronted by such a vast number of emaciated bodies starved not by nature but by men, one must notice a certain resemblance [to the Nazi Holocaust]," in *The Beauty Myth*). The same false statistic also appears in *Fasting Girls: The Emergence of Anorexia Nervosa as a Modern Disease*, by Joan Brumberg, former director of Women's Studies at Cornell, and hundreds of newspapers that carried Ann Landers's column. But the press never questioned this in spite of the figure being almost three times the number of dead in the entire 10 years of the Vietnam War (approximately 58,000) or in one year of auto accidents (approximately 48,000).

You might be tempted to compare this to the Super Bowl Sunday scare that went around in the early 1990s (the deliberate lie that more wives are beaten on Super Bowl Sunday than any other time). The original study only covered a very small portion of a select group—African Americans living in public housing in one particular part of one city. The author also later said that her report stated nothing of the kind, remarking that she had been trying to get the urban myth stopped for many months without success. She noted that the increase was considered "statistically insignificant" and could just as easily have been caused by bad weather that kept more people inside.

The broadcast and print media repeated it without even attempting to verify its accuracy, and even broadcasted public warning messages about it. But at least the Super Bowl scare was not obviously false on the face of it. And the press did do follow-up articles showing which groups created and knowingly spread a lie for political reasons.

1.2.3 Causation and Correlation

People forget that correlation is not cause and effect. A *necessary cause* is one that must be present for an effect to happen—a car has to have gas to run. A *sufficient cause* will bring about the effect by itself—dropping a hammer on your foot will make you scream in pain, but so will having your hard drive crash. A *contributory cause* is one that helps the effect along, but would not be necessary or sufficient by itself to create the effect. There are also *coincidences*, where one thing happens at the same time as another, but without a causal relationship.

A *correlation* between two measurements, say, X and Y, is basically a formula that allows you to predict one measurement given the other, plus or minus some error range. For example, if I shot a cannon locked at a certain angle, based on the amount of gunpowder I used, I could expect to place the cannonball within a 5-foot radius of the target most of the time. Once in awhile, the cannonball will be dead on target; other times it could be several yards away.

The formula I use to make my prediction could be a linear equation or some other function. The strength of the prediction is called the *coefficient of correlation* and is denoted by the variable r where $-1 \leq r \leq 1$, in statistics. A coefficient of correlation of -1 is absolute negative correlation—when X happens, then Y never happens. A coefficient of correlation of $+1$ is absolute positive correlation—when X happens, then Y also happens. A zero coefficient of correlation means that X and Y happen independently of each other.

The *confidence level* is related to the coefficient of correlation, but it is expressed as a percentage. It says that x % of the time, the relationship you have would not happen by chance.

The study of secondhand smoke (or environmental tobacco smoke, ETS) by the EPA, which was released jointly with the Department of Health and Human Services, is a great example of how *not* to do a correlation study. First they gathered 30 individual studies and found that 24 of them would not support the premise that secondhand smoke is linked to lung cancer. Next, they combined 11 handpicked studies that used completely different methods into one sample—a technique known as metanalysis, or more informally called the apples and oranges fallacy. Still no link. It is worth mentioning that one of the rejected studies was recently sponsored by the National Cancer Institute—hardly a friend of the tobacco lobby—and it also showed no statistical significance.

The EPA then lowered the confidence level from 98% to 95%, and finally to 90%, where they got a relationship. No responsible clinical study has ever used less than 95% for its confidence level. Remember that a confidence level of 95% says that 5% of the time, this could just

be a coincidence. A 90% confidence level doubles the chances of an error.

Alfred P. Wehner, president of Biomedical and Environmental Consultants Inc. in Richland, Washington, said, "Frankly, I was embarrassed as a scientist with what they came up with. The main problem was that statistical handling of the data." Likewise, Yale University epidemiologist Alvan Feinstein, who is known for his work in experimental design, said in the *Journal of Toxicological Pathology* that he heard a prominent leader in epidemiology admit, "Yes, it's [EPA's ETS work] rotten science, but it's in a worthy cause. It will help us get rid of cigarettes and to become a smoke-free society." So much for scientific truth versus a political agenda.

Another way to test a correlation is to look at the real world. For example, if ETS causes lung cancer, then why do rats who are put into smoke-filled boxes for most of their lives not have a higher cancer rate? Why aren't half the people in Europe and Japan dead from cancer?

There are five ways two variables can be related to each other. The truth could be that X causes Y. You can estimate the temperature in degrees Fahrenheit from the chirp rate of a cricket: degrees = (chirps + 137.22)/3.777, with $r = 0.9919$ accuracy. However, nobody believes that crickets cause temperature changes. The truth could be that Y causes X, case two.

The third case is that X and Y interact with each other. Supply and demand curves are an example, where as one goes up, the other goes down (*negative feedback* in computer terms). A more horrible example is drug addiction, where the user requires larger and larger doses to get the desired effect (*positive feedback* in computer terms), as opposed to habituation, where the usage hits an upper level and stays there.

The fourth case is that any relationship is pure chance. Any two trends in the same direction will have some correlation, so it should not surprise you that once in awhile, two will match very closely.

The final case is where the two variables are effects of another variable that is outside the study. The most common unseen variables are changes in a common environment. For example, severe hay fever attacks go up when corn prices go down. They share a common element—good weather. Good weather means a bigger corn crop and hence lower prices, but it also means more ragweed and pollen and hence more hay fever attacks. Likewise, spouses who live pretty much the same lifestyle will tend to have the same medical problems from a common shared environment and set of habits.

1.2.4 Testing the Model against Reality

The March 1994 issue of *Discovery* magazine had a commentary column entitled "Counting on Dyscalculia" by John Allen Paulos. His particular topic was health statistics since those create a lot of "pop dread" when they get played in the media.

One of his examples in the article was a widely covered lawsuit in which a man alleged a causal connection between his wife's frequent use of a cellular phone and her subsequent brain cancer. Brain cancer is a rare disease that strikes approximately 7 out of 100,000 people per year. Given the large population of the United States, this is still about 17,500 new cases per year—a number that has held pretty steady for years.

There are an estimated 10 million cellular phone users in the United States. If there were a causal relationship, then there would be an increase in cases as cellular phone usage increased. On the other hand, if we found that there were less than 70 cases among cellular phone users we could use the same argument to "prove" that cellular phones prevent brain cancer.

Perhaps the best example of testing a hypothesis against the real world was the bet between the late Julian Simon and Paul Ehrlich (author of *The Population Bomb* and a whole raft of other doomsday books) in 1980. They took an imaginary $1,000 and let Ehrlich pick commodities. The bet was whether the real price would go up or down, depending on the state of the world, in the next 10 years. If the real price (i.e., adjusted for inflation) went down, then Simon would collect the adjusted real difference in current dollars; if the real costs went up, then Ehrlich would collect the difference adjusted to current dollars.

Ehrlich picked metals—copper, chrome, nickel, tin, and tungsten—and "invested" $200 in each. In the fall of 1990, Ehrlich paid

Simon $576.07 and did not call one of his press conferences about it. What was even funnier is that if Ehrlich had paid off in current dollars, not adjusted for inflation, he would still have lost!

1.3 Models versus Reality

A model is not reality, but a reduced and simplified version of it. A model that was more complex than the thing it attempts to model would be less than useless. The term "the real world" means something a bit different than what you would intuitively think. Yes, physical reality is one "real world," but this term also includes a database of information about the fictional worlds in *Star Trek*, the "what if" scenarios in a spreadsheet or discrete simulation program, and other abstractions that have no physical forms. The main characteristic of "the real world" is to provide an authority against which to check the validity of the database model.

A good model reflects the important parts of its reality and has predictive value. A model without predictive value is a formal game and not of interest to us.

The predictive value does not have to be absolutely accurate. Realistically, Chaos Theory shows us that a model cannot ever be 100% predictive for any system with enough structure to be interesting and has a feedback loop.

1.3.1 Errors in Models

Statisticians classify experimental errors as Type I and Type II. A Type I error is accepting as false something that is true. A Type II error is accepting as true something that is false. These are very handy concepts for database people, too.

The classic Type I database error is the installation in concrete of bad data, accompanied by the inability or unwillingness of the system to correct the error in the face of the truth. My favorite example of this is a classic science fiction short story written as a series of letters between a book club member and the billing computer. The human has returned an unordered copy of *Kidnapped* by Robert Louis Stevenson and wants it credited to his account.

When he does not pay, the book club computer turns him over to the police computer, which promptly charges him with kidnapping Robert Louis Stevenson. When he objects, the police computer investigates, and the charge is amended to kidnapping and murder, since Robert Louis Stevenson is dead. At the end of the story, he gets his refund credit and letter of apology after his execution.

While exaggerated, the story hits all too close to home for anyone who has fought a false billing in a system that has no provision for clearing out false data.

The following example of a Type II error involves some speculation on my part. Several years ago a major credit card company began to offer cards in a new designer color with higher limits to their better customers. But if you wanted to keep your old card, you could have two accounts. Not such a bad option, since you could use one card for business and one for personal expenses.

They needed to create new account records in their database (file system?) for these new cards. The solution was obvious and simple: copy the existing data from the old account without the balances into the new account and add a field to flag the color of the card to get a unique identifier on the new accounts.

The first batch of new card orders came in. Some orders were for replacement cards, some were for the new card without any prior history, and some were for the new "two accounts" option.

One of the fields was the date of first membership. The company thinks that this date is very important since they use it in their advertising. They also think that if you do not use a card for a long period of time (one year), they should drop your membership. They have a program that looks at each account and mails out a form letter to these unused accounts as it removes them from the database.

The brand new accounts were fine. The replacement accounts were fine. But the members who picked the "two card" option were a bit distressed. The only date that the system had to use as "date of last card usage" was the date that the original account was opened. This was almost always more than one year, since you needed a good credit history with the company to get offered the new card.

Before the shiny new cards had been printed and mailed out, the customers were getting drop letters on their new accounts. The

switchboard in customer service looked like a Christmas tree. This is a Type II error—accepting as true the falsehood that the last usage date was the same as the acquisition date of the credit card.

1.3.2 Assumptions about Reality

The purpose of separating the formal model and the reality it models is to first acknowledge that we cannot capture everything about reality, so we pick a subset of the reality and map it onto formal operations that we can handle.

This assumes that we can know our reality, fit it into a formal model, and appeal to it when the formal model fails or needs to be changed.

This is an article of faith. In the case of physical reality, you can be sure that there are no logical contradictions or the universe would not exist. However, that does not mean that you have full access to all the information in it. In a constructed reality, there might well be logical contradictions or vague information. Just look at any judicial system that has been subjected to careful analysis for examples of absurd, inconsistent behavior.

But as any mathematician knows, you have to start somewhere and with some set of primitive concepts to be able to build any model.

Entities, Attributes, Values, and Relationships

Perfection is finally attained not when there is no longer anything to add but when there is no longer anything to take away.
—Antoine de Saint Exupery

What primitives should we use to build a database? The smaller the set of primitives, the better a mathematician feels. A smaller set of things to do is also better for an implementor who has to turn the primitives into a real computer system. We are lucky because Dr. Codd and his relational model are about as simple as we want to get, and they are very well defined for us.

Entities, attributes, values, and relationships are the components of a relational model. They are all represented as tables made of rows, which are made of columns in SQL and the relational model, but their semantics are very different. As an aside, when I teach an SQL class, I often have to stress that a table is made of rows, and not rows *and* columns; rows are made of columns. Many businesspeople who are learning the relational model think that it is a kind of spreadsheet, and this is not the case. A spreadsheet is made up of rows and columns, which have equal status and meaning in that family of tools. The cells of a spreadsheet can store data or programs; a table stores only data and constraints on the data. The spreadsheet is active, and the relational table is passive.

2.1 Entities

An *entity* can be a concrete object in its reality, such as a person or thing, or it can be a relationship among objects in its reality, such as a marriage, which can handled as if it were an object. It is not obvious that some information should always be modeled as an entity, an attribute, or a relationship. But at least in SQL you will have a table for each class of entity, and each row will represent one instance of that class.

2.1.1 Entities as Objects

Broadly speaking, *objects* are passive and are acted upon in the model. Their attributes are changed by processes outside of themselves. Properly speaking, each row in an object table should correspond to a "thing" in the database's reality, but not always uniquely. It is more convenient to handle a bowl of rice as a single thing instead of giving a part number to each grain.

Clearly, people are unique objects in physical reality. But if the same physical person is modeled in a database that represents a company, they can have several roles. They can be an employee, a stockholder, or a customer.

But this can be broken down further. As an employee, they can hold particular positions that have different attributes and powers; the boss can fire the mail clerk, but the mail clerk cannot fire the boss. As a stockholder, they can hold different classes of stock, which have different attributes and powers. As a customer, they might get special discounts from being a customer-employee.

The question is, Should the database model the reality of a single person or model the roles they play? Most databases would model reality based on roles because they take actions based on roles rather than based on individuals. For example, they send paychecks to employees and dividend checks to stockholders. For legal reasons, they do not want to send a single check that mixes both roles.

It might be nice to have a table of people with all their addresses in it, so that you would be able to do a change of address operation only once for the people with multiple roles. Lack of this table is a nuisance, but not a disaster. The worst you will do is create redundant work and perhaps get the database out of synch with the reality. The real problems can come when people with multiple roles have conflicting powers and actions within the database. This means that the model was wrong.

2.1.2 Entities as Relationships

A *relationship* is a way of tying objects together to get new information that exists apart from the particular objects. The problem is that the relationship is often represented by a token of some sort in the reality.

A marriage is a relationship between two people in a particular legal system, and its token is the marriage license. A bearer bond is also a legal relationship where either party is a lawful individual (i.e., people, corporations, or other legal creations with such rights and powers).

If you burn a marriage license, you are still married; you have to burn your spouse instead (generally frowned upon) or divorce them. The divorce is the legal procedure to drop the marriage relationship. If you burn a bearer bond, you have destroyed the relationship. A marriage license is a token that identifies and names the relationship. A bearer bond is a token that contains or is itself the relationship.

You have serious problems when a table improperly models a relationship and its entities at the same time. We will discuss this problem in section 2.5.1.

2.2 Attributes

Attributes belong to entities and define them. Leibniz even went so far as to say that an entity is the sum of all its attributes. SQL agrees with this statement and models attributes as columns in the rows of tables that can assume values.

You should assume that you cannot ever show in a table all the attributes that an entity has in its reality. You simply want the important ones, where "important" is defined as those attributes needed by the model to do its work.

2.3 Values

A *value* belongs to an attribute. The particular value for a particular attribute is drawn from a domain or has a datatype. There are several schools of thought on domains, datatypes, and values, but the two major schools are the following:

1. Datatypes and domains are both sets of values in the database. They are both finite sets because all models are finite. The datatype differs by having operators in the hardware or software so the database user does not have to do all that work. A domain is built on a subset of a datatype, which inherits some or all of its operators from the original datatype and restrictions, but now the database can have user-defined operators on the domain.

2. A domain is a finite or infinite set of values with operators that exists in the database's reality. A datatype is a subset of a domain supported by the computer the database resides on. The database approximates a domain with a subset of a datatype, which inherits some or all of its operators from the original datatype and other restrictions and operators given to it by the database designer.

Unfortunately, SQL-92 has a `CREATE DOMAIN` statement in its data declaration language (DDL) that refers to the approximation, so I will refer to database domains and reality domains.

In formal logic, the first approach is called an extensional definition, and the second is an intentional definition. Extensional definitions give a list of all valid values; intentional definitions give a rule that determines if a value is in the domain or not. You have seen both of these approaches in elementary set theory in the list and rule notations for defining a set. For example, the finite set of positive even numbers less than 16 can be defined by either

$A = \{2, 4, 6, 8, 10, 12, 14\}$

or

$B = \{i : (\mathrm{MOD}(i, 2) = 0) \text{ AND } (i > 0) \text{ AND } (i < 16)\}$

Defining the infinite set of all positive even numbers requires an ellipsis in the list notation, but the rule set notation simply drops restrictions, thus:

C = {2, 4, 6, 8, 10, 12, 14, . . .}

D = {*i* : MOD(*i*, 2) = 0}

While this distinction can be subtle, an intentional definition lets you move your model from one database to another much more easily. For example, if you have a machine that can handle integer datatypes that range up to (2^{16}) bits, then it is conceptually easy to move the database to a machine that can handle integer datatypes that range up to (2^{32}) bits because they are just two different approximations of the infinite domain of integers in the reality. In an extensional approach, they would be seen as two different datatypes without a reference to the reality.

For an abstract model of a DBMS, I accept a countably infinite set as complete if I can define it with a membership test algorithm that returns TRUE or FALSE in a finite amount of time for any element. For example, any integer can be tested for evenness in one step, so I have no trouble here.

But this breaks down when I have a test that takes an infinite amount of time, or where I cannot tell if something is an element of the set without generating all the previous elements. You can look up examples of these and other such misbehaved sets in a good math book (fractal sets, the $(3 * n + 1)$ problem, generator functions without a closed form, and so forth).

The $(3 * n + 1)$ problem is known as Ulam's conjecture, Syracuse's problem, Kakutani's problem, and Hasse's algorithm in the literature, and it can be shown by this procedure (see Lagarias 1985 for details).

```
FUNCTION ThreeN (i INTEGER IN, j INTEGER IN) RETURNS INTEGER;
LANGUAGE SQL
BEGIN
DECLARE k INTEGER;
SET k = 0;
```

```
WHILE k <= j
 LOOP
 SET k = k + 1;
 IF i IN (1, 2, 4)
 THEN RETURN 0 -- answer is False, not a member
 ELSE IF MOD (i, 2) = 0
      THEN ThreeN((i / 2), k)
      ELSE ThreeN((3 * i + 1), k);
 END LOOP;
RETURN 1 -- answer is True
END WHILE;
```

We are trying to construct a subset of all the integers that test true according to the rules defined in this procedure. If the number is even, then divide it by two and repeat the procedure on that result. If the number is odd, then multiply it by three, add one, and repeat the procedure on that result. You keep repeating the procedure until it is reduced to one.

For example, if you start with 7, you get the sequence (7, 22, 11, 34, 17, 52, 26, 13, 40, 20, 10, 5, 16, 8, 4, 2, 1, . . .), and seven is a member of the set. Bet that took longer than you thought!

As a programming tip, observe that when a result becomes 1, 2, or 4, the procedure hangs in a loop, endlessly repeating that sequence. This could be a nonterminating program, if we are not careful!

An integer, *i*, is an element of the set K(*j*) when *i* fails to arrive at one on or before *j* iterations. For example, 7 is a member of K(17). By simply picking larger and larger values of *j*, you can set the range so high that any computer will break. If the *j* parameter is dropped completely, it is not known if there are numbers that never arrive at one. Or to put it another way, is this set really the set of all integers?

Well, nobody knows the last time I looked. I have to qualify that statement this way, because in my lifetime I have seen solutions to the four-color map theorem and Fermat's Last theorem proven. But Gödel proved that there are always statements in logic that cannot be proven to be TRUE or FALSE, regardless of the amount of time or the number of axioms you are given.

2.4 Relationships

Relationships exist among entities. We have already talked about entities as relationships and how the line is not clear when you create a model.

2.5 ER Modeling

In 1976 Peter Chen invented entity-relationship (ER) modeling as a database design technique. The original diagrams used a box for an entity, a diamond for a relationship, and lines to connect them. The simplicity of the diagrams used in this method have made it the most popular database design technique in use today. The original method was very minimal, so other people have added other details and symbols to the basic diagram.

There are several problems with ER modeling:

1. ER does not spend much time on attributes. The names of the columns in a table are usually just shown inside the entity box, without datatypes. Some products will indicate which column(s) are the primary keys of the table. Even fewer will use another notation on the column names to show the foreign keys.

   I feel that people should spend more time actually designing data elements, as you can see from the number of chapters in this book devoted to data.

2. Although there can be more than one normalized schema from a single set of constraints, entities, and relationships, ER tools generate only one diagram. Once you have begun a diagram, you are committed to one schema design.

3. The diagram generated by ER tools tends to be a planar graph. That means that there are no crossed lines required to connect the boxes and lines. The fact that a graph has crossed lines does not make it nonplanar; it might be rearranged to avoid the crossed lines without changes to the connections (see Fig. 2.1).

Fig. 2.1

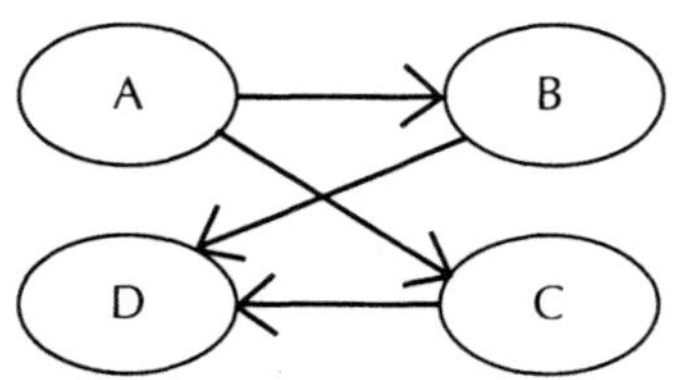

(a) Original diagram

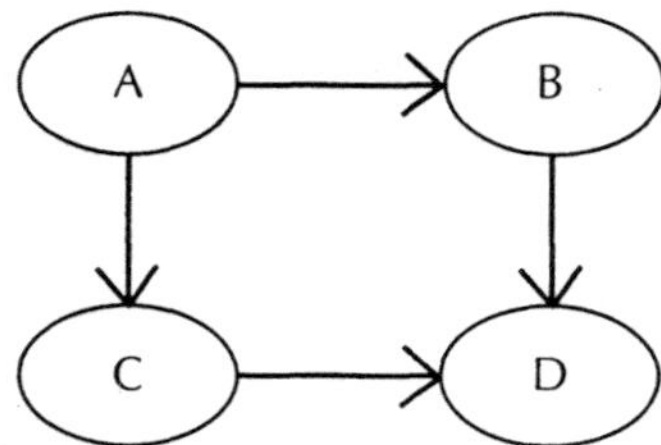

(b) Planar version

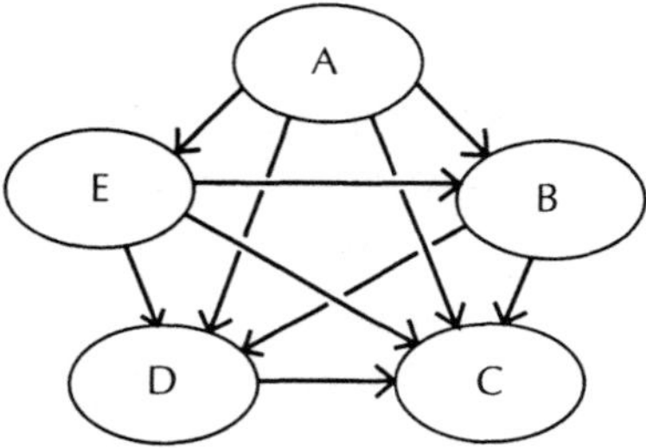

(c) Nonplanar graph

A planar graph can also be subject to another graph theory result called the "four-color map theorem," which says that you only need four colors to color a planar map so that no two regions with a common border have the same color.

4. ER diagrams cannot express certain constraints or relationships. For example, in the versions that use only straight lines between entities for relationships, you cannot easily express an *n*-ary relationship ($n > 2$).

   Furthermore, you cannot show constraint among the attributes within a table. For example, you cannot show the rule that "An employee must be at least 18 years of age" with a constraint of the form `CHECK ((hiredate - birthdate) >= INTERVAL 18 YEARS)`.

As an example of the possibility of different schemas for the same problem, consider a database of horse racing information. Horses are clearly physical objects, and we need information about them if we are going to calculate a betting system. This modeling decision could lead to a table that looks like this:

```
CREATE TABLE Horses
(horsename CHAR(30) NOT NULL,
 track CHAR(30) NOT NULL,
 race INTEGER NOT NULL CHECK (race > 0),
 racedate DATE NOT NULL,
 position INTEGER NOT NULL CHECK (position > 0),
 finish CHAR(10) NOT NULL
   CHECK (finish IN ('win', 'place', 'show', 'ran', 'scratch')),
 PRIMARY KEY (horsename, track, race, racedate));
```

The track column is the name of the track where the race was held, racedate is when it was held, race is the number of each race, position is the starting position of the horse, and finish is how well the animal did in the race. Finish is an attribute of the entity "horses" in this model. If you do not bet on horse races ("play the ponies"), "win" means first place; "place" is first or second place; "show" is first, second, or third place; "ran" is having been in the race, but not in first, second, or third place; and "scratch" means the horse was removed from the race in which it was scheduled to run. In this model, the finish attribute should have the highest value obtained by the horse in each row of the table.

Now look at the same reality from the viewpoint of the bookie who has to pay out and collect wagers. The most important thing in his model is the outcome of races, and detailed information on individual horses is of little interest. He might model the same reality with a table like this:

```
CREATE TABLE Races
(track CHAR(30) NOT NULL,
 racedate DATE NOT NULL,
 race INTEGER NOT NULL CHECK (race > 0),
```

```
win CHAR(30) NOT NULL REFERENCES Horses(horsename),
place CHAR(30) NOT NULL REFERENCES Horses(horsename),
show CHAR(30) NOT NULL REFERENCES Horses(horsename),
PRIMARY KEY (track, date, race));
```

The columns have the same meaning as they did in the Horses table, but now there are three columns with the names of the horse that won, placed, or showed for that race ("finished in the money"). Horses are values of attributes of the entity "races" in this model.

2.5.1 Mixed Models

We defined a mixed model as one in which a table improperly models both a relationship and its entities in the same column(s). When a table has a mixed model, you probably have serious problems. For example, consider the common adjacency list representation of an organizational chart:

```
CREATE TABLE Personnel
(emp_name CHAR(20) NOT NULL PRIMARY KEY,
 boss_name CHAR(20) REFERENCES Personnel(emp_name),
 dept_no CHAR(10) NOT NULL REFERENCES departments(dept_no),
 salary DECIMAL (10,2) NOT NULL,
 . . . );
```

in which the column boss_name is the emp_name of the boss of this employee in the company hierarchy. This column has to allow a `NULL` because the hierarchy eventually leads to the head of the company, and he or she has no boss.

What is wrong with this table? First of all, this table is not normalized. Consider what happens when a middle manager named `'Jerry Rivers'` decides that he needs to change his name to `'Geraldo Riviera'` to get minority employment preferences. This change will have to be done once in the emp_name column and *n* times in the boss_name column of each of his immediate subordinates. One of the defining characteristics of a normalized database is that one fact appears in one place, one time, and one way in the database.

Next, when you see `'Jerry Rivers'` in the emp_name column, it is a value for the name attribute of a Personnel entity. When you see

`'Jerry Rivers'` in the boss_name column, it is a relationship in the company hierarchy. In graph theory, you would say that this table has information on both the nodes and the edges of the tree structure in it.

There should be a separate table for the employees (nodes), which contains only employee data, and another table for the organizational chart (edges), which contains only the organizational relationships among the personnel.

2.6 Semantic Methods

Another approach to database design that was invented in the 1970s is based on semantics instead of graphs. There are several different versions of this basic approach, such as NIAM (Natural-language Information Analysis Method), BRM (Binary Relationship Modeling), ORM (Object-Role Modeling), and FORM (Formal Object-Role Modeling). The main proponent of ORM is Terry Halpin, and I strongly recommend getting his book (Halpin 1995) for details of the method. What I do not recommend is using the diagrams in his method. In addition to diagrams, his method includes the use of simplified English sentences to express relationships. These formal sentences can then be processed and used to generate several schemas in a mechanical way.

Most of the sentences are structured as subject-verb-object, but the important thing is that the objects are assigned a role in the sentence. For example, the fact that "Joe Celko wrote *Data and Databases* for Morgan Kaufmann Publishers" can be amended to read "AUTHOR: Joe Celko wrote BOOK: 'Data and Databases' for PUBLISHER: Morgan Kaufmann," which gives us the higher level, more abstract sentence that "Authors write books for publishers" as a final result, with the implication that there are many authors, books, and publishers involved. Broadly speaking, objects and entities become the subjects and objects of the sentences, relationships become verbs, and the constraints become prepositional phrases.

A major advantage of the semantic methods is that a client can check the simple sentences for validity easily. An ER diagram, on the other hand, is not easily checked. One diagram looks as valid as another, and it is hard for a user to focus on one fact in the diagram.

Data Structures

DATA STRUCTURES HOLD data without regard to what the data is. The difference between a physical and an abstract model of a data structure is important, but often gets blurred when discussing them.

Each data structure has certain properties and operations that can be done on it, regardless of what is stored in it. Here are the basics, with informal definitions.

Data structures are important because they are the basis for many of the implementation details of real databases, for data modeling, and for relational operations, since tables are multisets.

3.1 Sets

A *set* is a collection of elements of the same kind of thing without duplicates in it. There is no ordering of the elements in a set. There is a special set, called the empty or null set. Since the term "null" sounds and looks like the NULL missing value token in SQL, I will use the term "empty set."

The expression "same kind of thing" is a bit vague, but it is important. In a database, the rows of a table have to be instances of the same entity; that is, a Personnel table is made up of rows that represent individual employees. However, a grouped table built

from the Personnel table, say, by grouping of departments, is not the same kind of element. In the grouped table, the rows are aggregates and not individuals. Departmental data is a different level of abstraction and cannot be mixed with individual data.

The basic set operations are the following:

- *Membership:* This operation says how elements are related to a set. An element either is or is not a member of a particular set. The symbol is $\in$.

- *Containment:* One set A contains another set B if all the elements of B are also elements of A. B is called a *subset* of A. This includes the case where A and B are the same set, but if there are elements of A that are not in B, then the relationship is called *proper containment.* The symbol is $\subset$; if you need to show "contains or equal to," a horizontal bar can be placed under the symbol ($\subseteq$).

  It is important to note that the empty set is not a proper subset of every set. If A is a subset of B, the containment is proper if and only if there exists an element *b* in B such that *b* is not in A. Since every set contains itself, the empty set is a subset of the empty set. But this is not proper containment, so the empty set is not a proper subset of every set.

- *Union:* The union of two sets is a single new set that contains all the elements in both sets. The symbol is $\cup$. The formal mathematical definition is

  $\forall x: x \in A \vee x \in B \Rightarrow$
  $x \in (A \cup B)$

- *Intersection:* The intersection of two sets is a single new set that contains all the elements common to both sets. The symbol is $\cap$. The formal mathematical definition is

  $\forall x: x \in A \wedge x \in B \Rightarrow$
  $x \in A \cap B$

- *Difference:* The difference of two sets A and B is a single new set that contains elements from A that are not in B. The symbol is a minus sign.

$\forall x: x \in A$
$\wedge \neg (x \in) B \Rightarrow$
$x \in (A - B)$

- *Partition:* The partition of a set A divides the set into subsets, A1, A2, . . . , A*n*, such that

  $\cup A[i] = A$
  $\wedge \cap A[i] = \varnothing$

3.2 Multisets

A *multiset* (also called a *bag*) is a collection of elements of the same type with duplicates of the elements in it. There is no ordering of the elements in a multiset, and we still have the empty set. Multisets have the same operations as sets, but with extensions to allow for handling the duplicates.

Multisets are the basis for SQL, while sets are the basis for Dr. Codd's relational model.

The basic multiset operations are derived from set operations, but have extensions to handle duplicates:

- *Membership:* An element either is or is not a member of a particular set. The symbol is $\in$. In addition to a value, an element also has a degree of duplication, which tells you the number of times it appears in the multiset.

  Everyone agrees that the degree of duplication of an element can be greater than zero. However, there is some debate as to whether the degree of duplication can be zero, to show that an element is not a member of a multiset. Nobody has proposed using a negative degree of duplication, but I do not know if there are any reasons not to do so, other than the fact that it does not make any intuitive sense.

  For the rest of this discussion, let me introduce a notation for finding the degree of duplication of an element in a set:

  dod(<multiset>, <element>) = <integer value>

- *Reduction:* This operation removes redundant duplicates from the multiset and converts it into a set. In SQL, this is the effect of using a `SELECT DISTINCT` clause.

  For the rest of this discussion, let me introduce a notation for the reduction of a set:

  red(<multiset>)

- *Containment:* One multiset A contains another multiset B if
  1. $\text{red}(A) \subset \text{red}(B)$
  2. $\forall x \in B: \text{dod}(A, x) \geq \text{dod}(B, x)$

  This definition includes the case where A and B are the same multiset, but if there are elements of A that are not in B, then the relationship is called proper containment.

- *Union:* The union of two multisets is a single new multiset that contains all the elements in both multisets. A more formal definition is

  $$\forall x: x \in A \lor x \in B \Rightarrow$$
  $$x \in A \cup B$$
  $$\land$$
  $$\text{dod}(A \cup B, x) = \text{dod}(A, x) + \text{dod}(B, x)$$

  The degree of duplication in the union is the sum of the degree of duplication from both tables.

- *Intersection:* The intersection of two multisets is a single new multiset that contains all the elements common to both multisets.

  $$\forall x: x \in A \land x \in B \Rightarrow$$
  $$x \in A \cap B$$
  $$\land$$
  $$\text{dod}(A \cap B, x) = \text{ABS}\ (\text{dod}(A, x) - \text{dod}(B, x))$$

  The degree of duplication in the intersection is based on the idea that you match pairs from each set in the intersection.

- *Difference:* The difference of two multisets A and B is a single new multiset that contains elements from A that are not in B after pairs are matched from the two multisets. More formally:

$\forall x: x \in A$
$\land \neg (x \in) B \Rightarrow$
$x \in (A - B)$
$\land \text{dod}((A - B), x) = (\text{dod}(A, x) - \text{dod}(B, x))$

- *Partition:* The partition of a multiset A divides it into a collection of multisets, A1, A2, . . . , A*n*, such that their multiset union is the original set and their multiset intersection is empty.

Because sets are so important in the relational model, we will return to them in chapter 4 and go into more details.

3.3 Simple Sequential Files

Simple files are a linear sequence of identically structured records. There is a unique first record in the file. All the records have a unique successor except the unique last record. Records with identical content are differentiated by their position in the file. All processing is done with the current record.

In short, a simple sequential file is a multiset with an ordering added. In a computer system, these data structures are punch cards or magnetic tape files; in SQL this is the basis for CURSORs. The basic operations are the following:

- *Open the file:* This makes the data available. In some systems, it also positions a read-write head on the first record of the file. In others, such as CURSORs in SQL, the read-write head is positioned just before the first record of the file. This makes a difference in the logic for processing the file.
- *Fetch a record:* This changes the current record and comes in several different flavors:
  1. *Fetch next:* The successor of the current record becomes the new current record.
  2. *Fetch first:* The first record becomes the new current record.
  3. *Fetch last:* The last record becomes the new current record.
  4. *Fetch previous:* The predecessor of the current record becomes the new current record.

5. *Fetch absolute:* The *n*th record becomes the new current record.
6. *Fetch relative:* The record *n* positions from the current record becomes the new current record.

   There is some debate as to how to handle a fetch absolute or a fetch relative command that would position the read-write head before the first record or after the last record. One argument is that the current record should become the first or last record, respectively; another opinion is that an error condition should be raised.

   In many older simple file systems and CURSOR implementations, only fetch next is available. The reason was obvious with punch card systems; you cannot "rewind" a punch card reader like a magnetic tape drive. The reason that early CURSOR implementations had only fetch next is not so obvious, but had to do with the disposal of records as they were fetched to save disk storage space.

- *Close the file:* This removes the file from the system.
- *Insert a record:* The new record becomes the current record, and the former current record becomes its successor.
- *Update a record:* Values within the current record are changed. The read-write does not change position.
- *Delete a record:* This removes a record from the file. The successor of the current record becomes the current record. If the current record was the last record of the file, the read-write head is positioned just past the end of the file.

3.4 Lists

A *list* is a sequence of elements, each of which can be either a scalar value called an *atom* or another list; the definition is recursive. The way that a list is usually displayed is as a comma-separated list within parentheses, as for example, ((Smith, John), (Jones, Ed)).

A list has only a few basic operations from which all other functions are constructed. The `head()` function returns the first element of a list, and the `tail()` function returns the rest of it. A constructor function builds a new list from a pair of lists, one for the head and one for the tail of the new list.

While the abstract data structure does not depend on any particular implementation, you will see the phrase "linked list" used as a synonym for lists in computer literature. This method uses pairs of pointers to represent lists in a computer, where the pair points to the head and tail of a list. The pointers can link to either another pointer pair, to an atom, or to a special pointer value called a `NIL`. The `NIL` pointer points to nothing and is used as an end-of-list marker.

Lists are important in their own right, and the LISP programming language is the most common way to manipulate lists. However, we are interested in lists in databases because they can represent complex structures in a fast and compact form and are the basis for many indexing methods.

List programming languages also teach people to think recursively, since that is usually the best way to write even simple list procedures. As an example of a list function, consider `Member()`, which determines if a particular atom is in a list. It looks like this in pseudocode:

```
BOOLEAN PROCEDURE Member (a ATOM IN, l LIST IN)
IF l IS ATOMIC
THEN RETURN (a = l)
ELSE IF member(a, hd(l))
     THEN RETURN TRUE
     ELSE RETURN member(a, tl(l));
```

The predicate `<list> IS ATOMIC` returns TRUE if the list expression is an atom.

3.5 Arrays

Arrays are collections of elements accessed by using indexes. This terminology is unfortunate because the "index" of an array is a simple integer list that locates a value within the array, and not the index used on a file to speed up access. Another term taken from mathematics for "index" is "subscript," and that term should be favored to avoid confusion.

Arrays appear in most procedural languages and are usually represented as a subscript list after the name of the array. They are usually implemented as contiguous storage locations in host languages, but linked lists can also be used. The elements of an array can be records or scalars. This is useful in a database because it gives us a structure in the host language into which we can put rows from a query and access them in a simple fashion.

3.6 Graphs

Graphs are made up of nodes connected by edges. They are the most general abstract data structure and have many different types. We do not need any of the more complicated types of graphs in a database and can simply define an edge as a relationship between two nodes. The relationship is usually thought of in terms of a traversal from one node to another along an edge.

The two types of graphs that are useful to us are directed and undirected graphs. An edge in a directed graph can be traversed in only one direction; an edge in an undirected graph can be traversed in both directions. If I were to use a graph to represent the traffic patterns in a town, the one-way streets would be directed edges and the two-way streets would be undirected edges. However, a graph is never shown with both types of edges—instead, an undirected graph can be simulated in a directed graph by having all edges of the form (a,b) and (b,a) in the graph.

Graph theory is a branch of mathematics in its own right. Since graphs are so general, they are often used for high-level modeling of databases, computer networks, transportation networks, and so forth. We need a way of representing different kinds of graphs in a database, so we can model all of those things, too.

3.7 Trees

A *tree* is a special case of a graph. There are several equivalent definitions, but the most useful ones are the following:

- A tree is a graph with no cycles. The reason that this definition is useful to a database user is that circular references can cause a lot of problems within a database.
- A tree is made up of a node, called a *parent,* that points to zero or more other nodes, its *children,* or to another tree. This definition is recursive and therefore very compact, but another advantage is that this definition leads to a nested-sets model of hierarchies.

Trees are the basis for indexing methods used in databases. The important operations on a tree are locating subtrees and finding paths when we are using them as an index. Searching is made easier by having rules to insert values into the tree. We will discuss this when we get to indexes.

Relational Philosopher

The creator of the relational model talks about his never-ending crusade.

Interviewing Dr. Edgar F. Codd about databases is a bit like interviewing Einstein about nuclear physics. Only no one has ever called the irascible Codd a saint. In place of Einstein's publications on the theory of relativity, you have Codd's ground-breaking 1970 paper on relational theory, which proposed a rigorous model for database management that offered the beguiling simplicity of the rows and columns of tables. But there was more to it than that. Codd's work was firmly grounded in the mathematical theory of relations of arbitrary degree and the predicate logic first formulated by the ancient Greeks. Moreover, it was a complete package that handled mapping the real world to data structures as well as manipulating that data—that is, it included a specification for a normal form for database relations and the concept of a universal data sublanguage.

Almost as important to its success, Codd's relational theory had Codd backing it. The former World War II Royal Air Force pilot made sure word got out from his IBM research lab to the world at large. In those early years he had to struggle against the political forces aligned behind IBM's strategic database product, IMS, and came to work each day "wondering who was going to stab me in the back next." Codd parried often and well, although observers say some of the blows Codd returned over the years were imagined or had even been struck for Codd's own relational cause.

Codd won the great database debate and, with it, such laurels as the 1981 ACM (Association for Computing Machinery) Turing Award "for fundamental and continuing contributions to the theory and practice of database management systems."

Like Einstein, Codd has played a very public role in the days since his research and advocacy first let the genie out of the bottle. In place of Einstein's political activism on behalf of peaceful uses of nuclear energy, Codd has aggressively campaigned to make sure "relational" is more than an advertising buzzword. Many a careless user of the word (and even some rather careful experts in the field) found themselves on the end of a scathing "Coddgram" for what Codd deemed their public misstatements. Some say his ComputerWorld articles of 1985 brought two major nonrelational database vendors to the verge of bankruptcy and then takeover.

Whereas Einstein's work lead [sic] to the nuclear age, Codd's work has lead [sic] to what might be called the relational age. Yet Codd is not resting or turning to new pursuits. He says his goal of protecting users of large databases from knowing how data is actually organized in the machine has been realized only in part. He says errors in the implementation of DBMS engines and the dominant data sublanguage, SQL, jeopardize data integrity and make it too hard to frame a very complex query and get back a usable answer.

Codd's new book, *The Relational Model for Database Management: Version 2,* defines just how far he thinks we still have to go. It is highly recommended reading.

Whereas Code loves to elucidate the practical benefits of relational theory, things get dicey when talk ventures onto nonrelational grounds.

Einstein resisted new research done on quantum theory. Codd, in turn, resists nonrelational rumblings from the research community and DBMS vendors. Codd does not think much of work that extends the relational model (or skirts it) in order to deal more efficiently with data that doesn't look like the text and numeric data of the SUPPLIER-PARTS-SUPPLY example popularized by Codd. His new book dismisses practically all database research of the last ten years in a brief chapter.

For Einstein, the practical predictive value of quantum theory never overcame his fundamental objection to it: "God doesn't play dice with the universe." Codd says his objection to the new directions in database research has no such element of the theological. The real problem, he says, is that the new work lacks a satisfactory theoretical foundation. Worse, he says, it violates the principals [sic] laid down in the theoretical foundations of the relational model.

If relational systems can't deal effectively with the complex data found in applications like CAD, CASE, and office automation, Codd says, it is because their implementation of the relational model is lacking, not their underlying theory. The point may be moot, however: Users and vendors are succumbing to the heady performance improvements offered by nonrelational (or imperfectly relational) alternatives.

What follows is an edited transcript of *DBMS* Editor in Chief Kevin Strehlo's recent discussion with Dr. Codd.

DBMS: What got you started down the road toward those first papers on relational theory?

CODD: Well, a couple of things. Before I moved out to San Jose in '68, I attended a talk in Poughkeepsie given by a small software firm from Los Angeles, and they were describing the firm's DBMS. Now, in predicate logic, the two main quantifiers are the existential and the universal. I asked him to what extent the product supported the existential quantifier. He said, "Well I get some funny questions, but this is the first time I've been asked about support for existential philosophy." So right there, I knew that he didn't know a damn thing about predicate logic.

DBMS: I guess for him it wasn't an an [sic] intuitive leap to connect predicate logic to the management of data. But you made that leap somehow?

CODD: I felt that it was a natural thing to do. I did my studies in logic and mathematics and it occurred to me as a natural thing for queries. Then it occurred to me—and I can't say why ideas occurred to me, but they keep doing so, and I'm not short of them even now, I can tell you—why limit it to queries? Why not take it to database management in general? Some work had already gone on in special-purpose query systems that were software on top of and separate from a database management system. It occurred to me that predicate logic could be applied to maintaining the logical integrity of the data.

DBMS: Can you quickly try to give *DBMS* readers a grasp for existential quantifiers in particular and predicate logic in general in case they don't have one?

CODD: Sometimes I use this example: Statement A is *strictly stronger* in the logical sense than statement B if A logically implies B, but B does not logically imply A. Clearly, given a set of things and a property P that may or may not hold for each member of the set, the statement "P holds for *all* members of the set" is stronger than the statement "P holds for *some* members of the set." In predicate logic the former statement involves the universal quantifier, while the latter involves the existential quantifier.

Mathematicians are looking for generality, for results that apply to all numbers of some kind, like all integers, or all real numbers, or all complex numbers so that they don't have to keep making up theorems. That's the beauty of something like Pythagoras' theorem from ancient Greek times. It still applies to all right angle triangles, whether you're using it for surveying or for navigating a ship. How the Greeks got on to the things they did—there was no need for surveying, or things of that nature, at that time—is amazing to me.

Excerpt from *DBMS* interview with Edgar F. Codd, "Relational Philosopher." *DBMS,* Dec. 1990, pgs. 34–36. Reprinted with permission from *Intelligent Enterprise Magazine.* This and related articles can be found on *www.intelligententerprise.com.*

Relational Tables

SQL IS CLASSIFIED as a set-oriented language, but in truth it did not have a full collection of classic set operations until the SQL-92 standard, and even then actual products were slow to implement them.

We discussed the formal properties of multisets (or bags, to use a term I find less attractive), which included

1. A multiset is a collection of things (elements) of the same kind.
2. A multiset has no ordering to its elements.
3. A multiset may have duplicates in the collection.

A relational table has more properties than its simple data structure. It is far too easy for a beginner SQL programmer to think that a table is a file, a row is a record, and a column is a field. This is not true at all.

A table can exist only within a database schema, where it is related to the other tables and schema objects. A file exists in its own right and has no relationship to another file as far as the file system is concerned.

A file is passive storage whose structure is defined by the program that reads it. That is, I can read the same file in, say, Fortran several different ways in different programs by using different FORMAT statements. A file (particularly in Fortran, Cobol, and other older 3GL languages) is very concerned with the physical representation of the data in storage.

A table never exposes the physical representation of the data to the host program using it. In fact, one part of the SQL-92 standard deals with how to convert the SQL datatypes into host language datatypes, so the same table can be used by any of several standard programming languages.

A table has constraints that control the values that it can hold, while a file must depend on application programs to restrict its content. The structure of the table is part of the schema.

The rows of a table are all identical in structure and can be referenced only by name. The records in a file are referenced by position within the file and can have varying structure. Examples of changing record structures include arrays of different sizes and dimensions in Fortran, use of the OCCURS clause in Cobol, the variant records in Pascal, and `struct` declaration in C.

Perhaps more importantly, a row in a properly designed table models a member of a collection of things of the same kind. The notion of "things of the same kind" is a bit vague when you try to formalize it, but it means that the table is a set and whatever property applies to one row should apply to all rows.

The notion of kind also applies to the level of aggregation and abstraction used. For example, a Personnel table is a set of employees. A department is made up of employees, but it is not an aggregation of the employees. You can talk about the salary of an employee, but it makes no sense to talk about the salary of a department. A department has a budget allocation that is related to the salaries. At another level, you can talk about the average salary of an employee within a department.

This is not always true with files. For example, imagine a company with two types of customers, wholesale and retail. A file might include fields for one type of customer that do not apply to the other and inform the program about the differences with flags in the records. In a proper database schema, you would need a table for each kind of customer, although you might have a single table for the data common to each kind.

A field within a record is located by its position. That is why a statement like `READ(x, y, z)` will not produce the same results in a 3GL program as `READ(z, x, y)`. Columns can only be accessed by their name; the database system locates them physically.

A column can have constraints that restrict the values it can contain in addition to its basic datatype; a field is limited only by the datatype that the host program is expecting. This lack of constraints has led to such things as `'LATER'` being used in a field that is supposed to hold a date value.

A field can be complex and have its own internal structure, which is exposed to the application program. The most common example of this is Cobol, where a field is made up of subfields. For example, a date has year, month, and day as separate fields within it. There is nothing in Cobol per se to prevent a program from changing the day of the month to 99 at the subfield level, even though the result is an invalid date at the field level.

A properly designed column is always a scalar value. The term "scalar" means that the value is taken from a scale of some sort. It measures one attribute and only one attribute. We will discuss scales and measurement theory later in the book. In SQL, a date is a datatype in its own right, and that prevents you from constructing an invalid value.

4.1 Subsets

The name pretty much describes the concept—a subset is a set constructed from the elements of another set. A proper subset is defined as not including all the elements of the original set.

We already discussed the symbols used in set theory for proper and improper subsets. The most important property of a subset is that it is still a set. SQL does not have an explicit subset operator for its tables, but almost every single table query produces a subset. The `SELECT DISTINCT` option in a query will remove the redundant duplicate rows.

Standard SQL has never had an operator to compare tables against each other for equality or containment. Several college textbooks on relational databases mention a CONTAINS predicate, which does not exist in SQL-89 or SQL-92. This predicate existed in the original System R, IBM's first experimental SQL system, but it was dropped from later SQL implementations because of the expense of running it.

4.2 Union

The union of two sets yields a new set whose elements are in one, the other, or both of the original sets. This assumes that the elements in the original sets were of the same kind, so that the result set makes sense. That is, I cannot union a set of numbers and a set of vegetables and get a meaningful result.

SQL-86 introduced the UNION and the UNION ALL operators to handle the multiset problems. The UNION is the classic set operator applied to two table expressions with the same structure. It removes duplicate rows from the final result; the UNION ALL operator leaves them in place.

The fact that two table expressions have the same structure does not mean that they have the same kind of elements, and SQL-92 is not really able to check this. The classic example is a table of *x*, *y* coordinates and a table of polar coordinates. Both have two columns of REAL numbers, and both give a location on a map. The UNION makes no sense unless you convert one system of coordinates into the other.

In SQL-89, the columns of the result set did not have names, but you could reference them by a position number. This position number could only be used in a few places because the syntax would make it impossible to tell the difference between a column number and an integer. For example, does 1 + 1 mean "double the value in column one," "increment column one," or the value two?

In SQL-92, the use of position numbers is "deprecated," a term in the standards business that means that it is still in the language in this standard, but that the next version of the standard will remove it. The columns of the result set do not have names unless you explicitly give the columns names with an AS clause.

```
(SELECT a, b, c FROM Foo)
UNION [ALL]
(SELECT x, y, z FROM Bar) AS Foobar(c1, c2, c3)
```

In practice, actual SQL products have resolved the missing names problem several different ways: use the names in the first table of the operation, use the names in the last table of the operation, or make up system-generated names.

4.3 Intersection

The intersection of two sets yields a new set whose elements are in both of the original sets. This assumes that the datatypes of the elements in the original sets were the same, so that the result set makes sense.

If the intersection is empty, then the sets are called disjoint. If the intersection is not empty, then the sets have what is called a proper overlap.

SQL-92 introduced the `INTERSECT` and the `INTERSECT ALL` operators to handle the multiset problems. The `INTERSECT` is the classic set operator applied to two table expressions with the same structure. It removes duplicate rows from the final result; the `INTERSECT ALL` operator matches identical rows from one table to their duplicates in the second table. To be more precise, if R is a row that appears in both tables T1 and T2, and there are m duplicates of R in T1 and n duplicates of R in T2, where $m > 0$ and $n > 0$, then the `INTERSECT ALL` result table of T1 and T2 contains the minimum of m and n duplicates of R.

4.4 Set Difference

The set difference of two sets, shown with a minus sign in set theory, yields a subset of the first set, whose elements exclude the elements of the second set—for example, the set of all employees except those on the bowling team. Again, redundant duplicates are removed if `EXCEPT` is specified.

If the `EXCEPT ALL` operator is specified, then the number of duplicates of row R that the result table can contain is the maximum of $(m - n)$ and 0.

4.5 Partitioning

A partitioning of a set divides the set into subsets such that

1. No subset is empty.
2. The intersection of any combination of the subsets is empty.
3. The union of all the subsets is the original set.

In English, this is like slicing a pizza. You might have noticed, however, that there are many ways to slice a pizza.

4.5.1 Groups

The `GROUP BY` operator in SQL is a bit hard to explain because it looks like a partition, but it is not. The SQL engine goes to the `GROUP BY` clause and builds a partitioned working table in which each partition has the same values in the grouping columns. `NULL`s are grouped together, even though they cannot be equal to each other by convention.

Each subset in the grouped table is then reduced to a single row that must have only group characteristics. This result set is made up of a new kind of element, namely, summary information, and it is not related to the original table anymore.

The working table is then passed to the `HAVING` clause, if any, and rows that do not meet the criteria given in the `HAVING` clause are removed.

4.5.2 Relational Division

Relational division was one of the original eight relational operators defined by Dr. Codd. It is different from the other seven because it is not a primitive operator, but can be defined in terms of the other operators. The idea is that given one table with columns (a,b), called the *dividend,* and a second table with column (a), called the *divisor,* we can get a result table with column (b), called the *quotient.* The values of (b) that we are seeking are those that have all the values of (a) in the divisor associated with them. To make this more concrete, if you have a table of pilots and the planes they are certified to fly called PilotSkills, and a table with the planes in our hangar, when you divide the PilotSkills table by the hangar table, you get the names of the pilots who can fly every plane in the hangar.

As an analog to integer division, there is the possibility of a remainder (i.e., pilots who have certifications for planes that are not in the hangar leave those extra planes as a remainder). But if you want to draw an analogy between dividing by an empty set and division by zero, you have to be careful depending on the query you used. You can get all the pilots, even if they do not fly any planes at all, or you can get an empty result set (see my other book, *SQL for Smarties,* for more details).

The idea of Codd's original division operator was that it would be an inverse of the `CROSS JOIN` or Cartesian product. That is, if you did a `CROSS JOIN` on the divisor and the quotient, you would get the rows found in the dividend table.

A relational division operator proposed by Stephen Todd is defined on two tables with common columns that are joined together, dropping the join column and retaining only those nonjoin columns that meet a matching criteria.

Again, it is easier to explain with an example. Let's use Chris Date's classic tables and assume we have JobParts(jobno, partno) and SupParts(supno, partno), which show us suppliers, the parts that they provide, and the jobs that use those parts. We want to get the (supplier, job) pairs such that the supplier supplies all of the parts needed for the job. This is not quite the same thing as getting the supplier-and-job pairs such that job *jn* requires all of the parts provided by supplier *sn*.

4.6 Duplicates

Entities are a state of mind. No two people agree on what the real world view is.—Mexaxides

. . . an n*-ary relation R has the following properties: . . . (3) All rows are distinct. . . —E. F. Codd*

The idea of a key on a table is central to the relational model. The purpose of a key is to identify each row uniquely, and, from that property, you can build the rules for the normal forms. The terminology has changed a bit since Codd's first papers. All of the things that

Codd was calling primary keys now have more precise terms: All possible keys in a table are called *candidate keys;* the chosen one is the *primary key,* and the unchosen ones are the *alternate keys.* The ideas of duplication and uniqueness are central to the way that people think and deal with the world, so your database model should handle these concepts if it is going to reflect the real world.

In the real world, no two entities are exactly alike, but you ignore the differences in order to construct classes and reason with abstractions. You can build the classes using some criteria for matching entities against each other. There are several ways to do this:

- *Identity:* "Clark Kent is Superman!" You have two or more names for exactly the same entity. This is the strongest form of matching.
- *Equality:* "Five kilograms of rubber weigh the same as five kilograms of gold." You have an attribute in both entities that has the same value according to some test or scale. However, the entities are separate and might not match on other attributes, such as current market price or electrical conductivity.
- *Equivalency:* "One teaspoon of concentrate makes one cup of formula." One entity can be transformed into the other in some well-defined manner. This is not quite the same as equality because some outside agency is needed for the transformation. In this case, you must add water to the concentrate.
- *Substitutability:* "We don't have beer. Would you like a glass of wine?" One entity can replace the other in some operation, but it has a distinct identity of its own and is not transformed and does not have to have an exact match on an attribute (i.e., beer and wine do not taste alike, but both are in the superclass of potables).

Relational databases are built on the assumptions of identity or equality. How you treat duplicates in a relational database depends on whether you use identity or equality. I'll explain this statement by looking at the three methods used in relational database models to handle duplication:

1. Remove duplicates automatically.
2. Allow duplicates.
3. Reduce duplicates to a count of the members in the class.

4.6.1 Allow Duplicates

This is the SQL solution. The rationale for allowing duplicate rows was best defined by David Beech in an internal paper for the ANSI X3H2 committee and again in a letter to *Datamation* (Beech 1989). This is now referred to as the "cat food argument" in the literature. The name is taken from the example of a cash register slip, where you find several rows, each of which lists a can of cat food at the same price. To quote from the original article:

> For example, the row 'cat food 0.39' could appear three times [on a supermarket checkout receipt] with a significance that would not escape many shoppers. . . . At the level of abstraction at which it is useful to record the information, there are no value components that distinguish the objects. What the relational model does is force people to lower the level of abstraction, often inventing meaningless values to be inserted in an extra column whose purpose is to show what we knew already, that the cans of cat food are distinct.

All cans of cat food are interchangeable, so they have no natural unique identifier. The alternative of tagging every single can of cat food in the database with a unique machine-readable identifier preprinted on the can or keyed in at the register is not only expensive and time-consuming, but it adds no real information to the data model. In the real world, you collect the data as it comes in on the cash register slip, and consolidate it when you debit the count of cans of cat food in the inventory table. The cans of cat food are considered equivalent, but they are not identical.

You also encounter this situation when you do a projection on a table and the result is made up of nonkey columns. Counting and grouping queries also implies that duplicate rows exist in a "separate but equal" way; that is, you treat them as a class or a multiset. Let's make this more concrete with the following two tables:

```
CREATE TABLE Personnel
(emp CHAR(30) NOT NULL PRIMARY KEY,
 dept CHAR(8) NOT NULL);

CREATE TABLE Automobiles
(owner CHAR(30) NOT NULL,
 tag CHAR(10) NOT NULL,
 color CHAR(5) NOT NULL,
 PRIMARY KEY(owner, tag));
```

You can use these tables to answer the question: "Do more employees in the accounting department than in the advertising department drive red cars?" You can answer this quickly with the following query:

```
SELECT dept, COUNT(*)
 FROM Personnel, Automobiles
 WHERE owner = emp
  AND color = 'red'
  AND dept IN ('acct', 'advert')
GROUP BY dept;
```

Try to do this without knowing that people can own more than one car and that a department has more than one employee! Duplicate values occur in both projections and joins on these tables.

4.6.2 Disallow Duplicates

This is Chris Date's relational model. Date has written several articles on the removal of duplicates (e.g., Date 1990, 1994). Date's model says that values are drawn from a particular domain, which is a set of scalars. This means that when a column defined on the color domain uses the value "red", it is using "red" in the domain and it occurs once. There might be many occurrences of references to "red" or "3" or "1996-12-25", but they are pointing to the only red, the only integer three, and the only Christmas Day in 1996. Domains are based on an identity concept and disallow duplicate values. This is the same argument that mathematicians get into about pure numbers.

Date's example of the problems of duplicates uses the following two tables:

Parts

pno	pname
p1	screw
p1	screw
p1	screw
p2	screw

SupParts

supno	pno
s1	p1
s1	p1
s1	p2

and then attempts to write SQL to comply with the criterion "List the part numbers of screws or parts that come from supplier s1 (or both)." He produces a dozen different queries that are all different, and all produce a different number of answers. For example, if you assume that a part must have one supplier, you can write

```
SELECT P.pno
 FROM Parts AS P, SupParts AS SP
 WHERE (SP.supno = 's1'
       AND SP.pno = P.pno)
   OR P.pname = 'screw';
```

which gives the result:

pno	
p1	
p1	
p1	
p1	
p1	
p1	*9 duplicates*
p1	
p1	
p1	
p2	
p2	*3 duplicates*
p2	

However, the more direct query that translates an OR into a UNION would give

```
SELECT pno
 FROM Parts
 WHERE pname = 'screw'
UNION
SELECT pno
 FROM SupParts
 WHERE supno = 's1';
```

with the desired results:

pno
p1
p2

The real problem is that you can assign no meaning to the duplicates of (p1, screw) and (s1, p1) rows. If the Parts table models a list of shipments as they come in, then each row would be a shipment (which is what you did with cat food). But if you assume that SupParts is a similar shipment list, then each row in Parts would have to map to a row in SupParts. They don't match up, so the data is wrong. Even if they did match up, you would have put one fact in two places, which is always an incorrect model.

To answer the question "Which supplier sent us the most screws?" you must have an explicit quantity column in Date's relational model. This is consistent with the idea that any property of an entity should be shown as an explicit column in a table.

In SQL, you can get the effects of duplicate elimination with SELECT DISTINCT and aggregate functions with the DISTINCT option, the UNION operator, and careful design of queries around joins on UNIQUE and PRIMARY KEY columns. It is also possible for an optimizer to eliminate duplicates in certain subquery predicates, such as the IN predicate.

4.6.3 Consolidate Duplicates

Dr. Codd sent a paper to the ANSI X3H2 Database Standards Committee several years ago in which he proposed a "degree of duplication" function, which I will show as dod(*), in keeping with SQL syntax conventions. He wanted the function to return the number of duplicates as part of the results when you execute a query that produces duplicate rows, instead of dropping them. This function could produce the same results as GROUP BY and COUNT(*) in SQL, but in a different manner. Let's do the automobile problem ("Do more employees in the accounting department than in the advertising department drive red cars?") in relational algebra, with a dod(*) function:

```
Q1:= PROJECT Automobiles(owner, color, dod(*))
       WHERE color = 'red';
Q2:= PROJECT Personnel(emp, dept)
       WHERE dept = 'acct' OR dept = 'advert';
Q3:= Q1 JOIN Q2 ON emp = owner;
Q4:= PROJECT Q3(dept, dod(*));
```

Assume you have the following data:

Automobiles

owner	tag	color
'John'	123	'red'
'John'	122	'green'
'Sam'	111	'red'
'Mary'	345	'red'
'Mary'	678	'red'

Personnel

emp	dept
'John'	'advert'
'Sam'	'acct'
'Mary'	'acct'
'Mel'	'sales'

The intermediate steps look like this:

Q1—get the 'red' car owners

owner	color	dod(*)
'John'	'red'	1
'Sam'	'red'	1
'Mary'	'red'	2

Q2—get the employees

emp	dept
'John'	'advert'
'Sam'	'acct'
'Mary'	'acct'

Q3—join them

owner	color	dod(*)	emp	dept
'John'	'red'	1	'John'	'advert'
'Sam'	'red'	1	'Sam'	'acct'
'Mary'	'red'	2	'Mary'	'acct'

Q4—retain departments and counts

dod(*)	dept
1	'advert'
1	'acct'
2	'acct'

Oops, the `dod(*)` cannot operate like a regular function value in joins and projections! You need a rule that says that rows differing by only a `dod(*)` column are replaced automatically with a single row containing the sum of their `dod(*)` columns. In this case, what you want is

dod(*)	dept
1	'advert'
3	'acct'

I am not going to try to figure out all the rules for those cases in which a `JOIN` produces two or more `dod(*)` columns in intermediate result tables, or in which you try to join two intermediate results on their respective `dod(*)` columns.

This approach recognizes that there are occurrences of values, but it puts them into a single collection. That is, where SQL sees three separate but equivalent cans of cat food, Date's model sees a single class of canned cat food, and Codd's model sees a collection of three cans of cat food.

4.6.4 Uniqueness

There is a rule of thumb in SQL database design that says that all base tables should have a primary key. This will avoid a lot of the problems involved with duplicates and will make your SQL database look more like a pure relational database. However, there is a little problem in that a primary key in relational database theory means one chosen from several candidate keys. In SQL, the keywords PRIMARY KEY (I will capitalize the keywords to differentiate the SQL from the relational theory term) imply other things.

In SQL, I might not want to have a PRIMARY KEY, but instead use multiple candidate keys (shown by NOT NULL and UNIQUE constraints) because many systems will see the keywords PRIMARY KEY and set up access based on those columns. The PRIMARY KEY is the default target for the FOREIGN KEY. . .REFERENCES constraint clause, and many SQL products will set up special index structures (clustering, hashing, inverted lists, and so on) to favor joins and accesses on the PRIMARY KEY for the referencing table to those columns. Consider a table for a school schedule:

```
CREATE TABLE Schedule
(period INTEGER NOT NULL,
 teacher CHAR(15) NOT NULL,
 room INTEGER NOT NULL,
 CONSTRAINT tr UNIQUE (teacher, room), - candidate keys
 CONSTRAINT pr UNIQUE (period, room),
 CONSTRAINT pt UNIQUE (period, teacher),
 CONSTRAINT ptr UNIQUE (period, teacher, room));
```

Yes, the rules imposed by the UNIQUE constraints are a bit weird, but bear with me. The following is one possible solution set that does not violate any of the four constraints:

Schedule

period	teacher	room
1	'Curly'	101
1	'Larry'	102
1	'Moe'	103
2	'Curly'	102
2	'Larry'	101
3	'Curly'	103
3	'Moe'	101

I constructed this table by attempting to insert all 27 possible rows (3 teachers, 3 rooms, and 3 periods) into the table. This is a handy, if inelegant, testing trick for a table with multiple constraints.

Which `UNIQUE` constraint should be made into the `PRIMARY KEY`? And how did you decide? The relational model does not have to worry about performance, but you do. At first glance, it looks like the ptr constraint implies the other three constraints, but it does not. The ptr constraint by itself would allow all 27 possible rows to appear in the table.

Using the ptr constraint as a `PRIMARY KEY` violates another rule of thumb: a `PRIMARY KEY` should not be a super key. A super key is defined as a set of columns that is a key and also contains a subset that is a key (in other words, it's too fat). This rule of thumb has the practical advantage of leading the designer toward shorter keys, which will become smaller indexes, which will search faster. It sounds good so far.

If you follow this rule, which of the two column constraints do you use as the `PRIMARY KEY`? Unless I have a good reason, I would assume that searches are equally likely to use any pair or all three columns. That means I would use all four constraints, but not declare any of them to be the `PRIMARY KEY`. Yes, updates and insertions would be slow, but my searches would have the best average search time possible.

The usual next step is to try to break this table into smaller tables and then reconstruct the original table from them. However, this does not work. Break the table into three two-column tables, each of which uses a two-column constraint as its PRIMARY KEY, and insert some legal rows into each of them.

```
CREATE TABLE period_teacher
(period INTEGER NOT NULL,
 teacher CHAR (15) NOT NULL,
 PRIMARY KEY (period, teacher));
 INSERT INTO period_teacher
 VALUES (1, 'Curly'),
        (1, 'Larry'),
        (1, 'Moe'),
        (2, 'Curly'),
        (2, 'Larry'),
        (3, 'Larry'),
        (3, 'Moe');
```

Now execute a query to join the three tables together, replacing the ptr constraint with a SELECT DISTINCT. (I have used a GROUP BY instead to get the count of the duplicates for each row.)

```
CREATE TABLE period_room
(period INTEGER NOT NULL,
 room INTEGER NOT NULL,
 PRIMARY KEY (period, room));

 INSERT INTO period_room
 VALUES (1, 101),
        (1, 102),
        (1, 103),
        (2, 101),
        (2, 102),
        (3, 101),
        (3, 103);

CREATE TABLE teacher-room
(teacher CHART(15) NOT NULL,
 room INTEGER NOT NULL,
 PRIMARY KEY (teacher, room));
 INSERT INTO teacher-room
```

```
VALUES ('Curly', 101),
       ('Curly', 102),
       ('Curly', 103),
       ('Larry', 101),
       ('Larry', 102),
       ('Moe', 101),
       ('Moe', 103);
```

The idea is to reconstruct the original table from these three derived tables. But your query will not work, and you will get a lot of false data that did not exist in the original table. In fact, you can try the other three possible table joins and you still will not avoid false data.

As an aside, many first-time SQL database designers working with entity-relationship modeling tools think that "if it is a table, then it is an entity." Look at the Schedule table: there is nothing that implies an entity in the possible keys; rather, it holds nothing but relationships among three entities.

4.6.5 Levels of Aggregation

Chuck Reinke wrote to C. J. Date in response to his column in *Database Programming & Design* magazine and argued against the cat food example with another example. He was interested in lab rats and ratlets. Whenever there is a new litter, he wanted to create an entry for each new ratlet. When just born, they are indistinguishable, but tattooing is out of the question. Yet, as they grow, he can distinguish certain ones by color or behavior, and at that time, we need to assign them a unique key. This is usually done with colored markers on their tails.

Mr. Reinke argued that Chris should not record the ratlets prior to the stage when they become distinguishable from their litter mates. Assigning each ratlet an arbitrary unique key implies nonexistent information that the ratlets are distinguishable (in the mind of God, perhaps).

Chris Date responded with the following design for the ratlets problem:

```
CREATE TABLE Litters
(litter_id INTEGER NOT NULL PRIMARY KEY,
 ratlet_tally INTEGER NOT NULL);

CREATE TABLE Ratlets
(ratlet_id CHAR(15) NOT NULL PRIMARY KEY,
 litter_id INTEGER NOT NULL
           REFERENCES Litters(litter_id));
```

When there's a new litter, we make the obvious entry in litters. When an individual ratlet becomes "interesting" (unlike Reinke, Date did not like the word "distinguishable" because distinguishability presupposes identity), we make the obvious entry in ratlets.

Let's consider what we are actually doing in this case. One table is viewing a litter of ratlets as a single entity to be modeled in a table, while the other table is breaking the litter into its individual members. The Litter table is a set based on a collective noun, and the Ratlet table is based on a singular noun, if you want to think of it in those terms.

You see this same model in the GROUP BY operator, which creates a set at a higher level of aggregation from existing data. It is not a bad thing per se, but you need to be aware of it and not mix levels of aggregation in a query or in the same table.

4.7 VIEWs

According to the SQL-92 standard, VIEWs are virtual tables that act as if they are materialized when their name appears. In practice, however, we try to avoid materializing VIEWs because this would require a temporary working table and would not allow the optimizer to make certain decisions.

SQL-92 introduced the concept of a derived table that has the form

```
<table subquery> AS <table name>[<column list>]
```

that matches the VIEW definition syntax:

```
CREATE VIEW <table name>[<column list>] AS <select statement>
```

The difference is that the derived table is lost after the execution of the SELECT statement in which it is used. VIEWs are persistent schema objects.

VIEWs serve several purposes:

1. *Security:* Users can be given access to only those rows and columns for which they have authorization.

2. *Hiding complexity:* Rather than have programmers write the same complex query over and over, they can be given a VIEW that has the query in it. This has the added advantage that everyone will do it the same way—something that was impossible to guarantee if all programmers began their work from scratch each time.

3. *Optimization:* This is possible in certain SQL products where the optimizer looks for common subexpressions across multiple queries and statements. By definition, a VIEW that is used in several statements is a common subexpression and does not need to be parsed any further.

4.7.1 Updatable VIEWs

The updatability of a given VIEW should be a semantic issue, not a syntactic one. This is simply not true in SQL, however. For example, the following two VIEW definitions, taken from Date and McGoveran (1994b), are semantically identical:

```
CREATE VIEW V1
AS SELECT *
     FROM Personnel
    WHERE dept_nbr = 'D1'
       OR salary > 33000.00;

CREATE VIEW V2
AS SELECT *
     FROM Personnel
    WHERE dept_nbr = 'D1'
   UNION
   SELECT *
```

```
  FROM Personnel
 WHERE salary > 33000.00);
```

Obviously, both of these VIEWs should be updatable because they both create the same table, and that table contains the primary key of the base table from which it is derived. However, the SQL-92 standard, and most SQL products, will let you update Personnel via VIEW V1, but not via VIEW V2.

The SQL-92 standard is actually very conservative about what VIEWs are updatable:

1. The VIEW must be derived from a SELECT statement on one and only one base table; this can go through several layers of VIEWs on top of VIEWs, however.
2. The VIEW must include all the columns of a key (i.e., a UNIQUE or PRIMARY KEY constraint) in the base table.
3. All columns not shown in the VIEW must have default values or be NULLable (if you think about it for a minute, this lets you construct and insert a complete row into the base table).

The whole idea is that an updatable VIEW looks and behaves pretty much like a base table, but slightly restricted as to what you can see. One row in the VIEW maps to exactly one row in the base table from which it is drawn.

However, other views are updatable, and some vendors support more than the basic version given in the SQL-92 standard. The VIEW must have an INSERT, UPDATE, and DELETE rule under the covers that maps its rows back to a single row in the base table(s).

Nathan Goodman (1990) discusses the conditions required for updating the following types of VIEWs:

1. Projection from a single table
2. Selection/projection from a single table
3. Unioned VIEWs
4. Set difference VIEWs
5. One-to-one joins
6. One-to-one outer joins

7. One-to-many outer joins
8. Many-to-many joins
9. Translated and coded fields

Another feature, which is not used enough, is the WITH CHECK OPTION clause on a VIEW. This can be a bit tricky (I have a section in *SQL for Smarties* that discusses this feature in detail).

In 25 words or less, WITH CHECK OPTION requires the VIEW to reevaluate the WHERE clause in the defining query every time a row is changed. For example, let's build a VIEW of the salesmen in an imaginary company.

```
CREATE VIEW Salesmen
AS SELECT name, title, quota
     FROM Personnel
    WHERE title = 'salesman'
WITH CHECK OPTION;
```

and now let's assume I am a salesman who wants to make myself the president of the company by changing the database. The WITH CHECK OPTION prevents the following attempts:

```
UPDATE Salesmen
   SET title = 'president'
 WHERE name = 'Joe Celko';
INSERT INTO Salesmen
VALUES ('Joe Celko', 'president', NULL);
```

These fail because I can only work with salesmen. The new image of my row in the Personnel table would have failed the test (title = 'salesman') if it had been allowed.

If I decide to eliminate the current president, I cannot do so because his job title is not in my VIEW. This would hold true even without the WITH CHECK OPTION clause:

```
DELETE FROM Salesmen
 WHERE title = 'president';
```

There is more to the feature than this, but that is more of a detailed programming issue.

Access Structures

DATA ACCESS METHODS are not part of the SQL standard, so each vendor is free to do anything they want as a vendor extension. When the ANSI X3H2 Database Standards Committee (now called NCITS H2) decided to exclude index creation from the SQL-86 standard, the reason given was that indexing and accessing data was too physical for a standard that was trying to be as abstract as possible. There was also some debate in the committee that introducing a CREATE INDEX command would also require us to introduce a CREATE HASH command, a CREATE LINK command, and assorted CREATE commands for an endless list of access methods.

However, in the real world, it is vital to have some method to improve access to the data— simple sequential file access would be too slow to be practical. The X/Open Consortium came up with this syntax, based on the most common vendor syntax in use at the time, for handling indexing:

```
CREATE INDEX <index name> ON <table name>(<column list>);
DROP INDEX <index name>;
```

This basic syntax can then have additional product-specific clauses and keywords that modify the index in some way. However,

every product agrees that the user can only CREATE and DROP an index. The SQL engine handles any references to the access without requiring the user to code for them in SQL, though the product might provide ways of forcing the use of a particular access path.

The important questions concerning access methods in a given SQL implementation are

- Do users have the ability to specify the type of access method used in their schema declaration? Or does the system decide this?
- How many kinds of access methods (hashing, B-trees, bit mapping, inverted lists, etc.) are available?
- If there is a multicolumn access method, will the system use part of the column list when only a subset of those columns appears in the query? Or do you have to declare separate access structures for each subset to improve performance?
- Does the order of the columns in the access structure make a difference in the access method's performance?
- Can the product detect and avoid identical access structures that have been given different names? More generally speaking, does the database detect redundant structures and operations so they can be removed?

5.1 Simple Indexes

The simplest thing you can do to search a table is to just use the CREATE TABLE command and nothing else. In most SQL implementations, the rows will be stored in a file structure with a sequential access method of some kind. This saves the storage that would have been used for another access method, but will cost access time. SQL is not assumed to order the rows in a table, so every query to the table will have to do a complete linear search to be sure that it checked every row. While this is not really an index at all, it is leading up to the idea of an index.

What if instead of reading the table sequentially, I put the search results in another, smaller data structure that had the search value and the location of the matching row in it? This will cost me some extra storage, but I will get better search times because my little list will be so much smaller than the original table. That is the idea of an index!

The most basic form of index consists of a file made up of the key column value(s) from all the base table's rows and a pointer to the physical address where each row is located in the table. If you need a physical analogy for this method, look at the doorbell board in a large apartment building. The index is the list of names and apartment numbers (usually sorted on apartment numbers) and the doorbell button is the pointer that fetches the data (person) you sought.

Since this kind of index usually has the primary key in it and it is used to ensure uniqueness, it is often called a primary index. However, you can use this method to ensure other uniqueness constraints on other keys, too.

In the case of a multiple-column key in the table, the key column in the index is usually constructed by concatenating the base table column values together. The search is then done not on the values per se, but on a binary string. A variance of this is to replace simple concatenation of the columns with a rearrangement of the bytes involved. The idea is to increase the granularity of the index by getting more variation in the front of the string.

This approach is based on the observation that words and encoding schemes tend to vary more in the middle and the end than at their start. For example, let's take a short list of names, picked at random, that start with the letter *A* and average 5 to 6 characters in length. Now we split the name at different positions, swap the pieces, and concatenate them back to give a new string, thus:

```
CREATE TABLE Foobar (name VARCHAR (25) NOT NULL);

INSERT INTO Foobar
VALUES ('Adrian'), ('Adrienne'), ('Al'), ('Alan'), ('Alex'),
       ('Alpharetta'), ('Amanda'), ('Amber'), ('Amy'),
```

```
        ('Andrea'), ('Angeles'), ('Angie'), ('Annette'), ('Anya'),
        ('Asya'), ('Atlanta'), ('Avery'), ('Avondale');

SELECT name,
        SUBSTRING(name FROM 4 FOR LENGTH(name))
            || SUBSTRING(name FROM 1 FOR 3) AS pivot4,
        SUBSTRING(name FROM 5 FOR LENGTH(name))
            || SUBSTRING(name FROM 1 FOR 4) AS pivot5,
        SUBSTRING(name FROM 6 FOR LENGTH(name))
            || SUBSTRING(name FROM 1 FOR 5) AS pivot6,
        SUBSTRING(name FROM 7 FOR LENGTH(name))
            || SUBSTRING(name FROM 1 FOR 6) AS pivot7
  FROM Foobar;
```

name	pivot4	pivot5	pivot6	pivot7
Adrian	ianAdr	anAdri	nAdria	Adrian
Adrienne	ienneAdr	enneAdri	nneAdrie	neAdrien
Al	Al	Al	Al	Al
Alan	nAla	Alan	Alan	Alan
Alex	xAle	Alex	Alex	Alex
Alpharetta	harettaAlp	arettaAlph	rettaAlpha	ettaAlphar
Amanda	ndaAma	daAman	aAmand	Amanda
Amber	erAmb	rAmbe	Amber	Amber
Amy	Amy	Amy	Amy	Amy
Andrea	reaAnd	eaAndr	aAndre	Andrea
Angeles	elesAng	lesAnge	esAngel	sAngele
Angie	ieAng	eAngi	Angie	Angie
Annette	etteAnn	tteAnne	teAnnet	eAnnett
Anya	aAny	Anya	Anya	Anya
Asya	aAsy	Asya	Asya	Asya
Atlanta	antaAtl	ntaAtla	taAtlan	aAtlant
Avery	ryAve	yAver	Avery	Avery
Avondale	ndaleAvo	daleAvon	aleAvond	leAvonda

Now look at the first two letters of each pivoted string. The reason for using two letters is that this gives us two bytes, or 16 bits, which is a common word size in many machines. We get the following granularities:

no pivot = 7 cases

pivot at position 4 = 15 cases

pivot at position 5 = 15 cases

pivot at position 6 = 13 cases

pivot at position 7 = 12 cases

Although not very scientific, it demonstrates the principle that words vary more toward the middle and end than toward the beginning. And it also demonstrates that a pivot position near the average length will usually be optimal or near-optimal.

You can also expect the database engine to have an upper length in bytes for an index structure. The system will maintain the sorted order in a primary index, but the table itself might be stored in any order.

To use the index to obtain a row in the indexed base table, the search engine finds the key value(s) in the first field of the index that match the search value(s), then uses the pointer in the second field to read the physical location where the corresponding row is located.

Since the index is smaller than the original table and it is in sorted order, searching it is fairly quick and easy compared to reading the entire table sequentially. The trade-off for faster search time is slower update, insert, and delete times because when a row in the base table changes, all the indexes also have to be changed. An old rule of thumb was that more than five indexes will give you too large a performance hit for a database doing heavy transaction processing, but you need to judge this for your particular situation.

Secondary indexes are made on nonunique columns in the base table and therefore must allow duplicate values. If there is a record in the index for every row in the base table, then the index is dense; if not, then the index is sparse. Using a secondary index is almost exactly like using a primary index.

A sparse index does not have a record for each row in the base table. Instead, the physical storage for the base table is kept in sorted order, so that the sparse index needs to only have the values(s) of the

first (or last) row on each physical page of storage. For example, if the first index entry is the name 'Adams' and the second entry is 'Brown', then we know that 'Adcock' is on the first page of storage, if such a row exists at all. If you need to think of a physical analog to this method, look at a large unabridged dictionary with a notch or thumb index in its side.

The database engine can then fetch the page to which the index points, bring it into main storage, and perform a search on it. Obviously, a table can have only one such index, since it is impossible to sort a physical file more than one way.

However, you might want to ask if your particular implementation can split out the original columns of a compound index. That is, if you had declared

```
CREATE INDEX Xfoo3 ON Foobar (a, b, c);
```

does the database engine know how to use this index to simulate other indexes based on the front part of the concatenation, so that in effect you have "virtual indexes" like this:

```
CREATE INDEX Xfoo2 ON Foobar (a, b);
CREATE INDEX Xfoo1 ON Foobar (a);
```

5.2 Tree-Structured Indexes

Now, let's go back to the original unindexed table for a minute. If the table is kept in sorted order, then I use a binary search to locate a particular row or a subset of the rows based on the columns used for sorting. If you have (n) rows in the table, then the binary search will take at most $\log_2(n)$ disk reads to locate a row. The trade-off will be in keeping the tables in order when new rows are inserted. The only thing SQL-92 says about an inherent sorting order is that all NULLs must sort together either before or after all values.

Just as we viewed the simple index as putting a linear search into a persistent data structure, we can think of a tree-structured index as putting a binary (or n-ary) search into a persistent data structure.

There are many different types of tree-structured indexes, but they all have the same motivation. As a simple index gets bigger and bigger, it starts to require longer and longer search times. The obvious solution is to build a sparse index on the original index, in which the sparse index points to the pages of the original index. Then build another sparse index on the index to the original index, and so forth. When this process stops, we have a tree structure that starts at a root node. In practice, all these layers of indexing are kept in one file and not in separate files. Furthermore, the levels of the tree are arranged so that they can be searched by reading the index file sequentially.

The most popular family of tree-structured indexes in database products is the B-trees. They have the best average performance in most real situations and are well understood. In most B-trees, each node of the tree has four or five pointers to other nodes.

Instead of going into the details for an actual B-tree, let me explain the concepts with the much simpler binary search tree as an index. In a binary tree, each node has two points; the left pointer points to the node for all the values that are less than the value of this node, and the right pointer points to the node for all the values that are greater than or equal to the value of this node (see Fig. 5.1).

The worst-case search involves searching four levels of this tree, with an average of 2.3 reads. The original table had a worst case of 16 reads, with an average of 8 reads per search.

Now if you add a node for 23, you would first look for it by going down the tree following the path (21, 22, 30, 28, 23).

5.3 Covering Indexes

An index can answer an `EXISTS()` or `NOT EXISTS()` predicate for its base table immediately if the column(s) upon which it is built are used in the query. The index will contain at least one occurrence of a value of that attribute if and only if it is in the base table. A dense index is also able to perform aggregate functions on its base table column(s) quickly because all of the value(s) are physically contiguous in the index file. The base table itself is never read.

A sparse index can sometimes answer an `EXISTS()` predicate for its base table value(s) immediately, if you got lucky and asked for one of the indexed values. But most of the time, you have to read the base table itself.

Fig. 5.1

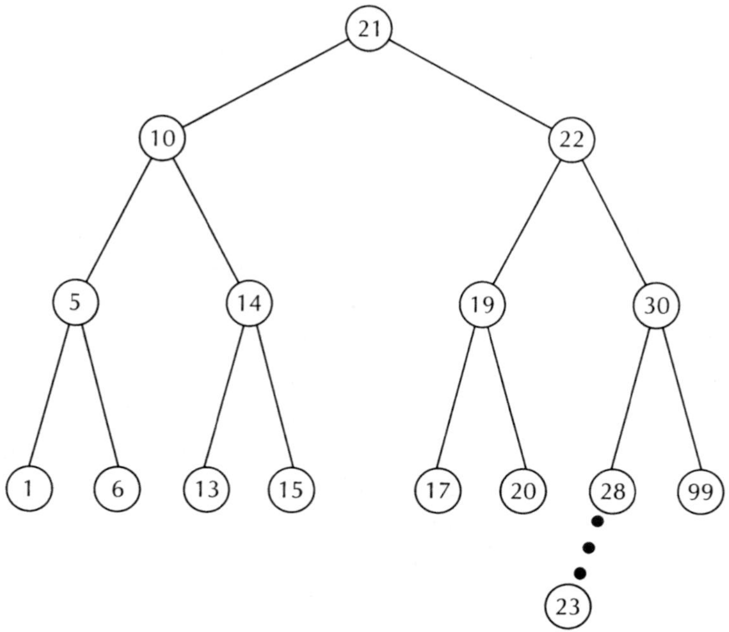

A covering index is an index built on multiple columns that are all used in a query. A common example is (last name, first name) in tables that deal with people. Queries might be done on just the last name, but the display is almost always of both first and last name together. In this case, you are depending on the indexing method to allow the first part of the index, the last name, to be searched so that the first name will be brought along with it.

5.4 Hashing Functions

Hashing functions take a very different approach to finding data. These functions take the value of the column(s) used in the search and convert them into a number that maps into an address in physical data storage. This mapping is handled with an internal data structure called a hash table (not to be confused with a database table!), which has the actual disk address in it.

The disk drive can then be positioned directly to that physical address and read the data. Since doing calculations inside the main processor is many orders of magnitude faster than reading a disk drive, hashing is the fastest possible access method for a single row in a table. The trade-off is "speed for space," as it often is in computing.

Unify's Unify SQL and Centura's (nee Gupta) SQLBase products both have a `CREATE HASH` command. Teradata uses proprietary hashing algorithms to handle large sets of data. But even outside the world of computers, hashing is not as exotic as you might think. If you place a telephone order with Sears or J. C. Penney, they will ask you the last two digits of your telephone number. That is their hashing function for converting your name into a two-digit number (if you have no telephone, then they use 00).

The trick in a `CREATE HASH` command is how good the hashing algorithm is. A good hashing algorithm will minimize collisions (also called "hash clash")—where two different input values hash to the same location in the hash table. A good algorithm also will minimize the size of the hash table. The hash table is often bigger than an index, but it will work faster because it can locate a tuple in fewer execution cycles on average.

While there are many exotic hashing functions, the major algorithms fall into four types:

1. *Digit selection:* Pick a subset of the bits, characters, or digits that make up the input value. That is what the telephone number trick we just discussed does.

2. *Division:* The input is treated as a number that is divided by a second number, and the remainder is used as the hash. That is, Hash(x) = MOD (x, m). It is important that m be a prime number for reasons we will discuss later.

3. *Multiplication:* The input is treated as a number that is multiplied by a second number, and then a subset of digits (usually in the middle of the result) is used as the hash. The second number can be derived from the first number, such as by squaring it. If you are going to use a constant, c, then it is important that c be an irrational number represented to a large number of decimal places.

4. *Folding:* The digits of the input value are broken into subsets and then added to each other. This method is usually used with division or multiplication.

5.4.1 Uniform Hashing Function

The reason that Sears and J. C. Penney use the last two digits of your telephone number as their hashing function is that if they filed orders by the last names, they would get too many collisions in the *J* and *S* pigeonholes and not fill up the *Q* and *X* pigeonholes. Telephone numbers tend to be uniformly distributed, unlike last names, which favor "Johnson" and "Smith" over "Quixby" and "Xavier" in English-speaking countries.

This property is called *uniform distribution*, or just uniformity for short. It will let us keep all the buckets the same size, and let us expect that they will fill at approximately the same rate. We will get to the problems with hash collisions shortly, but minimizing them is very important if you are going to get any speed out of this access method.

5.4.2 Perfect Hashing Function

A perfect hashing function is one that takes n distinct input values and assigns them to $n + k$ buckets, without any hash clash. Obviously, the input values cannot have duplicates. Such functions are hard to find unless you know all the possible input values in advance.

In the real world, we use imperfect hashing functions that have the property that several inputs map to the same result. This is called a "collision" or "hash clash," and it has to be resolved in some manner. To make this easier to understand, let's use what has to be the world's worst hashing function. Going back to the list of names used in the indexing examples, take the first three letters, assign each letter its position in the alphabet, and multiply this triplet. Take that result modulus five and get an answer between 0 and 4 as the hash:

```
Hash ('Adrian')     = MOD ((1 * 4 * 18), 5)  = 2
Hash ('Adrienne')   = MOD ((1 * 4 * 18), 5)  = 2
Hash ('Al')         = MOD ((1 * 12 * 0), 5)  = 0
```

Hash ('Alan')	= MOD ((1 * 12 * 1), 5)	= 2
Hash ('Alex')	= MOD ((1 * 12 * 5), 5)	= 0
Hash ('Alpharetta')	= MOD ((1 * 12 * 16), 5)	= 2
Hash ('Amanda')	= MOD ((1 * 13 * 1), 5)	= 3
Hash ('Amber')	= MOD ((1 * 13 * 2), 5)	= 1
Hash ('Amy')	= MOD ((1 * 13 * 25), 5)	= 0
Hash ('Andrea')	= MOD ((1 * 14 * 4), 5)	= 1
Hash ('Angeles')	= MOD ((1 * 14 * 7), 5)	= 3
Hash ('Angie')	= MOD ((1 * 14 * 7), 5)	= 3
Hash ('Annette')	= MOD ((1 * 14 * 14), 5)	= 1
Hash ('Anya')	= MOD ((1 * 14 * 25), 5)	= 0
Hash ('Asya')	= MOD ((1 * 19 * 25), 5)	= 0
Hash ('Atlanta')	= MOD ((1 * 20 * 12), 5)	= 0
Hash ('Avery')	= MOD ((1 * 22 * 5), 5)	= 0
Hash ('Avondale')	= MOD ((1 * 22 * 15), 5)	= 0

Each of the results, 0 through 4, identifies a numbered hash bucket. If we assume that the original bucket size was five addresses, then we can see that bucket #4 is empty, buckets #1 and #3 have three addresses apiece, and bucket #2 has four. The problem is that bucket #0 is running over, with a total of eight addresses. How do we handle the extra three addresses?

There are two basic approaches to handling overflow. The first is to set up an overflow area that will catch the extra addresses from the buckets. There are many variations on this basic approach, so I will not go into details.

The second method is to rehash the input value again, using a second hashing function. If this second hashing also leads to a collision, then a third hashing is done and so forth until a bucket is found or the system crashes. These hashing functions are usually related to each other in some way so that the *n*th attempt is not likely to skew toward the previous attempts. Perhaps they share a basic formula that is modified slightly each time a rehashing is performed.

Notice that, in general, you have no idea that a probe (the term for using a hashing function to locate data) has failed until you attempt it with a disk read. This is why it is important to minimize hash clash.

5.4.3 Minimal Hashing Functions

You might have noticed that given five buckets of five addresses each, we have preallocated 25 units of storage for 18 addresses. If the set of values being hashed is exactly equal to the total size of the buckets allocated, this is called a minimal hashing function. Just as a perfect hashing function is difficult to discover, so is a minimal hashing function. In practice, most hashing schemes try to allow a "little extra room" so that they do not have to worry about bucket overflow. The "little extra room" can actually be fairly large as a percentage of the total storage allocation, perhaps as much as 50% over the minimal amount needed. This is a classic trade-off of "speed for space" since a larger bucket size costs you main storage, but avoids collisions.

Is it possible for an algorithm to be both minimal and perfect? That is, is it possible for a hashing function to take the *n* values and put them into exactly *n* contiguous buckets, without any hash clash? Yes, it is! R. J. Cichelli (1980) presented such a minimal perfect hashing algorithm. His example used the reserved words in standard Pascal. But he admitted that in some cases his algorithm could fail. Thomas J. Sager (1985) then developed an improved perfect hashing algorithm, based on Cichelli's original work, that covers the cases where that one fails.

5.4.4 Multicolumn Hashing Functions

Just as indexes usually handle multiple columns by concatenating the values together to make bit patterns, so do hashing functions.

It would be nice if a hashing function had the same properties that an index on multiple columns has, namely, that you could search for one of the columns in the set. This would imply that there is an accumulation operator, ⊕, with the property that

$$\text{Hash}(c_1 \,||\, c_2 \,||\, \ldots \,||\, c_N) = \text{Hash}(c_1) \oplus \text{Hash}(c_2) \oplus \ldots \oplus \text{Hash}(c_N)$$

Unfortunately, that property is not enough for a good hashing function. For example, if the accumulation operator is addition, and there is an additive relationship among the columns involved (i.e., $c_1 = c_2 + c_3$, or whatever), you will get a lot of collisions. A good accumulation operator should also have these properties:

- *Nonadditive:* $\text{Hash}(c_1) \oplus \text{Hash}(c_2) <> \text{Hash}(c_1) + \text{Hash}(c_2)$
- *Commutative:* $\text{Hash}(c_1) \oplus \text{Hash}(c_2) = \text{Hash}(c_2) \oplus \text{Hash}(c_1)$
- *Associative:* $(\text{Hash}(c_1) \oplus \text{Hash}(c_2)) \oplus \text{Hash}(c_3) = \text{Hash}(c_1) \oplus (\text{Hash}(c_2) \oplus \text{Hash}(c_3))$

These properties are possible, and in fact exist in Teradata's proprietary hashing algorithms.

5.5 Inverted Files

In the early days of relational databases, the consensus of ignorance was that an implementation would have to use fully inverted files. In an inverted file, every column in a table has an index on it. It is called an inverted file structure because the columns become files. Imagine a file where each record starts with a value, followed by a list of row numbers. This means that you could then throw away the tables, since they can be reconstructed from the row numbers. `NULL` values have a natural representation by not having a row number in the record for them.

Inserting, updating, and deleting on a fully indexed table is very slow, since many different index files have to be searched to find and reconstruct each row. But searching for groups of rows with a common value is very fast. Doing a `GROUP BY` operation is a matter of merging the index files for the columns in the grouping and seeing what records overlap.

The Model 204 database is based on the inverted file model. It is very good at picking a small subset from a much larger set and has been favored by the U.S. government for certain agencies, such as the CIA and NSA.

5.6 Bit Vector Indexes

FoxPro and Nucleus are two examples of products that use different bitmap schemes, but they have some basic features in common. Imagine an array with table row numbers or pointers on its columns and values for that column on its rows.

If a table row has that value in that position, then the bit is set; if not, the bit is zeroed. A search is done by doing bitwise ANDs, ORs, and NOTs on the bit vectors.

This might be easier to explain with an example of the technique. Assume we have Chris Date's Parts table, which has columns for the attributes "color" and "weight."

Parts

pno	pname	color	weight	city	
'p1'	'Nut'	'Red'	12	'London'	—Physical row #3
'p2'	'Bolt'	'Green'	17	'Paris'	—Physical row #4
'p3'	'Cam'	'Blue'	12	'Paris'	—Physical row #7
'p4'	'Screw'	'Red'	14	'London'	—Physical row #9
'p5'	'Cam'	'Blue'	12	'Paris'	—Physical row #11
'p6'	'Cog'	'Red'	19	'London'	—Physical row #10

The bit indexes are built by using the physical row and the values of the attributes in an array, thus:

INDEX Parts (color)

Rows	1	2	3	4	5	6	7	8	9	10	11
Blue	0	0	0	0	0	0	1	0	0	0	1
Green	0	0	0	1	0	0	0	0	0	0	0
Red	0	0	1	0	0	0	0	0	1	1	0

INDEX Parts (weight)

Rows	1	2	3	4	5	6	7	8	9	10	11
12	0	0	1	0	0	0	1	0	0	0	1
17	0	0	0	1	0	0	0	0	0	0	0
14	0	0	0	0	0	0	0	0	1	0	0
19	0	0	0	0	0	0	0	0	0	1	0

To find a part that weighs 12 units and is red, you would perform a bitwise AND to get a new bit vector as the answer:

Red	0	0	1	0	0	0	0	0	1	1	0
AND											
12	0	0	1	0	0	0	1	0	0	0	1
Answer	0	0	1	0	0	0	0	0	0	0	0

To find a part that weighs 12 units or is colored red, you would perform a bitwise OR and get a new bit vector as the answer:

Red	0	0	1	0	0	0	0	0	1	1	0
OR											
12	0	0	1	0	0	0	1	0	0	0	1
Answer	0	0	1	0	0	0	1	0	1	1	0

Searches become a combination of bitwise operators on the indexes before any physical access to the table is done.

The Nucleus database engine, which stores the database as bit vectors in dedicated hardware, uses a sophisticated version of this approach. Imagine a spreadsheet that represents an attribute with values represented by the columns and entities by the rows. To show that a given entity has a particular value, just insert a bit into the spreadsheet at the proper coordinate. If you look across the columns, you see the values for each entity. If you look down the rows, you see the entities for each value of the attribute. You can then represent each attribute as a vector by going to three dimensions, and so forth.

The final effect is automatic full indexing on all columns, and a database that is smaller than the original flat files from which it was built. Since all relational operations are done on long bit vectors with special hardware, the speed of a query can be several orders of magnitude faster than a conventional system. It also lets you ask queries such as "What kind of red things do we have in the database?" that cannot be easily asked in other relational databases.

The trade-off is in reconstructing the data in a conventional format, since the engine returns the query result a column at a time, instead of a row at a time. Certain statistical distributions of values over attributes also perform better than others in the Nucleus engine.

5.7 Mixed Access Methods

No single access method will work best for all tables. Access depends too much on the current data and the current queries made against it to generalize. The MARIS project at Grady Hospital in Atlanta, Georgia, under Henry Camp used a unique self-adjusting access method to get around this problem. This system was a medical research statistical database used by doctors. It would track the queries being made against its files and analyze them. Then during downtime, it would pick the best access method from a set of about a dozen options and reorganize the files. Users never saw this, but they would notice that response time was better after letting the system rest.

This is one of the great strengths of SQL: a change in the database access method does not invalidate all the code that has already been written. But it is also a problem because we become like the detached mathematician in that classic joke: we tend to shove the mere details of performance onto our engineer and physicist, in the form of the database administrator. We should worry about them, too, because that is where our next meal is coming from.

5.8 Multiple Table Access Structures

Declarative referential integrity (DRI) in SQL-92 gives vendors the opportunity to add structures that in effect "prejoin" the tables involved in a foreign key relationship. This might be easier to see with a small example. Let's create two tables and note where they physically store their rows:

```
CREATE TABLE Foo
(fookey INTEGER NOT NULL PRIMARY KEY,
 description CHAR(25) NOT NULL);
```

```
INSERT INTO Foo
VALUES (1, 'This is one'),        — goes to address 101
       (2, 'This is two');        — goes to address 102

CREATE TABLE Bar
(barkey CHAR(2) NOT NULL PRIMARY KEY,
 foo_stuff INTEGER NOT NULL
           REFERENCES Foo(fookey),
 . . . );

INSERT INTO Bar
VALUES  ('a1', 1),    — goes to address 4001
        ('a2', 1),    — goes to address 4007
        ('b1', 2),    — goes to address 4011
        ('b2', 2);    — goes to address 4003
```

In this case, Foo is the *referenced* table and bar is the *referencing* table. Those words are easy to confuse when you just hear them, so I stressed the relationship.

The table Foo needs a primary index to enforce the uniqueness of its primary key, fookey. Likewise, the table Bar needs a primary index to enforce the uniqueness of its primary key, barkey.

However, I can also construct something like this, with pointers to the rows in both tables:

value	referenced row address	referencing row address
1	101	4001
1	101	4007
2	102	4003
2	102	4011

The join between Foo and Bar is already done! I can also check the uniqueness of the key in the referenced table column by seeing that each value has one and only one address in the referenced column of this table. Furthermore, I could add more "referencing row" columns to the table and extend this structure easily. In a real database engine,

the system would probably not use a table, but would opt for a linked list of some sort.

Sybase's SQL Anywhere (nee WATCOM SQL) has an internal structure like the one we have discussed. They allow the programmer to specify what they call a "key join" that will force the database engine to use the structure.

Oracle has used a method somewhat like this, which they call "clustering" (not to be confused with an index type in Sybase products). They break multiple tables into subsets and put pieces of the tables on the same page of physical storage. The usual method is to keep rows from one table on the same page of physical storage. However, if two or more tables are frequently joined together, having the related rows read into main storage at the same time can increase performance greatly.

The other alternative to a multitable indexing structure is to keep a primary index on the PRIMARY KEY in the referenced table and then decide if you wish to have an index on the FOREIGN KEY in the referencing table.

Let's first examine the approach where there is no index on the FOREIGN KEY. An INSERT INTO or UPDATE of a referencing table will lock the referenced table's PRIMARY KEY index. This will prevent the reference from being changed by another user and will give this user access to allowable values for the FOREIGN KEY.

Likewise, an UPDATE or DELETE FROM of a row in the referenced table will need to lock the referencing table. This is not as obvious as the first case. The rules are that when a transaction is rolled back, the database is returned to the state it was in before the transaction began *and* that this state be consistent with all constraints. Assume that table T1 references table T2 on column x:

```
CREATE TABLE T2
(x INTEGER NOT NULL PRIMARY KEY,
 stuff CHAR(15) NOT NULL);

INSERT INTO T2 (x, stuff)
VALUES (1, 'this is one'),
       (2, 'this is two'),
       (3, 'this is three');
```

```
CREATE TABLE T1
(keycol_1 CHAR(2) NOT NULL PRIMARY KEY,
 x INTEGER NOT NULL REFERENCES T2(x),
 . . .);

INSERT INTO T1 (keycol_1, x)
VALUES ('a', 1),
       ('b', 2),
       ('c', 3);
```

Now play this series of changes to the database without locking:

User A: `INSERT INTO T1 VALUES (4, 'this is four');`

User B: `UPDATE T2 SET x = 4 WHERE keycol_1 = 'a';`

User B: `COMMIT WORK;`

User A: `ROLLBACK WORK;`

User B got a phantom match that was never committed by user A, but user B did a COMMIT on his work anyway. User A has to be able to do a ROLLBACK on her own work, but if she does, then the database will have constraint violations. User A cannot do a ROLLBACK on someone else's work. DRI is now out of synch, and the database is corrupted.

Now let's examine the approach where there is an index on the FOREIGN KEY. An UPDATE to the PRIMARY KEY column(s) or a DELETE FROM on the referenced table will both lock the referencing table's FOREIGN KEY index. Again, the UPDATE or DELETE FROM statement on the referenced table would have to wait until the transaction accessing the referencing table and causing the locks on the referencing table's FOREIGN KEY index has committed.

In both cases, an INSERT INTO statement on the referencing table does not affect the referenced table directly, but you have to ensure that you are not caught by changes to the referenced table.

In the case of referential actions, you must assume that there will be an action in the referencing table, so it is very handy to have established locks and gotten access to both tables.

5.9 An Informal Survey of Database Products

I conducted an informal survey of the indexing methods used in actual database products in 1998 on my CompuServe forum. Here is the simple list of questions I asked and the answers I got back:

1. Do users have the ability to specify the type of indexing used in their declaration?
2. How many kinds of indexing are available?
3. If there is a "`CREATE INDEX Xfoo3 ON Foobar(a,b,c)`", will the system use the part of the index when a subset of the columns appears in the query? Or do you have to also declare "`CREATE INDEX Xfoo2 ON Foobar(a,b)`"?
4. Is there a difference between "`CREATE INDEX XfooA ON Foobar(a,b)`" and "`CREATE INDEX XfooB ON Foobar(b,a)`"? If so, what?
5. Can the product detect and avoid redundant indexing? That is, given "`CREATE INDEX Xfoo1 ON Foobar(a,b)`" and "`CREATE INDEX Xfoo2 ON Foobar(a,b)`", does it know that `Xfoo2` is a waste of time and resources and warn you or refuse to do it ?

Oracle 7 and 8:

1. Yes.
2. Hashing (via clusters), B-trees, bitmapping, inverted lists, and other options including index-organized tables (the table itself is a B-tree index).
3. Can use the combinations (a,b) and (a), but not (b,c) or (c) from the index.
4. There is a difference. The columns are concatenated for index generation.
5. Yes. This is error "`ORA -01408: such column list already indexed`".

R:Base v4.5+ through v6.1:

1. Indexes are built with B-trees. The user can specify what is indexed and whether to use hashed data. The command syntax is

```
CREATE INDEX indexname ON <table> (<column list>) [UNIQUE]
[ASC | DESC] [SIZE <integer>] [CASE]
```

   R:Base indexes can be built with data from up to eight columns.

   UNIQUE constrains the column definition to unique values. CASE preserves case sensitivity in text values. ASC|DESC specifies index order, default is ASCENDING. SIZE n specifies how many text characters to preserve in the index data.

   (*Note:* A PRIMARY KEY or a UNIQUE constraint in the table definition will automatically generate an index. A FOREIGN KEY will generate an index by default, but the user has the option not to index a FOREIGN KEY.)

2. Only B-trees. The data may be hashed as specified.
3. Can use the combinations (a,b) and (a), but not (b,c) or (c) from the index.
4. There is a difference. The columns are concatenated for index generation.
5. Yes. Refuses with message "Error duplicate indexes are not allowed".

Centura's SQLBase:

1. Specified by the user as CREATE INDEX or CREATE CLUSTERED HASHED.
2. Hashed and B-tree indexes.
3. Any subset of columns.
4. No.
5. No.

Oracle RDB, v7.0:

1. Yes.
2. `HASHED ORDERED`, `HASHED SCATTERED`, `SORTED RANKED`, and `SORTED`. Sorted indexes (whether ranked or not) are B-trees. In addition, it is possible to use one of the indexes on a table so as to place the data in a nearly clustered fashion.
3. For hashed indexes, the answer is no; each query must use all the columns in the index in order to benefit from the index.

   For sorted indexes, the answer is yes; it will use the index provided that the query is specifying the first key column.

   In the case presented, both indexes have the same first column, so it is unnecessary to declare `Xfoo2`, provided that `Xfoo1` is `SORTED`.
4. Yes, for B-trees. No, for hashed indexes.
5. No.

Numeric Data

NUMBERS ARE EVEN trickier than people think. Most people do not make a distinction between a number and a numeral in everyday conversation. A number is the abstraction represented by the numeral, which is a written symbol. Roman numerals, Chinese numerals, Mayan numerals, and hundreds of other systems have existed to represent numbers in a written form so that they could be recorded or manipulated.

The Hindu-Arabic numerals and place value notation have proven so useful that they have replaced all other systems today. Because Hindu-Arabic numerals are on every computer printer, are universally understood, and linguistically neutral, we use Hindu-Arabic numerals for many different purposes, and we are not always clear about the distinctions. The three uses for the numerals in a database are for cardinal numbers, ordinal numbers, and tag numbers.

6.1 Tag Numbers or Absolute Scales

A tag number or absolute scale is simply a list of names for the elements of a set. The advantage of using numbers instead of names is that a computer can store them more compactly, they are

linguistically neutral, and there are simple rules for generating an unlimited number of such values. This is discussed in some detail in chapter 12, so we will not go into that concept here.

6.2 Cardinal Numbers

The usual definition of a cardinal number is something that represents a quantity or magnitude (0, 1, 2, 3, . . .), and it is what people mean most of the time when they think of numbers. Or I should say that it is what they think they are thinking of when they think of numbers. The truth is that people do not like to think of quantity as an abstraction; they want to think of a quantity of *something*, even if the nature of the something is abstract.

Children learn to count with sets of uniform objects—rods, plastic chips, or whatever. Gradually, they learn to mentally remove attributes from the objects until all that is left is the number of the set. For example, a child will tell you that he has five red plastic squares, three plastic yellow circles, and two red plastic triangles. When you ask him, "How many red things do you have?" it is a mental effort for him to remove the shape and see only the color. When you ask for the number of plastic shapes, the child must construct a still more abstract set, until eventually the child thinks of pure numbers not attached to any objects.

Two sets have the same cardinality if you can do a one-to-one mapping from one set to the other and vice versa. One set is less than another if there is a one-to-one mapping from it onto a subset of the other set, but no one-to-one mapping in the other direction.

Mappings are the basis for counting in Stone Age cultures. For example, Hottentots have only the words for "one," "two," "three," and "many" in their language. To compare two sets of things, say, beads and animal skins, they place one bead on one skin. When they have finished doing this, they know if there are more beads, more skins, or if they are equal in number. In fact, they will know to some extent how much greater one set is than the other (e.g., "one more bead than skins" or "many more beads than skins").

Natural numbers are integers greater than zero, while zero is a cardinal number because it can represent the number of elements in a set, namely, the empty set.

6.3 Ordinal Numbers

An ordinal number represents a position (first, second, third, . . .) in an ordering. An ordinal number also implies a corresponding cardinal number (1, 2, 3, . . .), but knowing the ordinal position does not tell you about the cardinality of the set; in English, knowing that you are the third person in line for a promotion does not tell you how many candidates there were for the job.

This question of position leads to another debate: Is there such a thing as the zeroth ordinal number? Computer people like to have a zeroth position because it is handy in implementing data structures with relative positioning. For example, in the C language and many versions of BASIC, arrays start with element zero. This allows the compiler to locate an array element with the displacement formula:

<base address> + (<element size> * <array index>)

The idea of a zeroth ordinal number is a mild mathematical heresy. To be in the zeroth position in a queue is to have arrived in the serving line before the first person in the line.

6.4 Arithmetic with Ordinals, Cardinals, and Tags

Arithmetic differs with ordinals, cardinals, and tag numbers. Moreover, you often have to convert from one type of number to another, and this is a source of errors.

Consider consecutively numbered theater tickets. If I buy the block of seats from two to eight, I have 8 – 2 + 1 = 7 tickets, not 8 – 2 = 6 tickets. Arithmetic with tag numbers makes no sense at all—you cannot add flight #123 to flight #456 to get flight #579.

6.5 Computer Representations

The SQL standard has a very wide range of numeric types. The idea is that any host language can find an SQL numeric type that matches one of its own.

You will also find some vendor extensions in the datatypes, the most common of which is `MONEY`. This is really a `DECIMAL` or `NUMERIC` datatype, which also accepts and displays currency symbols in input and output.

6.5.1 Exact Numeric Representations

An exact numeric value has a precision, P, and a scale, S. The precision is a positive integer that determines the number of significant digits in a particular radix (formerly called a base of a number system). The standard says the radix can be either binary or decimal, so you need to know what your implementation does. The scale is a nonnegative integer that tells you how many decimal places the number has. An integer has a scale of zero. The datatypes `NUMERIC`, `DECIMAL`, `INTEGER`, and `SMALLINT` are exact numeric types. `DECIMAL(P,S)` can also be written `DEC(P,S)`, and `INTEGER` can be abbreviated `INT`. For example, `DECIMAL(8,2)` could be used to hold the number 123456.78, which has eight significant digits and two decimal places.

The difference between `NUMERIC` and `DECIMAL` is subtle. `NUMERIC` specifies the exact precision and scale to be used. `DECIMAL` specifies the exact scale, but the precision is implementation-defined to be equal to or greater than the specified value.

Mainframe Cobol programmers can think of `NUMERIC` as a Cobol picture numeric type, whereas `DECIMAL` is like a BCD. Personal-computer programmers these days probably have not seen anything like this. You may find that many small-machine SQLs do not support `NUMERIC` or `DECIMAL` because the programmers do not want to have Cobol-style math routines that operate on character strings or internal decimal representations.

6.5.2 Approximate Numeric Representations versus the Continuum

A point is defined in mathematics as an indivisible position in some space. A continuum is defined as being made up of parts that are always further divisible. If you look at a line in geometry (or a number in analysis, an event in time, etc.), we speak about geometric points on a geometric line (or a number on the number line, a duration in time, etc.), and we regard the line (numbers, time) as being a continuum. Look at the number line: clearly, given a segment on the number line, such as (1, 2), we can always further divide the segment into smaller segments, such as (1.1, 1.5) and repeat this process forever. The same thing applies to geometric lines and to time.

This leads to a paradox. If a continuum is infinitely divisible, how can an indivisible point be a part of a continuum?

I will let you worry about this and tell you that we do not worry about it in real databases. Instead, we have learned to live with approximate numeric values and a certain amount of inherent error.

An approximate numeric value consists of a mantissa and an exponent. The mantissa is a signed numeric value; the exponent is a signed integer that specifies the magnitude of the mantissa. An approximate numeric value has a precision. The precision is a positive integer that specifies the number of significant binary digits in the mantissa. The value of an approximate numeric value is the mantissa multiplied by 10 to the exponent. `FLOAT(P)`, `REAL`, and `DOUBLE PRECISION` are the approximate numeric types. There is a subtle difference between `FLOAT(P)`, which has a binary precision equal to or greater than the value given, and `REAL`, which has an implementation-defined precision.

Most SQL implementations use the floating-point hardware in their machines rather than trying to provide a special floating-point package for approximate numeric datatypes.

In recent years, IEEE has introduced a floating-point hardware standard that can work quite well with SQL. As more vendors adopt it, query results will become more uniform across platforms. Please note that uniform results are not the same thing as correct results.

The IEEE floating-point standard also has certain bit configurations, called NaNs (Not a Number), to represent overflow, underflow, errors, and missing values; these provide a way to implement `NULL`s as well as to capture errors.

6.6 Zero, NULL, and Math

The `NULL` in SQL is only one way of handling missing values. The usual description of `NULL`s is that they represent currently unknown values that might be replaced later with real values when we know something. This actually covers a lot of territory. The Interim Report 75-02-08 to the ANSI X3 (SPARC Study Group 1975) showed 14 different kinds of incomplete data that could appear as the results of operations or as attribute values. They included such things as

arithmetic underflow and overflow, division by zero, string truncation, raising zero to the zeroth power, and other computational errors, as well as missing or unknown values.

The NULL is a global creature, not belonging to any particular datatype but able to replace any of their values. This makes arithmetic a bit easier to define. You have to specifically forbid NULLs in a column by declaring the column with a NOT NULL constraint. But in SQL-92 you can use the CAST function to declare a specific datatype for a NULL, such as CAST (NULL AS INTEGER). The reason for this convention is practical: it lets you pass information about how to create a column to the database engine.

6.6.1 Division

The basic rule for math with NULLs is that they propagate. An arithmetic operation with a NULL will return a NULL. That makes sense; if a NULL is a missing value, then you cannot determine the results of a calculation with it. However, the expression (NULL/0) is not consistent in SQL implementations. The first thought is that a division by zero should return an error; if NULL is a true missing value, there is no value to which it can resolve and make that expression valid. However, almost all SQL implementations propagate the NULL and do not even issue a warning about division by zero when it appears as a constant in an expression. A non-NULL value divided by zero will cause a runtime error, however.

I asked people on CompuServe to try a short series of SQL commands on different products for me. The DDL was very simple:

```
CREATE TABLE GotNull (test INTEGER);
INSERT INTO GotNull VALUES (NULL);

CREATE TABLE GotOne (test INTEGER);
INSERT INTO GotOne VALUES (1);

CREATE TABLE GotZero (test INTEGER);
INSERT INTO GotZero VALUES (0);
```

They sent me the results of three queries that had explicit divisions by zero in them. This is as opposed to a runtime division by zero.

```
SELECT test / 0 FROM GotNull;
SELECT test / 0 FROM GotOne;
SELECT test / 0 FROM GotZero;
```

The results are shown below:

product	NULL/0	1/0	0/0
Ingres 6.4/03	NULL	float point error, no data	float point error, no data
Oracle 6.0	NULL	divide by 0 error, no data	divide by 0 error, no data
Progress 6.2	NULL	NULL	NULL
R:Base 4.0a	NULL	divide by 0 error, no data	divide by 0 error, no data
Rdb	truncation at runtime divide by 0	truncation at runtime divide by 0	truncation at runtime divide by 0
SQL Server 4.2	NULL	NULL & error	NULL & error
SQLBase 5.1.	NULL	plus infinity	plus infinity
Sybase 4.9	NULL	NULL & error	NULL & error
WATCOM SQL	NULL	NULL	NULL
XDB 2.41	NULL	divide by 0 error, no data	divide by 0 error, no data

Everyone agrees that NULLs always propagate, but everyone has another opinion on division by zero. Getting a floating-point error from integer math is a violation of the standard, as is not giving a division-by-zero error. The positive infinity in SQLBase is also a floating-point number that is all nines. Other products return NULLs for all three cases, but with and without error messages.

Since host languages do not support NULLs, the programmer can elect either to replace them with another value that is expressible in the host language or to use indicator variables to signal the host program to take special actions for them.

SQL-92 specifies two functions, NULLIF() and the related COALESCE(), that can be used to replace expressions with NULL and vice versa. These functions are not yet present in most SQL implementations, but you will often find something like them.

6.6.2 Powers

While SQL-92 is weak on arithmetic functions, a common vendor extension is to add powers to the usual four-function arithmetic, sometimes as a function call or as an infixed operator.

This leaves us with another question: What does 0^0 equal? The schools of thought are that this expression is equal to one, that it is undefined, or that it is an "indeterminate form," meaning that in some cases it has one value, and in other cases it has another.

The discussion goes back to Euler, who argued for $0^0 = 1$ since $x^0 = 1$ for x <> 0, and this convention would avoid making zero an exception. This is enforced by the fact that the limit of x^x as $x \rightarrow 0$ is 1. The function $f(x,y) = x^y$ cannot be assigned values for x and y that will make it continuous at (0,0), since the limit along the line $x = 0$ is 0, and the limit along the line $y = 0$ is 1.

However, you can argue that giving a value to a function with an essential discontinuity at a point, such as x^y at (0,0), should not be done.

Donald Knuth thought that we must define $x^0 = 1$ for all x, if the binomial theorem is to be valid when $x = 0$, $y = 0$, and/or $x = -y$. This is an important theorem, but the function 0^x is quite unimportant.

6.7 Rounding and Truncating

Rounding and truncation have the effect of changing the granularity of an approximate number. You have to state how many places in the higher magnitudes you are going to retain in the rounded or truncated number.

Truncation cuts off the lower magnitudes of the number. Truncation is usually defined as truncation toward zero; this means that 1.5 would truncate to 1, and –1.5 would truncate to –1. This is not true for all programming languages; everyone agrees on truncation toward zero for the positive numbers, but you will find that negative numbers may truncate away from zero (i.e., –1.5 would truncate to –2).

Rounding changes the lower magnitudes of the number to a higher magnitude. There are two major types of rounding in computer programming.

6.7.1 Applied to Individual Values

The scientific method looks at the digit in the position to be removed. If this digit is 0, 1, 2, 3, or 4, you drop it and leave the higher-order digit to its left unchanged. If the digit is 5, 6, 7, 8, or 9, you drop it and increment the digit to its left.

This method works with single numbers and is popular with scientists because the results will be only as precise as the worst measurement made in the set.

6.7.2 Applied to Sets of Values

The commercial method looks at the digit to be removed. If this digit is 0, 1, 2, 3, or 4, you drop it and leave the digit to its left unchanged. If the digit is 6, 7, 8, or 9, you drop it and increment the digit to its left. However, when the digit is 5, you want to have a rule that will round up about half the time. One rule is to look at the digit to the left: if it is odd, then leave it unchanged; if it is even, increment it. There are other versions of the decision rule, but they all try to make the rounding error as small as possible.

This method works well with a large set of numbers and is popular with bankers because it reduces the total rounding error in the entire set of numbers.

6.8 Addition and Summation Are Different

In SQL (and in other database languages before SQL), there has been a function for doing a summation—the `SUM()` aggregate function in SQL. You would think that it would be well understood. In June 1996 the DBMS forum on CompuServe had a lively thread (aka "religious war") on this topic. It seems that summation is not actually all that easy in a relational database model or in mathematics.

Addition and summation are closely related, but not quite the same thing. This is weird at first, but it is important. Addition is a binary operator shown by a plus sign (+) that has some algebraic properties like associativity and commutativity that we learned in high school algebra. You cannot add just one thing, and you cannot add an infinite set of things; the operation is simply not defined for either situation.

Summation is an aggregate or set valued function that has an index set. The index set can be finite or infinite, but it cannot be empty. Each term in the summation has a one-to-one relationship with each element of the index set. If you are old enough, you might remember the "big sigma" (Σ) notation from college math. The index is the subscript variable, usually i, j, or k, which ranges from a starting value to an ending value. If you wished the summation process to continue forever, you used the special symbol "infinity," shown as ∞.

The old figure-eight "infinity" notation is procedural and not functional in nature. That is, you can think of it as hiding a small computer program that looks like this:

```
BEGIN
DECLARE <datatype> sum;
sum := 0;
WHILE <index> < = <finish>
DO BEGIN
   <index> := <start>;
   sum := sum + <terms> [<index>];
   <index> := <index> + 1;
   END;
RETURN sum;
END;
```

When the <finish> value is infinity, you can think of the program as equivalent to

```
BEGIN
DECLARE <datatype> sum;
sum := 0;
WHILE TRUE  - the result of (<index> < = INFINITY)
DO BEGIN
   <index> := <start>;
   sum := sum + <terms> [<index>];
   <index> := <index> + 1;
   END;
RETURN sum;
END;
```

Every programmer knows that this has some problems because we have all written an endless loop sometime in our careers. The answer in mathematics was to invent limits. The idea of a limit is that there is a value that the sum never exceeds, no matter how many iterations of the loop are executed.

What happens if the index set is empty? Let's modify the original program again:

```
BEGIN
DECLARE <datatype> sum;
sum := 0;
WHILE FALSE — the result of having no <index> values
DO BEGIN
   <index> := <start>;
   sum := sum + <terms> [<index>];
   <index> := <index> + 1;
   END;
RETURN sum;
END;
```

Thus, we might conclude that the summation of an empty set is zero, the identity element of addition. I am going to make several arguments that this is not the case.

First, the zero we are getting back from this program is something we created that was never in the original set of terms. There is a philosophical principle *ab nullo, ex nullo* ("from nothing, comes nothing"), which makes me feel uncomfortable about creating a result, zero, from an empty set.

Second, look at another way to write the procedural code, given an array called `<terms>` and the `<start>` and `<finish>` values:

```
BEGIN
DECLARE <datatype> sum;
sum := <terms> [<start>];
DO BEGIN
   <index> := <index> + 1;
   sum := sum + <terms> [<index>];
   END;
```

```
UNTIL <index> < <finish>
RETURN sum;
END;
```

In this code, no values that were not in the original summation are created. The empty set would result in a program failure on the first executable statement because the initial term is not defined.

The third argument needs a little background about what has happened in mathematics since 1820. The current preferred notation is to show the index set as a set; you can see examples of this notation in Graham, Knuth, and Patashnik (1994). There is no ordering as there was in the old notation.

A set is a completed, bound thing that can be treated as a unit of operation in itself. You cannot do this with a process. Without going into the painful details, mathematical proofs are completely different in those two cases. Since the relational model and SQL are both set-oriented languages, I will argue that the set-oriented approach is better than a procedural one.

It is much easier to specify a complicated set using logical predicates than it is to write a complicated index expression inside a term. For example, I can simply define an index to be the set of all prime numbers, but nobody knows how to write an expression that will generate the series of all prime numbers.

Let's create a simple Personnel table having just the employee's name and their salary and their lottery winnings in each row. The lottery tickets are the employee retirement plan at this company; we knew it would come to this someday. We will model lottery tickets that have not been checked against the winning numbers as a NULL. The value of the lottery winnings will probably resolve to zero, but you don't know that yet.

```
CREATE TABLE Personnel
(emp CHAR (5) NOT NULL PRIMARY KEY,
 salary DECIMAL (8,2) NOT NULL,
 lottery DECIMAL (8,2));
INSERT INTO Personnel VALUES ('Tom', 500.00, 200.00);
INSERT INTO Personnel VALUES ('Dick', 700.00, NULL);
INSERT INTO Personnel VALUES ('Harry', 800.00, NULL);
```

Now consider the straightforward statement to report the payroll:

```
SELECT emp, (salary + lottery) AS total_pay
 FROM Personnel;
```

Result

emp	total_pay
'Tom'	700.00
'Dick'	NULL
'Harry'	NULL

The total_pay will be a NULL for all employees who have not scratched their tickets yet because NULLs propagate in addition in SQL. This is probably not what you wanted as a result.

Now look at the SUM( ) aggregate function in the statement

```
SELECT emp, SUM(salary + lottery) AS total_pay
  FROM Personnel
 GROUP BY emp;
```

Again, when I come to an employee, the addition in the parameter of the SUM( ) function will be NULL, but the SUM( ) in SQL is really the summation of all known values in its parameter set, and the function will drop that computed NULL from the total. So I get the same results, which feels right because we were grouping on the PRIMARY KEY for the table. Grouping a table on a key will put one row into each group, so in effect this query is like putting parentheses around the terms in a summation. We don't want it to change the results.

Now, look at this query:

```
SELECT emp,
  (SUM(salary) + SUM(lottery)) AS total_pay
 FROM Personnel
 GROUP BY emp;
```

Result

emp	total_pay
'Tom'	700.00
'Dick'	700.00
'Harry'	800.00

We have a different result from the previous queries. This happens because the index set for the SUM( ) aggregate function in SQL is all the non-NULL values in the parameter expression.

What if you actually wanted SUM( ) to behave like "+" and propagate NULLs? Just use a fancy expression to see if any NULLs exist in your expression, thus:

```
SELECT emp,
      (SUM(salary + lottery)
         * CASE WHEN COUNT (*) = COUNT (salary + lottery)
                THEN 1
                ELSE NULL END) AS total_pay
 FROM Personnel
 GROUP BY emp;
```

What should the result of a SUM( ) function on an empty table be? Chris Date has advocated returning a zero, using the procedural code argument (Date 1993a). The zero result has also been a convention in mathematics since the days of the procedural notation. This convention made writing the indexing expressions easier in many cases because the zero would not matter in the final result, but was known to be formally incorrect (see Graham, Knuth, and Patashnik 1994, chapter 2, p. 62, exercise 1, for other situations where the sequence is not well defined). Zero is called the identity element for addition—if you add zero to something, it does not change.

The reason that it is incorrect is that there is nothing in the index set to create a term in the summation. There is no one-to-one mapping from the index to the terms of the summation. Fourier did not have the idea of sets, empty or otherwise, much less mappings, in 1820 when he invented this notation. He was doing quite well to come up with a procedural approach.

The argument for the NULL result was that there is a fundamental difference between an empty set and a nonempty set that totals to zero. Imagine that you are guarding a flock of sheep, and I ask you how many sheep jumped over the fence into the other field; you answer, "Zero." Now I ask you how many pink elephants jumped over the fence into the other field; would you answer, "Zero," or "I ain't got no elephants! I'm a shepherd, not a circus!" to that question? Hence, summation ought to return an error message, a NULL, or some indication that a set is missing.

Another property that is hard to understand at first is how GROUP BY works on an empty set. Consider this query:

```
SELECT SUM(x) FROM Empty;
```

which returns a result table with a single NULL. Now, consider

```
SELECT SUM(x) FROM Empty GROUP BY x;
```

which returns an empty set result table (and probably a warning that no rows exist or satisfy the specified search criteria). The reason for the empty set result is that the GROUP BY partitions the table. A partitioning cuts the original set into a collection of subsets such that

1. All the subsets are nonempty.
2. The intersection of any distinct pair of the subsets is empty.
3. The union of all the subsets together forms the original set.

You can get this definition from any book on elementary set theory (see, for example, Gordon and Hindman 1975). In English, this is slicing up a pizza in a mathematical disguise—but not quite.

A grouped table is constructed from the subsets by reducing each subset to one row. You are now working at a different level of abstraction and thus with a different kind of element. Since an empty set (table) has no partitions, the GROUP BY cannot return a value. You could make an argument for an error message, but the convention in SQL is to return an empty result.

Another SQL convention is that if you get an empty result set in a subquery expression, it becomes a NULL. Since it is an expression, it

has to return something that can fit into a column in the result table. Since there is no value that would make sense, we use a NULL.

Partitions and summation act like parentheses and addition—they are both ways of grouping operands that do not affect the operator. That is, just as ((a + b) + (c + d)) = ((a) + (b) + (c) + (d)), so does

```
SELECT SUM(x)
FROM (SELECT SUM(x) FROM Pizza WHERE a = x1
      UNION
      SELECT SUM(x) FROM Pizza WHERE a = x2
      . . .
      UNION
      SELECT SUM(x) FROM Pizza WHERE a = xN)
      AS subtotal(x);
```

Another important property is that if you partition a table on a key, each group has exactly one element. The result of the SUM( ) for each singleton group is the single element in it. This is also the convention in the "big sigma" (Σ) notation when it has a single term and another reason why addition, a binary operator, is not the same as summation, an n-ary operator ($n > 0$).

Set theory has the Axiom of Choice, which can be expressed in many different ways. Without being too formal about it, the Axiom of Choice says that if you have a partitioning of a set, even an infinite set, you can choose an element from each partition and build a new set from it.

This leads to a fundamental problem: if you believe that the summation over an empty set is zero, then what partition(s) of the original set does that sum map into? Oops, there are no partitions for the mapping. This violates the Axiom of Choice and destroys induction and a bunch of other nice things in the system.

6.9 Exotic Numbers

That covers the basic datatypes that are used in most database products, but there are also other numbers that are not often used. However, many databases today have user-defined datatypes and are extensible, so these numbers might be found in packages that can be added to an existing database engine.

6.9.1 Fractions

Fractions of the form "a b/c" are found as an option on many pocket calculators. The calculations are usually handled internally as a binary number, then are converted to and from the fractional notation for display and input. The alternative is to have the fractional datatype package manipulate them as three component data elements.

Fractions are handy for input when the data is given that way, as for example, English measurements with fractional inches. But frankly, with the SI (metric) system in universal use, there is less and less need for this datatype. You are better off using a decimal fraction shown with as many decimal places as you need.

6.9.2 Repeating Decimals

The mathematical notation for repeating decimals is to put a bar over the digits in the decimal fraction that form the repeating group. The convention for the bar in a computer package might well be a bracket around the repeating group. You will also see the use of an ellipsis after the group in some books, following the convention used for a series or sequence.

Unlike fractions, there is no way to convert repeating decimals into floating-point or fixed decimal numbers without some loss. Instead, the datatype arithmetic package has to manipulate them as symbols. The rules are not the same as those for fractions kept as an internal datatype. This is one of many places where infinite and finite things behave differently. Consider this statement:

$1.0 = 0.99\ldots$

Proof: Let

$x = 0.99\ldots$

Therefore

$(10 * x) = 9.99\ldots$

Subtract x from both sides:

$(10 * x) - x = 9.99\ldots - 0.99\ldots$

Therefore

$$9 * x = 9$$
$$x = 1$$

There is no floating-point rounding error in this calculation.

6.9.3 Infinite Precision Numbers

SuperBase (*www.superbase.com*) is one of the few database products that has "infinite" precision numbers. This actually means that the database will store as many digits as you key into the column. This extension is quite handy for data encryption techniques that use large prime numbers (100 digits or more). Simple arithmetic is fairly fast, but you do lose a little speed in the complex functions.

6.9.4 Complex Numbers

Complex numbers are used only in scientific and engineering calculations. There are DataBlades for Informix that implement complex numbers, and DB2 and Oracle probably have similar packages for their products.

The real problem with complex numbers in a database is in the host language. Only Fortran and PL/I have native complex datatypes. In Fortran, the variables must be declared to be single or double precision complex numbers. In PL/I, a calculation can promote a real number to a complex number unexpectedly.

6.9.5 Coordinates

Coordinates are an important datatype for Geographical Information Systems (GIS) or geobases. Within this general datatype, you will find Cartesian coordinates, polar coordinates, longitude and latitude, and other spatial systems for three dimensions. Since geobases and spatial data are a separate topic in itself, with emerging standards, I will not discuss them in this book.

Data Warehousing Scope and Scale Enhanced

IBM First to Deliver Integrated Database Multimedia Extenders

SANTA CLARA, CA, June 12, 1996 . . . IBM today announced the delivery of three new multimedia database extenders for its award-winning DATABASE 2* (DB2*). They support complex multimedia data types, including video, audio, and images enabling customers to use their DB2 relational database to store, search, manipulate and distribute multimedia objects, ranging from voice annotations and photographs to music and video.

IBM also announced the general availability of the enhanced DB2 Parallel Edition* (DB2 PE*) Version 1.2. This new version offers customers up to a 50 percent improvement in query performance and a 200 percent increase in on-line transaction processing speed over previous versions.

The new video, audio, and image multimedia extenders are available for DB2 for AIX*, DB2 for OS/2* and DB2 for Windows NT** clients and servers, with additional client support for Windows 3.1** and Windows 95**. In addition, the DB2 Text Extender, shipping since January on the AIX platform, is now available on DB2 for OS/2 and DB2 for Windows NT.

"When you want a database that provides both robustness and powerful multimedia support, as well as scalability and openness, there is only one to consider—DB2," said Janet Perna, director, Database Technology, IBM Software Group. "DB2, with its object relational support, will allow customers to extract the maximum value from one of their most important business assets, data."

Seamless Integration

IBM's multimedia DB2 Extenders provide seamless integration between complex data types and more traditional structured data. Using the relational extenders, a retailer, for example, could obtain inventory items from a number of different suppliers, then store and search his inventory by attributes such as type of material, cost, style, manufacturer, as well as by image attributes such as color and texture.

"IBM is the only major database vendor shipping any integral object functionality and is way ahead of the game in adding support for complex data types," said Herb Edelstein, president, Two Crows Corporation.

"Southern New England Telephone (SNET) views the future of the Internet as a powerful platform for conducting commerce," said Tim Roy, project manager, SNET. News services such as Interactive Yellow Pages are a natural step towards this goal for SNET, our advertisers and our user community. We have been working closely with IBM to develop the solution. We expect the advanced search capabilities and the flexibility afforded by the DB2 Extenders to enhance the usability of our product to the user and, therefore, provide value to the advertiser."

Improved Warehousing Functionality, Performance

The enhancements to DB2 Parallel Edition Version 1.2 are in both functionality and performance. A new Outer Join capability enables simpler SQL coding for commonly used business queries, delivering fast, responsive queries against the database. Additionally, the new SQL Case statement functionality enables developers to create more powerful SQL applications with less repetitive programming.

"We are very pleased with IBM's responsive delivery of DB2 PE Version 1.2 and the partnership we have with IBM," said Sully McConnell, director of technology, Aetna Health Insurance. "In particular, Outer Join and Case expressions will prove extremely useful for us. Our application performance will get even better and our productivity will increase because of less SQL coding required."

*Indicates trademark or registered trademark of International Business Machines Corporation.
**Indicates trademark or registered trademark of respective companies.

Character String Data

CHARACTERS ARE REPRESENTED internally in the computer as bits, and there are several different systems for doing this. Almost all schemes use fixed-length bit strings. The three most common ones in the computer trade are ASCII, EBCDIC, and Unicode.

ASCII (American Standard Code for Information Interchange) is defined in the ISO 464 standard. It uses a byte (8 bits) for each character and is most popular on smaller machines.

EBCDIC (Expanded Binary Coded Digital Information Code) was developed by IBM by expanding the old Hollerith punch card codes. It also uses a byte (8 bits) for each character. EBCDIC is fading out of use in favor of ASCII and Unicode.

These two code sets are what is usually meant by `CHAR` and `VARCHAR` data in database products because they are what the hardware is built to handle. There is a difference in both the characters represented and their collation order, which can cause problems when moving data from one to the other.

7.1 National Character Sets

Unicode is what is usually meant by `NATIONAL CHARACTER` and `VARYING NATIONAL CHARACTER` datatypes in SQL-92, but this standard represents alphabets, syllabaries, and ideograms.

An alphabet is a system of characters in which each symbol has a single sound associated with it. The most common alphabets in use today are Roman, Greek, Arabic, and Cyrillic.

A syllabary is a system of characters in which each symbol has a single syllable associated with it. The most common syllabaries in use today are Korean and part of Japanese.

An ideogram system uses characters in which each symbol is a single word. Chinese is the only such system in use today; however, other Asian languages borrow from the Chinese character set.

Unicode is the result of an international effort to represent all the alphabets, syllabaries, and written language character sets in the world, including a few dead languages. Unicode uses 2 bytes per character (16 bits) and introduces a complete set of terminology for character names.

A "code point" is the place of a character within an encoding scheme. Thus, in all ISO standard character sets, uppercase A is encoded as 0 × 41 in hexadecimal—65 in decimal—so we say that A's code point is 65.

7.1.1 Latin-1

All the characters we are talking about do occur in Latin-1, that is, in the ISO 8859-1 standard. That is not to say that ISO 8859-1 is in general use throughout these areas. In fact, Germans could use any of the ISO 8859-x "Latin" character sets without requiring translation, since the code points for sharp *S* and diaeresised characters tend to be invariant in those sets. There is no plan to remove either accents or sharp *S*s in German. There is no need, since modern character sets do not restrict us to simple Latin letters (which is what I presume was meant by the term "Roman-1").

7.1.2 German Collation

There are three ways to sort German. Two of them are based on official German (DIN) standards; the third is an Austrian variant, which (apparently) is not standard but common. In all cases the sharp *S* sorts with *SS*. The differences have to do with vowels containing diaereses.

DIN-1 Standard

Ä sorts with *A*, *Ö* sorts with *O*, *Ü* sorts with *U*. This is the recommended standard for dictionaries, book indexes, or any lists of words. It is also used for name lists in Switzerland (for example, the Zurich phone book).

DIN-2 Standard

Ä sorts with *AE*, *Ö* sorts with *OE*, *Ü* sorts with *UE*. This is the recommended standard for phone books in Germany (but not in Austria or Switzerland), voter lists, or any lists of names (for example, the Hamburg phone book).

Austrian Nonstandard

Ä sorts after *A* (i.e., as a separate letter between *A* and *B*), *Ö* sorts after *O*, *Ü* sorts after *U*. This method seems to occur only in Austria (for example, the Vienna phone book).

Above is the primary sort order. The secondary (tie-breaking) rules are complex, but only one actually has an effect in everyday sorting: words with accents or ligatures appear after words without accents or ligatures.

7.1.3 Scandinavian

There are some special difficulties with the minor languages (Icelandic, Greenlandic, Lappish, Nynorsk). But the main ones—Danish, Norwegian, Swedish, Finnish—can be handled together if we employ a "unioned" set of letters. This combined Nordic set takes all the additional characters in all four of the languages and puts them in a common order. Thus, some of these rules are not necessary in Swedish (because the characters do not appear there), but in that case the rule does no harm.

The last letters of the unioned alphabet are:

U	(Danish)	(Norwegian)	(Swedish)	(Finnish)
V	(Danish)	(Norwegian)	(Swedish)	(Finnish)
W	(Danish)	(Norwegian)	(Swedish)	(Finnish)

X	(Danish)	(Norwegian)	(Swedish)	(Finnish)	
Y	(Danish)	(Norwegian)	(Swedish)	(Finnish)	
Ü = Y	(Danish)				obsolete?
Z	(Danish)	(Norwegian)	(Swedish)	(Finnish)	
Æ	(Danish)	(Norwegian)			
Ø	(Danish)	(Norwegian)			
Å	(Danish)	(Norwegian)	(Swedish)		
AA = *Å*	(Danish)				
Ä			(Swedish)	(Finnish)	
Ö			(Swedish)	(Finnish)	

There is a story that, when ISO 646 ("ASCII") was being considered, the six code points after *Z* were filled with unimportant characters (i.e., [\] ^ _). This was done specifically so that Scandinavians could add their own characters as above. Subsequently, Nordic union collation has been used by several compiler vendors including Microsoft. Again, the full (SIS) specification has many more rules; the ones here suffice only for most everyday purposes.

7.1.4 SQL-92 Collations

SQL-92 made a valiant attempt to allow for character set and collation specification, but some shortcomings were apparent:

1. Every collation should be associated with a particular character set, so if you have 10 collations and 10 character sets you need 10 × 10 = 100 `COLLATION` objects. (Luckily, you can force a different interpretation here.)
2. The fold functions `UPPER` and `LOWER` don't work for accented letters.
3. The qualification rules for collation and character set identifiers are different from the qualification rules for other objects such as tables.
4. At bottom, all essential decisions are left up to the implementor anyway. Though we here (at Ocelot) pride ourselves on

our degree of SQL-92 standardization, we had to stretch the rules considerably to implement character sets and collations in a practical way. The current SQL3 draft has many more options for CREATE COLLATION, but none of them work for German or Scandinavian languages.

7.2 Problems of String Equality

Different programming languages handle string comparisons differently. Some comparisons ignore the case of the letters; others do not. Some programming languages truncate the longer string; others pad the shorter string with blanks; and some refuse to compare strings of unequal length at all. For example, the Xbase family truncates, while SQL pads the shorter string, so 'Smith' and 'Smithsonian' are equal in Xbase and not equal in SQL.

Library filing conventions for matching strings perform semantic transforms on words, expanding abbreviations, replacing ligatures with letter pairs, and even accepting different spellings and transliterations from one alphabet to another.

7.3 Length

SQL-92 has three versions of the string length function: one that counts the bytes (octets), one that counts bits involved, and one that counts characters. Remember that with Unicode, it is no longer true that one character uses exactly one byte to represent it. The syntax is

```
<length expression> ::=
     <char length expression>
   | <octet length expression>
   | <bit length expression>
<char length expression> ::=
   { CHAR_LENGTH | CHARACTER_LENGTH }
       <left paren> <string value expression> <right paren>
<octet length expression> ::=
   OCTET_LENGTH <left paren> <string value expression> <right
   paren>
<bit length expression> ::=
   BIT_LENGTH <left paren> <string value expression> <right paren>
```

In practice, almost all SQL products implement only the CHAR_LENGTH() function, usually using the name LENGTH().

7.3.1 Empty String versus NULL String

In the ANSI/ISO SQL-92 standard, the NULL string is not the same as the empty string. The usual rule that "NULLs propagate" holds for strings as well as for numerics and temporal expressions.

Another interesting property is that CHAR(n) and VARCHAR(n) datatypes have to have $n \geq= 1$ and cannot be less than one character in length. Even a VARCHAR(n) string has to be padded out with blanks to bring it to the minimum length of one. Thus, any attempt to store an empty string in an SQL column will be padded out with a blank, and you cannot store an empty string in SQL.

Having said this, you will find that some versions of Access and Oracle have done it all wrong and do not handle the empty string properly.

7.4 Concatenation

Concatenation is the operation of attaching one string to another to produce a result. The SQL-92 standard notation is taken from the PL/I programming language and consists of the infixed operator ||. Since the rest of the string operators are function calls, concatenation has the lowest precedence. Interestingly, when the ANSI X3H2 Database Standards Committee (now the NCITS H2 Database Standards Committee) was debating this choice of notations, it was opposed by Phil Shaw, who was the IBM representative at the time, the company that invented PL/I.

The rules for concatenation of NULL, empty, and nonempty strings can be summarized in these examples:

```
'abc' || 'def' produces 'abcdef'
'abc' || NULL  produces NULL
'abc' || ''    produces 'abc'
```

7.5 Position

This function appears in many different forms in programming languages, but it is always designed to find the starting position of one string (usually called the *search string*) inside another string (usually called the *target string*). The other most common name for this function is `INDEX()`, but that conflicts with the use of the same word for an index on a table. You will also see `LOCATE()` and other words used.

The SQL-92 syntax for this function is

```
POSITION (<character value expression>
      IN <character value expression>)
```

and it returns a nonnegative integer result, with a zero meaning that the search string was not a substring of the target string. SQL has to add some more rules to handle `NULL`s and national character sets.

The rules for `POSITION` can be summarized in these examples:

```
POSITION ('abc' IN 'abcdef') produces  1
POSITION ('xyz' IN 'abcdef') produces  0
POSITION ('' IN 'abcdef')    produces  0
POSITION ('abc' IN '')       produces  0
POSITION ('' IN '')          produces  0
POSITION ('abc' IN NULL)     produces  NULL
POSITION (NULL IN 'abcdef')  produces  NULL
POSITION (NULL IN NULL)      produces  NULL
```

Let me state the rules more formally:

1. The character repertoires of the two `<character value expression>`s have to be the same. You cannot look for a Korean word inside an English sentence. This leads to some problems when you have text with a mixture of languages in it. The Japanese often use Latin characters with their native characters.

2. If either the target or the search string is `NULL`, then the result is `NULL`. Since the general principle in SQL is that "`NULL`s

propagate," this is no surprise. However, a large number of people think that a NULL and an empty string are the same thing and thus get confused.

3. If the search string has a length of 0 and the target string is not NULL, then the result is always 1.
4. If the search string is equal to an identical-length substring of contiguous characters in the target, then the result is 1 greater than the number of characters within the target string preceding the start of the first such substring. In English, this is the starting position of the first matching substring, counting from 1.
5. Otherwise, the result is 0.

7.6 Reversal

String reversal is a common vendor extension to standard SQL and appears in other programming languages. It reverses the order of the characters in the input string as its result.

7.7 Pattern Matching

SQL-92 has only one pattern matching predicate, the [NOT] LIKE Boolean operator. In simple terms, it uses three character strings to determine whether or not a character string "matches" a given "pattern" (also a character string). The characters '%' (percent) and '_' (underscore) have special meanings when they occur in the pattern. The optional third argument is a character string containing exactly one character, known as the "escape character," for use when a percent or underscore is required in the pattern without its special meaning. The syntax is

```
<like predicate> ::=
<match value> [NOT] LIKE <pattern>
[ESCAPE <escape character>]
```

The basic rules have no great surprises. The strings have to be in the same character repertoires. The expression "<match value> NOT LIKE <pattern>" is equivalent to "NOT (<match value> LIKE

<pattern>)", as with other SQL constructs. If any of the three strings is NULL, then the predicate returns an UNKNOWN as its result.

Formally defining LIKE is trickier than it would seem at first.

The ESCAPE character, if it is given, must be followed by a percent sign, an underscore, or another ESCAPE character. The leading ESCAPE character is ignored for matching purposes, and the character that follows it is now treated as a character literal with no special properties.

Each "unescaped" underscore character represents an arbitrary character specifier, and each "unescaped" percent character represents an arbitrary string specifier. All other characters represent whatever character they are.

If <match value> and <pattern> are character strings whose lengths are variable and if the lengths of both <match value> and <pattern> are 0, then the result is TRUE.

The LIKE predicate is TRUE if there exists a partitioning of <match value> into substrings such that

1. You can map every unescaped single character substring in the pattern to the same character in the <match value>.
2. You can map every underscore wildcard character substring in the pattern to some character in the <match value>.
3. You can map every percent wildcard character substring in the pattern to a substring of zero or more contiguous characters in the <match value>.
4. The number of substrings in the partition of <match value> is equal to the number of substring specifiers in <pattern>.
5. Otherwise, the result is FALSE.

The following examples might help make this clear:

'Book' LIKE 'B%k' is TRUE

because 'B' maps to 'B',
'%' maps to 'oo',
'k' maps to 'k'.

```
'Block' LIKE 'B%k' is TRUE
        because 'B' maps to 'B',
                '%' maps to 'loc',
                'k' maps to 'k'.
'Bk' LIKE 'B%k' is TRUE
        because 'B' maps to 'B',
                '%' maps to '',
                'k' maps to 'k'.
'Blob' LIKE 'B%k' is FALSE
        because 'k' has nothing to map onto.
'20% off' LIKE '20/% %' ESCAPE '/' is TRUE
        because '2' maps to '2',
                '0' maps to '0',
                '%' maps to '%' via an escape,
                ' ' maps to ' ',
                '%' maps to 'off'.
```

7.8 Language as Data

Natural language and text retrieval are topics in themselves. There are attempts to put text retrieval into SQL and to standardize this in SQL3. But a text retrieval problem is best handled with a text retrieval tool.

7.8.1 Syntax versus Semantics

Syntax has to do with the formal rules for manipulating the symbols in a language. Semantics has to do with what those symbols mean. The classic example of the difference is that "Green dreams swim furiously" is a perfectly good English sentence from a syntactic viewpoint. It has a subject ("green dreams") and a predicate ("swim furiously"), with an adjective ("green") and an adverb ("furiously") thrown in. The only problem is that it makes no sense.

Now consider "This sentence no verb." It is not a sentence at all because it lacks a verb. Yet that violation of syntax did not interfere with the meaning, did it?

You can program syntax into a computer for formal languages, but it is harder to handle the syntax of natural languages and virtually impossible to fully handle the semantics of natural languages.

This is part of what makes text searching so hard. The legal textbase service WestLaw offers free access to law students and has some search problems having to do with basic first-year U.S. constitutional law. They have found that students typically miss about 20% of what they needed and that 20% of what they did retrieve is unneeded.

Obviously, the best situation is where syntax supports semantics. This is why your English teacher was trying to get you to use good grammar.

7.8.2 Computerized Language Translation

Computerized language translation is still not fully realized, but it is much closer than at any other time. Much of the progress is due to cheap storage and faster processors and not as much to new and clever algorithms. It helps if you can find millions of sentence pattern templates almost instantly and match them to your input sentence. One proposal for using the supercomputers left over from the Cold War era is to put them on the Internet to do "really intense computing" for whomever logs on. Under the heading of "really intense computing" is natural language translation. The idea is that you would upload a text file, wait, and download emails with the text translated into several different languages. This would let you conduct chat rooms across language barriers, translate your website into another language, and so forth. Currently, there is a website in Korea that translates English language websites into Korean and posts them for Korean browsers.

Logic and Databases

LOGIC IN WESTERN thought started with Aristotle and pretty much stayed there until the 1800s. Logic was considered a branch of philosophy until George Boole wrote his book *An Investigation of the Laws of Thought* in 1854 and introduced the idea of "mathematical logic" as opposed to "philosophical logic." In the Dewey decimal system, logic still appears under philosophy, although virtually no philosophical logic books have been written in over a century. In this chapter, we will look at several different systems of logic that can be used with a database.

Although most programmers think that they know formal logic from writing program control structures (i.e., IF-THEN-ELSE, WHILE-DO, and so forth) in procedural languages, their logic skills are really pretty weak, and they do not realize how much they depend on the temporal aspect of their languages to hide what would have to be complex declarative statements.

This is the big difference: logic in an SQL database is declarative, while logic in a procedural programming language is for sequential control. That is, SQL's logic makes a general descriptive statement about the state of the data, while logic in a procedural programming language makes decisions about actions to be taken on one unit of data at a time, not a whole set.

In theory, anything that can be written in a procedural language (i.e., finite deterministic automata) can be written in a nonprocedural language (i.e., primitive recursive functions). I will give you the names of two formal systems in case you want to research the topic yourself, but I have to warn you that it is a lot of mathematics. The proof that finite automata and recursive functions are equivalent does not say how complex the nonprocedural code will be, however.

8.1 Boolean or Two-Valued Logic

George Boole's contribution was a system of logic derived from algebra in which there were only two constants—one meant TRUE and zero meant FALSE. The multiplication and addition operators were restricted to return only one or zero. Multiplication mapped to logical conjunction (the AND operator) and addition mapped to logical disjunction (the OR operator). The unary minus could not be used as logical negation, so Boole first used $(1 - x)$ to represent "NOT x" in his notation and later replaced it with a bar over the letter that represented a proposition. It took some time before people realized that you should be using other symbols for Boolean algebra and invented the modern notations.

Almost a century later, people built binary computers based on Boolean algebra. It is not too surprising that early programming languages that were designed much closer to the physical hardware had Boolean logic in them.

Fortran has a `LOGICAL` datatype, the Algol family (Algol, Pascal, Modula, etc.) has a `BOOLEAN` datatype, and the C family has direct access to machine-level bit operators. But SQL does not have a logical datatype of any sort. This deficiency seems a bit strange to procedural language programmers who miss being able to store the results of a logical operation in a local variable or a field in a file. But if you look at most actual programs, the logical variables are seldom used at all and are almost never stored in files in procedural languages.

The man most responsible for the renewed importance of logic in programming is Edsger Dijkstra, the father of structured programming and formal correctness proofs for programs.

8.2 Multivalued Logic

As David McGoveran has pointed out, technically speaking SQL does not have a system of logic. The formal definition of the SQL-92 language refers to "<search condition>" and "<predicate>" and defines the results of the logical operators with lookup tables. A system of formal logic needs to have rules of deduction or inference in addition to operators and logical terms. Although this deficiency might be lost on the nonmathematician, it is important. It is the difference between having algebraic laws and doing all your math with lookup tables.

But there is another problem with SQL. A `NULL` cannot be compared to another `NULL` or to a value with what Dr. Codd called a theta operator and what programmers call a comparison operator (equal, not equal, less than, greater than, and so forth). This results in a three-valued logic, which has an `UNKNOWN` value in addition to `TRUE` and `FALSE`.

Most programmers do not easily think in three values. If I execute

```
SELECT * FROM SomeTable WHERE SomeColumn = 2;
```

and then execute

```
SELECT * FROM SomeTable WHERE SomeColumn <> 2;
```

I expect to see all the rows of SomeTable between these two queries. This is what would happen in a traditional programming language. But in SQL, I need to also execute

```
SELECT * FROM SomeTable WHERE SomeColumn IS NULL;
```

to see all the rows.

`UNKNOWN` is a logical value and not the same as a `NULL`, which is a data value. That is why you have to say `x IS [NOT] NULL` in SQL and not use `x = NULL` instead. Theta operators are expressions of the form *x* <comp op> *y*; when *x* or *y* or both are `NULL`, theta operators will return an `UNKNOWN` and not a `NULL`.

8.2.1 Łukasiewicz and *n*-Valued Logics

Jan Łukasiewicz, the logician responsible for Polish notation, developed generalized multivalued logics; SQL is based on one of his schemes. The SQL standard still refers to Boolean operators rather than Łukasiewiczian operators, but nobody has complained about it, for the same reason that Hewlett-Packard never tried to market a "reverse Łukasiewiczian notation" calculator.

Łukasiewicz defined his logic systems around generalized implication and negation operators, from which he derived the other operators.

In standard first-order logic, implication is shown with a double-tailed arrow, defined by the following lookup table:

a	b	a ⇒ b
TRUE	TRUE	TRUE
TRUE	FALSE	FALSE
FALSE	TRUE	TRUE
FALSE	FALSE	TRUE

This operator is equivalent to NOT(NOT a AND b) or to (a OR NOT b) in Boolean algebra. Unfortunately, SQL is based on three-valued logic, in which these definitions would translate directly into this lookup table:

a	b	a IMPLIES b
TRUE	TRUE	TRUE
TRUE	FALSE	FALSE
TRUE	UNKNOWN	TRUE
FALSE	TRUE	FALSE
FALSE	FALSE	TRUE
FALSE	UNKNOWN	UNKNOWN
UNKNOWN	TRUE	UNKNOWN
UNKNOWN	FALSE	TRUE
UNKNOWN	UNKNOWN	UNKNOWN

8.2.2 SQL-92 and Three-Valued Logic

Here are the tables for the basic three logical operators that come with SQL. It is comforting to see that they have the same truth tables as the three-valued system of Łukasiewicz.

x	NOT
TRUE	FALSE
UNKNOWN	UNKNOWN
FALSE	TRUE

AND	TRUE	UNKNOWN	FALSE
TRUE	TRUE	UNKNOWN	FALSE
UNKNOWN	UNKNOWN	UNKNOWN	FALSE
FALSE	FALSE	FALSE	FALSE

OR	TRUE	UNKNOWN	FALSE
TRUE	TRUE	TRUE	TRUE
UNKNOWN	TRUE	UNKNOWN	UNKNOWN
FALSE	TRUE	UNKNOWN	FALSE

SQL-92 added a new predicate of the form

```
<search condition> IS [NOT] TRUE | FALSE | UNKNOWN
```

which will let you map any combination of three-valued logic to the two Boolean values. For example, `((age < 18) AND (gender = 'Female')) IS NOT FALSE` will return `TRUE` if `(age IS NULL)` or `(gender IS NULL)` and the remaining condition is not `NULL`.

IS	TRUE	UNKNOWN	FALSE
TRUE	TRUE	FALSE	FALSE
UNKNOWN	FALSE	TRUE	FALSE
FALSE	FALSE	FALSE	TRUE

IS NOT	TRUE	UNKNOWN	FALSE
TRUE	FALSE	TRUE	TRUE
UNKNOWN	TRUE	FALSE	TRUE
FALSE	TRUE	TRUE	FALSE

This gives us a complete set of logical operators.

8.3 Fuzzy Sets, Logic, and Math

The chief danger to our philosophy, apart from laziness and wooliness, is scholasticism, the essence of which is treating what is vague as if it were precise and trying to fit it into an exact logical category.—Frank Plumpton Ramsey

In traditional naive set theory an element is a member of a set or it is not. This is very convenient for a model, but the real world does not always fall into such neat pigeonholes. We tend to think "with adjectives"—that is, someone does not fall neatly into the categories "young" or "not young," but rather they are "young," "very young," "not so young", and so forth. Aristotle recognized the fact that categories are not always clear but decided to ignore it in his first book on logic.

In naive set theory, membership is tested by a characteristic function. Characteristic functions take a logical expression as their parameter and then return either a zero (FALSE) or a one (TRUE). Authors have used the symbols δ, ω, and X for these functions. In SQL-92, we use a CASE expression instead, and characteristic functions are a handy programming trick.

Lofti Zedah introduced the idea of fuzzy sets in a paper in 1965. The characteristic functions of a fuzzy set return a value *between* zero and one, which is the degree of membership in the set. For example, we can probably agree that someone between 0 and 5 years of age is "very young" and would score 1.0, while someone over 40 would score a 0.0, but what value do you assign someone who is 6 to 10 years of age? Let's say that they get a 0.9 score, someone between 11 and 15 years of age gets a 0.8, and so forth until we cut off at 40 years of age.

There are subtle differences among multivalued logic, fuzzy sets, and probability models. Let me explain the differences informally.

In a probability model, a 0.8 probability of finding an orange in the refrigerator means that when I open up 10 refrigerators, I expect to find an orange in 8 of them. Each actual event resolves to a yes or no situation, and the prediction from the probability model is useful when I repeat the experiment over and over. But I do not know which 8 refrigerators will test out beforehand. Probability is a group characteristic model of the world.

In a multivalued logic model, the statement that "there is an orange in the refrigerator" is UNKNOWN means that I never open the refrigerator and find out if it is TRUE or FALSE. Logic is a single-case characteristic model of the world.

In a fuzzy model, a membership degree of 0.8 orange means that when I open the refrigerator I will find eight-tenths of an orange on the shelf. Fuzzy theory is based on single cases, but with degrees of membership rather than categories or aggregates. There are some experimental databases with fuzzy logic databases, but they are not commercial products yet.

There are other fuzzy operators, but I will not deal with them. (Bojadziev and Bojadziev 1995 gives a clear set of rules with examples that can be used to write SQL code.)

Exactly how a Fuzzy SQL engine should be built is a research topic in itself. The result of a query in SQL-92 is a multiset, so it would seem reasonable to get a fuzzy set or multiset back from Fuzzy SQL. Perhaps we need a clause that says . . . `WITH FUZZY LEVEL (n)`, where `(n BETWEEN 0.00 AND 1.00)`, that could be attached to `SELECT` statements and other statements that produce result sets.

8.3.1 Fuzzy Logic Operators

Fuzzy logic operators follow directly from the union and intersection operators from fuzzy sets. A predicate in fuzzy logic is treated as the characteristic function of a set. The degree of truth of a statement is between 0.0 (FALSE) and 1.0 (TRUE). The fuzzy logical operators can then be defined by arithmetic operators on those values. For example, given the statement p = "John is young," we need to have a

fuzzy set defined by the characteristic function "x is young" so we can see how John rates against it. Using $\delta(x)$ as the fuzzy characteristic function, we can define

$\delta(\text{NOT } p) = 1.0 - \delta(p)$ which means "John is not young"

$\delta(\text{VERY } p) = \delta(p)^2$ which means "John is very young"

$\delta(\text{FAIRLY } p) = \sqrt{\delta(p)}$ which means "John is fairly young"

The basic logical operators are then defined as

$p \text{ AND } q = \text{LEAST } (\delta(p), \delta(q))$

$p \text{ OR } q = \text{GREATEST } (\delta(p), \delta(q))$

To add fuzzy logic to an SQL database, you would need to extend the logic database engine to handle the new predicates. Since SQL uses comparison operators for predicates, much of the fuzzy logic would have to be applied after a set of fuzzy math operators were defined in the engine. This leads us to the next topic.

8.3.2 Fuzzy Math Operators

Fuzzy numbers usually are shown as intervals instead of points on the number line. They are always expressed as ". . . plus or minus something" or as "in the neighborhood of . . ." in English. The bad news is that they tend to get "fuzzier" as you do more operations on them.

Fuzzy numbers need at least a high value and a low value to limit them. After that, the number may include a statistical distribution over the interval defined by those limits. One common distribution is a simple triangle defined by a third number that represents the expected value of the number. Informally, the triangular fuzzy number $x = (2,3,4)$ would be "three plus or minus one", and the fuzzy number $y = (2,3,8)$ would be "close to three, but could be as high as eight and no lower than two" in English. The "regular number" a is defined by the triplet (a,a,a); there is nothing fuzzy about it.

Addition is based on adding the upper and lower limits of the two numbers involved. For example, given $a = (a_1,a_2,a_3)$ and $b = (b_1,b_2,b_3)$

where the triplets are the lower, middle, and upper values, respectively, we define

$$a + b = ((a_1 + b_1), (a_2 + b_2), (a_3 + b_3))$$

Notice that some of the laws of arithmetic still hold and some do not:

$$a + b = b + a$$
$$a + 0 = a$$
$$a + (b + c) = (a + b) + c$$

We can define

$$\text{neg}(a) = (-a_1,-a_2,-a_3)$$

and then define

$$a - b = a + \text{neg}(b)$$

but then

$$(a - b) + b <> a$$

The distance formula for triangular fuzzy numbers $a = (a_1,a_2,a_3)$ and $b = (b_1,b_2,b_3)$ is defined by the formula

$$\text{distance } (a,b) = 0.5 * \text{GREATEST } (\text{ABS}(a_1 - b_1), (\text{ABS}(a_2 - b_2) + \text{ABS}(a_3 - b_3)))$$

I will not go into the definitions of multiplication and division, as they are a bit complicated and not really the topic of this book (see Kaufmann and Gupta 1985 for more details).

8.4 Constructionist Logic

In an attempt to resolve certain paradoxes in formal mathematics, L. E. J. Bouwer and others invented a system of theorem proving that came to be known as Intuitionist or Constructivist mathematics. This school of thought holds that the only valid proofs are those that construct an entity that has the desired properties and rejects proofs

based on contradiction. That is, they reject what Aristotle called the law of the excluded middle. In their system:

$a \vee \neg a$ is not always TRUE

This has the result that other classical logical forms are also not axioms:

$\neg \neg a$ is not always TRUE

$\neg \forall x: p(x) \Rightarrow \exists x: \neg p(x)$ is not always TRUE

However, you can prove

$\neg \exists x: p(x) \Leftrightarrow \forall x: \neg p(x)$

The axioms are

$a \Rightarrow (b \Rightarrow a)$

$(a \Rightarrow (b \Rightarrow c)) \Rightarrow ((a \Rightarrow b) \Rightarrow (a \Rightarrow c))$

$a \Rightarrow (b \Rightarrow (a \wedge b))$

$(a \wedge b) \Rightarrow a$

$(a \wedge b) \Rightarrow b$

$a \Rightarrow (a \vee b)$

$b \Rightarrow (a \vee b)$

$(a \Rightarrow c) \Rightarrow ((b \Rightarrow c) \Rightarrow (a \vee b \Rightarrow c))$

$(a \Rightarrow b) \Rightarrow ((a \Rightarrow \neg b) \Rightarrow \neg a)$

$\neg a \Rightarrow (a \Rightarrow b)$

$p(a) \Rightarrow \exists x: p(x)$

$x = x$

$\forall x: p(x) \Rightarrow p(a)$

$p(x) \wedge (x = y) \Rightarrow p(y)$ substitution

Rules of inference:

1. Given

   a

   $a \Rightarrow b$

   deduce b

2. Given

   $b \Rightarrow p(x)$

   b

   deduce

   $b \Rightarrow \forall x: p(x)$

3. Given

   x is not a free variable in b

   $p(x) \Rightarrow b$

   deduce

   $\exists x: p(x) \Rightarrow b$

A Chat with the Great Explainer

C.J. Date has made a career of explaining, teaching, and clearing up misunderstandings about the relational model.

Dr. E.F. Codd invented the relational model in the late '60s. But it has largely been C.J. Date who has explained it. The two are so closely linked that "Codd and Date" is a unitary phrase—they are the relational "Lewis and Clark."

Chris Date first heard about Codd's theories while working on database languages for IBM in England, and he was one of the first people to recognize the relational model's significance. He wrote to Codd, the two developed a correspondence, and Codd eventually invited him to the U.S. to give a series of presentations on the technology within IBM. Date has been explaining it quite ably ever since, yet the model continues to be misunderstood.

The reasons for this misunderstanding are, quite simply, beyond Date's ken. "I can draw parallels, but . . . ." The model seemed so obviously right to him that Date was surprised to find Ted Codd was very much a voice in the wilderness. "He was just one person, and very few people were listening to him." It had never occurred to Date that it would literally be years before the world would begin to appreciate the relational model.

Through the 13 long years between Codd's first external publication on the model and when IBM's work with the experimental System R came to fruition with the release of DB2 in 1983, Date explained relational theory. It turned out that people wanted to be educated in this new technology, and he was often invited to give presentations on relational technology in general, and System R in particular.

Date thinks of himself as an explainer. "Education is my thing. That's what I do." Yet even though Date generally characterizes Ted Codd as the "inventor" and himself as the teacher, Date also kept busy working on an IBM attempt to create a successor to System 370 architecture. Although the FS (Future System) project was killed before it made it to market, some of the ideas behind it—the single-level STORE, encapsulated objects, and built-in database functions—later surfaced in IBM's System 38.

Since leaving IBM in 1983, Date has continued explaining and teaching the relational model through The Relational Institute, the San Jose-based organization that presents such seminars as "rdb UPDATE '89", and the Codd and Date Consulting Group, both cofounded by Codd. Date's books include *An Introduction to Database Systems (Volumes I and II), Database: A Primer and Guide to DB2.* These textbooks helped to "spread the word" at numerous colleges and universities.

When *DBMS* Editor in Chief Kevin Strehlo visited Date, he found him taking a forced break from work on his latest book, *Relational Database Writings, 1985 to 1989*. Date owns a 128K Mac but does his writing on an original PC 1 running DOS 1.0 on 160K floppies, and one of those old drives had just gone south. This is an edited transcript of that conversation.

DBMS: Really? 1.0? 160K?

DATE: Yes, I'm afraid so.

DBMS: You are persistent, aren't you? It's a bit like you're defending and explaining and re-explaining the relational model—you've seen a need and just stuck to it. But isn't it a bit like beating your head against the wall?

DATE: *Everyone* just keeps doing the same thing over and over again until they get it right.

DBMS: Yeah, I suppose so. So what was the real significance of this System R?

DATE: IBM Research intended to build a relational prototype that would prove (1) that relational systems really were as user-friendly as the relational people said they ought to be, and (2) that you could build a relational system that could perform comparably with a non-relational system. The relational theoreticians had always said that there's no reason why you couldn't, but no one had done it. Well, System R did it. In many ways you can trace the success of

this field to the success of System R. After that, there were no longer technical barriers, but rather political barriers, vested interest barriers, that sort of thing.

DBMS: But System R wasn't the only thing going on back then, in the early days. There was Professor, uh . . .

DATE: Michael Stonebraker.

DBMS: Right. Stonebraker, who developed the Ingres DBMS at the University of California at Berkeley.

DATE: Yes, IBM and UC Berkeley's project went pretty much in parallel. Both have been incredibly influential, yet IBM's won in some sense. Most database professionals would readily tell you that the Ingres QUEL language is actually superior to IBM's SQL, but SQL is what we are seeing in the marketplace because SQL is what IBM implemented.

DBMS: There were 13 years between IBM's first public proposal in 1970 and when IBM announced DB2 in 1983. What was going on internally at IBM?

DATE: There was the technical problem of optimization to solve. The relational folks always believed it was solvable, but nobody had done it. The problem involves taking high-level database requests and converting them into code that's as good as a human programmer would come up with. System R proved you could build an optimizer that would do a credible job.

DBMS: I've heard the optimizer described as an expert system that knows enough about the internal workings of the data structure to turn high-level requests into an efficient low-level access strategy. In some sense, it's AI.

DATE: Some people would say that. But an expert system has to be rules driven, and you need a way of easily maintaining and changing the rules. Certainly the original System R wasn't that neatly structured. And although some vendors will claim that their optimizers use sophisticated AI techniques and so on, between you and me, I think that's rubbish. If there was an optimizer that could learn from its mistakes and do better next time, I'd agree that there was AI at work, and I'd be impressed. I don't think any commercial optimizers are like that. Yet there are some very good optimizers out now that generate extremely good code. Sometimes very weird code, too!

DBMS: Compilers sometimes generate weird code, too.

DATE: Yes, and so do human programmers. But the optimizer *is* like an expert system, in that, even though you can probably find some human expert who can do better than a given optimizer, on average the optimizer will do better than the average human expert.

DBMS: There's also the question of how much effort you need to expend to do better than the optimizer.

DATE: That's right. It's a simple cost equation. Human programmers are very expensive. Suppose a very smart human programmer invents a clever new way to do a JOIN. By definition there's only one of that person. If we fold the technique the guy invents into the optimizer, it's available for everybody. In other words, the vendor does it once and everybody benefits. Anyway, human programmers should be concentrating on real application problems.

DBMS: But the optimizer was only "sort of" a success. I'm saying, "sort of," because there was a perception that relational systems didn't perform as well as other systems. What's the basis of that perception?

DATE: Well, it was true of the earliest systems. If you took one of the early prototypes and queried it, you could wait an hour for the answer. But that's not the point, is it? If you didn't have the query facility, which is one of the main points of a relational system, then you'd have to write a COBOL program to do the job and it would be six *months* before you got an answer.

DBMS: Poor performance is just one of the misconceptions, isn't it? You've actually done a series of papers where you present an excerpt or quote from something published about relational technology and then explain why it promulgates a misconception. . . . What gave you the idea?

DATE: It seemed a useful thing to do. Ted Codd or I would find some misconception in an article and we'd get angry, and say, "Look at what this turkey's saying now."

Excerpt from *DBMS* interview with C. J. Date, "A Chat with the Great Explainer." *DBMS,* Sept. 1989, pgs. 26–29. Reprinted with permission from *Intelligent Enterprise Magazine.* This and related articles can be found on *www.intelligententerprise.com.*

Temporal Data

TEMPORAL DATA IS the hardest type of data for people to handle conceptually. Perhaps time is difficult because it is dynamic and all other datatypes are static, or perhaps because time allows multiple parallel events. To illustrate both points, let me tell two old jokes:

> A youngster gets his first nondigital watch. His father asks him, "What time is it?" The child replies, "I don't know. The hands never stop moving!"
>
> "Time is what keeps everything from happening at once."—tee shirt slogan.

Okay, the jokes were not very good, but let me convince you that you do not understand how to compute with time. This is an old puzzle that still catches people. If a hen and a half can lay an egg and a half in a day and a half, then how many hens does it take to lay six eggs in six days? Do not look at the rest of the page and try to answer the question in your head.

The answer is a hen and a half. People tend to get tripped up on the rate (eggs per hen per day) because they handle time wrong. For example, if a cookbook has a recipe that serves one and you want to serve 100 guests, you increase the amount of ingredients by 100, but you do not cook it 100 times longer.

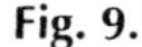

Fig. 9.1

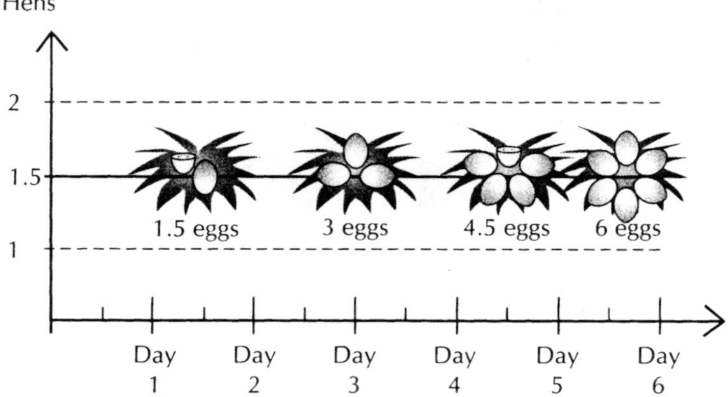

The algebra in this problem looks like this, where we want to solve for the rate in terms of "eggs per day," a convenient unit of measurement for summarizing the henhouse output:

$1\frac{1}{2}$ hens * $1\frac{1}{2}$ days * rate = $1\frac{1}{2}$ eggs

The first urge is to multiply both sides by $\frac{2}{3}$ and turn *all* of the $1\frac{1}{2}$s into 1s. But what you actually get is

1 hen * $1\frac{1}{2}$ days * rate = 1 egg; multiply by eggs per hen

$1\frac{1}{2}$ days * rate = 1 egg per hen; divide by the number of hens

rate = $\frac{2}{3}$ egg per hen per day; divide by $1\frac{1}{2}$ days

If you still don't get it, draw a picture (see Fig. 9.1).

9.1 Temporal Terminology

Another major problem with time is that it is both a physical concept and a legal concept. Let me first deal with the physical side of time, then move to the legal and social side.

Time in the real world seems to be continuous, and I will work from that assumption. There are arguments that time has quanta—discrete units, like the frames in an old motion picture film—in the real world, but that is a topic for a book on theoretical physics and not databases. What I do know is that the database has to store discrete units of temporal measurement.

The granularity of a scale is how fine a unit of measurement you keep. A calendar is calibrated to units of days. A wristwatch is calibrated to units of a second. A stopwatch is calibrated to units of 1/100 of a second. Laboratory atomic clocks resolve to even finer fractions of a second.

Time is infinite back into the past as well as into the future, but again the database model assumes that there is a minimum and maximum date and time that can be represented. We will spend more time on that topic when we get to the Gregorian calendar.

The next problem is that the same time words describe and measure events, durations, and intervals.

9.1.1 Events

An event is a single anchored moment in time, but it depends on the granularity used. Christmas day is an event if your level of granularity is one day (because you are using a wall calendar instead of a watch). The sentence "My English class starts at 15:00 Hrs" talks about an event and probably assumes a granularity of 15-minute intervals, since that is how class schedules are often posted.

In SQL-92, an event is represented by a `TIMESTAMP` datatype. This datatype has year, month, day, hours, minutes, seconds, and a decimal fraction of a second. The SQL-92 standard is mute on the precision required, but the FIPS-127 conformance tests looked for five decimal places.

9.1.2 Durations

A duration is a period of time without regard to when it starts and finishes. It is usually associated with an action or state of being. The sentence "My English class takes three hours" talks about the duration of the class and again probably assumes a granularity of minutes.

In SQL-92, a duration is represented by an `INTERVAL` datatype. There are two classes of intervals. One class, called year-month intervals, has an expressed or implied datetime precision that includes no fields other than `YEAR` and `MONTH`, though both are not required. The

other class, called day-time intervals, has an expressed or implied interval precision that can include any fields other than YEAR or MONTH; that is, HOUR, MINUTE, and SECOND.

9.1.3 Periods

A period is a duration with a fixed starting point in time. The sentence "My English class is third period" talks about both the duration and starting time of the class and again probably assumes a granularity of minutes.

In SQL-92, a period can be represented in two ways—by a pair of columns in which the first is a TIMESTAMP and the second is either another TIMESTAMP or an INTERVAL datatype.

The SQL model of time periods assumes that the starting time is in the period, but that the ending time is not. This use of open intervals is actually quite handy in calculations and produces a system of temporal arithmetic that has closure.

9.1.4 Time in Databases

Temporal databases have become a separate topic of academic study in themselves. Temporal database research literature identifies two main classes of time: transaction time and logical time. *Transaction time* is when a record of a transaction event is actually written to the database. *Logical time* is when the event that the database record models is intended to have effect. These two times do not have to be the same, so it is important to coordinate both of these in a database.

Relational database management systems leave some temporal problems unsolved. Most relational databases do not have mechanisms for triggering events based on an external time source, and the programmer has to put this code into an application program.

Another inherent problem with relational databases is the destruction of useful older data as new data is added. You must make a special effort to capture data over time in relational databases. The systems do include a log file, but the log is used to reconstruct the database to a point in time where it was consistent, not for the purpose of querying the history of the data.

Consider a bank account as an example. A bank account always has a balance, which must be the net result of all the deposit and withdrawal transactions done, in effective time sequence, since the account was opened, up to the current time. The current balance can always be recalculated at any time by adding up all the transactions, assuming that all these transactions are stored in the database.

There are external transactions caused by the owner of the account (a payroll deposit, a check cashed, etc.), and there are also internal system-generated transactions created by the bank (service charges, overdraft penalties, interest posting, etc.) for that type of account.

These system transactions, unlike external transactions, need not be stored, but could be regenerated by the database by replaying external transactions against the business rules, just as they were generated the first time. Thus the business rules, which can change from time to time, should also be stored and timestamped within the database.

Often the balance in an account will earn interest. In this case, if you ask the database for the balance some weeks later, the balance it reports should be increased by the interest earned, even if there were no intervening transactions. The amount of money in the account changes simply because of the passage of time.

If an external transaction updating an entity is later found to be incorrect, it can be reversed. A correct replacement transaction can be backdated into the correct effective time point in the sequence of stored transactions. Then the database replays all the transactions forward again to automatically recalculate a corrected new result for the entity.

An omitted or delayed external transaction can be entered, backdated with the correct effective time, and the data recalculated automatically. Likewise, a faulty business rule or operations error, such as running a job with the wrong date or data, can be corrected.

The database can query data "as of" any point in effective time, past, present, or future. The data reported this way is correct from the perspective of the current point in time. Lamentably, the data can be correct or consistent but often not both simultaneously. For example, a report for June run in August will not be consistent with the same

report for June run in October if there were backdated corrections effective for June and entered in September.

The database concept can be extended to allow the user to choose consistent reporting as a (per request or per user) alternative to correct reporting. This involves a parallel business rule implementing the enterprise understanding of consistency, and an alternate consistency view of the same base data.

Nobody has agreed on the proper display format, so most databases will give you several options. The usual ones are some mixture of a two- or four-digit year, a three-letter or two-digit month, and a two-digit day within the month. The three fields can be separated by slashes, dashes, or spaces. NATO at one time tried to use Roman numerals for the month to avoid language problems among members when the French were still members of the alliance; be grateful this failed.

The U.S. Army made a study back in World War II and found that the day, three-letter month, and four-digit year format was the least likely to be misread or miswritten. They have now switched to the four-digit year, three-letter month, and day format so that documents can be easily sorted by hand or by machine. This is the format I would recommend using for output on reports to be read by people for just those reasons; otherwise use the standard calendar format for transmissions.

Many programs use a year-in-century date format of some kind. This was supposed to save space in the old days when that sort of thing mattered (i.e., when punch cards only had 80 columns). They assumed that they would not need to tell the difference between the years 1900 and 2000 because they were too far apart. Old Cobol programs that did date arithmetic on these formats are already screwing up and returning negative results. If Cobol had a date datatype, instead of making the programmers write their own routines, then this would not have happened. Relational database user and 4GL programmers can gloat over this, since they have full date datatypes built into their products.

Hitchens (1991) and Celko (1981) discussed some of the problems with dates. There is even a newsletter on the subject (*tick, tick, tick;* Box #020538; Brooklyn, NY 11202).

The problem is more subtle than Hitchens implied in his article, which dealt with nonstandard date formats. Dates hide in other places, not just in date fields. The most common places are in serial numbers and computer-generated identifiers.

In the early 1960s, a small insurance company in Atlanta bought out an even smaller company that sold burial insurance policies to poor people in the Deep South. The burial insurance company used a policy number format identical to those of the larger company. The numbers began with the two digits of the year within century, followed by a dash, followed by an eight-digit sequential number.

The systems analysts charged with integrating the two files decided that the easiest way was to add 20 years to the first two digits of the newly acquired accounts. Their logic was that no customer would keep these cheap policies for 20 years—and the analyst who did this would not be working there in 20 years, so who cares? As the years passed, the company moved from a simple file system to a hierarchical database and was using the policy numbers for unique record keys. The system would simply generate new policy numbers on demand using a global counter in a policy library routine. No problems occurred for decades.

There were about 100 burial policies left in the database after 20 years. Nobody had written programs to protect against duplicate keys, since the problem had never occurred. Then one day, they created their first duplicate number. Sometimes the database would crash, but sometimes the child records would get attached to the wrong parent. This second situation was worse, since they started paying and billing the wrong people.

The company was lucky enough to have someone who recognized the old burial insurance policies when he saw them. It took months to clean up the problem because they had to manually search a warehouse to find the original policy documents. If the policies were still valid, then there were insurance regulations problems because these burial policies had been made illegal in the years in between, and they would owe the holders settlements.

In this case the date was being used to generate a unique identifier. But consider a situation where this same scheme is used starting in the year 1999 for a serial number. Once the company goes into the

year 2000, you can no longer select the largest serial number in the database and increment it to get the next one.

A quote in the July 1991 issue of *CFO* magazine says that ITT Hartford estimates the cost of adding the century years to dates in their computer systems will cost them up to $20 million. They also report that Colin Campbell at Hughes Aircraft Company was working on software to convert all dates over to the four-digit year format. They might have a good commercial product there.

9.2 A Short History of the Calendar

The Western world is and has been on a solar calendar. That means a year is defined as one revolution of the earth around the sun. Unfortunately, this revolution is not an even number of days (one solar year = 365.2422 days) and therefore solar calendars drift out of alignment unless corrected.

The Egyptian calendar drifted "completely around" approximately every 1,461 years and made two complete cycles from its introduction to the time of Julius Caesar. As a result, this calendar was useless for agriculture. The Egyptians relied on the stars to predict the flooding of the Nile.

Julius Caesar decreed that the year 708 AUC ("ab urbis conditae"—from the founding of the city of Rome, or 46 BCE) had 445 days in order to realign the calendar with the seasons. Leap years were referred to as bissextile years. Julius Caesar, on the advice of Sosigenes of Alexandria, also introduced leap years in 708 AUC (they did not exist in solar calendars prior to then). This calendar became known as the Julian calendar.

The year 46 BCE was called the "Year of Confusion" by the Romans. Over the next several centuries, months were added to the year, and days were added and subtracted from the months by assorted Romans, until the Christians had control over the calendar. The problem with the Julian calendar was that it used a simple four-year leap year cycle. It drifted by approximately 3 days every 400 years and had gotten 10 days out of step with the seasons by 1582. However, you might want to remember that a Roman calendar without a leap year would have drifted 'completely around' slightly more than once between 708 AUC and 2335 AUC (1582 CE).

The summer solstice, so important to planting crops, had no relationship to June 21 by 1582, so Pope Gregory took two weeks out of the month of October in 1582 to realign things. (A thousand years before Pope Gregory, the Aztecs and Mayans knew the number of days in a solar year to three decimal places.)

The Gregorian calendar is now properly known as the "Common Era" calendar to avoid religious references that might confuse non-Christians. What used to be "AD" and "BC" are now properly abbreviated as "CE" and "BCE."

The transition from the old Julian calendar to the Gregorian calendar took place at different times in different countries:

- The Italian duchies and kingdoms, Catholic parts of Switzerland, Spain, and Portugal (at that time under the same king, Philip II), including their colonies, skipped from 1582 October 4 to 1582 October 15.
- France (including its colonies) skipped from 1582 December 9 to 1582 December 20.
- Poland skipped from 1582 October 4 to 1582 October 15.
- German-Roman Empire (the Habsburgs in Austria): in 1583.
- German duchies with Catholic confession: in 1583.
- German duchies with Protestant confession skipped from 1700 February 18 to 1700 March 1.
- Netherlands: in 1700.
- Protestant parts of Switzerland: in 1701.
- Denmark and Norway skipped from 1700 February 18 to 1700 March 1.
- Sweden and Finland skipped from 1753 February 17 to 1753 March 1, but were one day apart from the old calendar between 1700 and 1712! (that is, 1700 February 28 was followed by 1700 March 1, and 1712 February 29 was followed by 1712 February 30, which was followed by 1712 March 1).

- Great Britain and its colonies skipped from 1752 September 2 to 1752 September 14.
- Russia and the former Soviet Union skipped from 1918 January 18 to 1918 February 1 (therefore, the October Revolution took place 1917 November 7 in the Gregorian calendar).
- The Balkan nations switched between 1918 and 1924.

9.3 The Julian Date

If you're going to use universal dates, think big and use Julian dates. The Julian date is a number set up by astronomers that currently is seven digits long. It ranges from 4713 January 01 BCE through 27,378 CE, which ought to be enough for any database application. The use of the starting date of 4713 January 01 BCE is related to solar and lunar cycles.

This format avoids some problems, such as finding the day of the week (take the Julian date modulo 7) and leap year conversions. Durations are calculated by simple subtraction and addition. Finding the phase of the moon, lunar eclipses, solar eclipses, and other astronomical facts is fairly simple algebra—which is why astronomers use it.

The downside is that existing systems, both legal and computer, would need to be rewritten.

9.4 ISO Temporal Standards

The International Standard ISO 8601 specifies numeric representations of date and time. These formats have several important advantages in databases over traditional date and time notations. The ISO time notation is the de facto, and in many cases, the de jure standard in almost all nations, and the date notation is becoming increasingly popular.

ISO 8601 has been adopted as European Standard EN 28601 and is therefore now a valid standard in all EU countries. All conflicting national standards have been changed accordingly.

The areas where people are most reluctant to part with traditional notation is in abbreviations for months and days of the week, and in their choice of display formats for a date or time.

9.4.1 ISO Date Formats

Using the ISO date formats is not a matter of choice anymore. Too many of the international standards, including SQL-92, specify the calendar date for transmission and storage of data. There are two broad categories of date formats, calendar and ordinal formats (day within year and week within year). The calendar dates are more for human readability and mirror the traditional Gregorian calendar, while the ordinal dates are easier to use in calculations.

Calendar Date Format

The ISO standard calendar date notation is a four-digit year, a two-digit month, and a two-digit day shown as a vector with the fields separated by hyphens: *yyyy-mm-dd*. The year is the usual Gregorian calendar, *mm* is the month of the year between 01 (January) and 12 (December), and *dd* is the day of the month between 01 and 31.

This notation is easy to read, write, and sort for software because you do not need a table to convert alphabetic codes and code to rearrange the date string. Another international advantage is that it is language independent and cannot be confused with local date notations. Date notations with the order "year, month, day" are already used in Denmark, Finland, Hungary, Japan, Korea, Sweden, and other countries.

This is the recommended primary standard notation, but ISO 8601 also specifies a number of alternative formats for use in applications with special requirements:

1. The hyphens can be omitted if compactness of the representation is more important than human readability.
2. For situations where information about the century is really not required, a two-digit year can be used.
3. If only the month or even only the year is of interest, the other fields can be dropped: 1999-02 or 1999.

Ordinal Date Format

The ISO ordinal date formats are described in ISO 2711-1973. The format is a four-digit year, followed by a digit day within the year (001-366). The year can be truncated to the year within the century. The ANSI date formats are described in ANSI X3.30-1971.

Week Format

Although not as common in the United States as it is in Europe, many commercial and industrial applications use the week within a year as a unit of time. Week 01 of a year is defined as the first week in that year that has a Thursday, which is equivalent to the week that contains the fourth day of January.

In other words, the first week of a new year is the week that has the majority of its days in the new year. Week 01 might also contain days from the previous year, and the week before week 01 of a year is the last week (52 or 53) of the previous year even if it contains days from the new year. The days of the week are numbered from 1 (Monday) through 7 (Sunday).

The standard notation uses the letter *W* to announce that the following two digits are a week number. The week number component of the vector can be separated with a hyphen or not, as required by space: 1999-W01 or 1999W01.

This notation can be extended by a single digit between 1 and 7 for the day of the week. For example, the day 1996-12-31, which is the Tuesday (day 2) of the first week of 1997, can be shown as 1997-W01-2 or 1997W012.

The ISO standard avoids explicitly stating the possible range of week numbers, but a little thought will show that the range is between 01 to 52 or between 01 to 53, depending on the particular year. There is one exception to the rule that a year has at least 52 weeks: the year 1753, when the Gregorian calendar was introduced, had less than 365 days and therefore less than 52 weeks.

9.5 The Year 2000 Problem

At this point you should have been hearing a lot about the "year 2000" or the "millennium" problem. There are whole books and a small software industry devoted to this single example of a bad encoding scheme. The major problems with the year 2000 representations in computer systems are the following:

1. The year 2000 has a lot of zeros in it.
2. The year 2000 is a leap year.
3. The year 2000 is a millennium year.
4. We have weird data in date fields.

9.5.1 The Odometer Problem

The "odometer problem" is in the hardware or at the system level. This is not the same as the millennium problem, where date arithmetic is invalid. If you are using a year-in-century format, the year 2000 is going to "roll over," like a car odometer that has reached its limit, and leave a year that is assumed to be 1900 (or something else other than 2000) by the application program.

This problem lives where you cannot see it in hardware and operating systems related to the system clock. Information on such problems is very incomplete, so you will need to keep yourself posted as new releases of your particular products come out.

Another subtle form of the zero problem is that some hashing and random number generators use parts of the system date as a parameter. Zero is a perfectly good number until you try to divide by it and your program aborts.

The problem is in mainframes. For example, the Unisys 2200 system will fail on the first day of 2036 because the eighth bit of the year field—which is a signed integer—will go to 1. The vendor has some solutions. Do you know what other hardware uses this convention? You might want to look.

The real killer will be with Intel-based PCs. When the odometer wraps around, DOS jumps to 1980 most of the time, and sometimes to 1984, depending on your BIOS chip. Windows 3.1 jumps to 1900 most of the time. Since PCs are now common as stand-alone units and as workstations, you can test this for yourself. Set the date and time to 1999-12-31 at 23:59:30 Hrs and let the clock run. What happens next depends on your BIOS chip and version of DOS.

The results can be that the clock display shows "12:00 AM" and a date display of "01/01/00" so you think you have no problems. However, you will find that you have newly created files dated in 1984 or in 1980. Surprise!

This problem is passed along to application programs, but not always the way that you would think. Quicken version 3 for the IBM PC running on MS-DOS 6 is one example. As you expect, directly inputting the date 2000-01-01 results in the year resetting to 1980 or 1984 off the system clock. But strangely enough, letting it wrap from 1999-12-31 into the year 2000, Quicken interprets the change as 1901-01-01 and not as 1900.

9.5.2 The Leap Year Problem

You might remember being told in grade school that there are 365.25 days per year and that the accumulation of the fractional day creates a leap year every four years. Once more, your teachers lied to you; as I've already mentioned, there are really 365.2422 days per year and every 400 years the fraction of the fractional day that was left over from the leap years accumulates, too. Since most of us are not over 400 years old, we have not had to worry about this until now. The correct test for leap years in Pascal is

```
FUNCTION isleapyear (year: INTEGER): BOOLEAN;
BEGIN
IF ((year MOD 400) = 0)
THEN isleapyear := TRUE
ELSE IF ((year MOD 100) = 0)
     THEN isleapyear := FALSE
     ELSE IF ((year MOD 4) = 0)
          THEN isleapyear := TRUE
          ELSE isleapyear := FALSE;
END;
```

Note that century years are leap years only if they are divisible by 400 (the year 2000 is a leap year, but the year 1900 is not). Lots of programs were written by people who did not know this algorithm. I do not mean Cobol legacy programs in your organization; I mean packaged programs for which you paid good money. The date functions in the first releases of Lotus, Excel, and Quatro Pro did not handle the day 2000 February 29 correctly. Lotus simply made an error, and the others followed suit to maintain "Lotus compatibility" in their products. Currently, MS Excel for Windows, version 4, shows correctly that the next day after 2000-02-28 is February 29. However, it thinks that the next day after 1900-02-28 is also February 29 instead of March 1. MS Excel for Macintosh doesn't handle the years 1900–1903.

Have you checked all of your word processors, spreadsheets, desktop databases, appointment calendars, and other off-the-shelf packages for this problem yet? Just key in the date 2000-02-29, then do some calculations with date arithmetic and see what happens.

With networked systems, this is going to be a real nightmare. All you need is one program on one node in the network to reject leap year day 2000 and the whole network is useless for that day, and transactions might not reconcile for some time afterwards. How many nodes do you think there are in the ATM banking networks in North America and Europe?

9.5.3 The Millennium Problem

This problem is the best-known one in the popular and computer trade press. We programmers have not been keeping true dates in data fields for a few decades. Instead, we have been using one of several year-in-century formats. These will not work in the last year of this millennium (the second millennium of the Common Era calendar ends in the year 2000 and the third millennium begins with the year 2001—that is why Arthur C. Clarke used it for the title of his book).

If only we had been good programmers and not tried to save storage space at the expense of accuracy, we would have used ISO standard formats (see section 9.4.1) and not have these problems today.

Programs have been doing arithmetic and comparisons based on the year-in-century and not on the year. A 30-year mortgage taken out in 1992 will be over in the year 2022, but when you subtract the two year-in-centuries, you get (22 – 92) = –70 years—a very early payoff of a mortgage!

Inventory retention programs are throwing away good stock, thinking it is outdated. Lifetime product warranties are now being dishonored because the service schedule dates and manufacturing dates cannot be resolved correctly. One hospital has already sent geriatrics patients to the children's ward because they only keep two digits of the birth year. Imagine your own horror story.

According to Benny Popek of Coopers & Lybrand LLP (Xenakis 1995):

> This problem is so big that we will consider these bugs to be out of the scope of our normal software maintenance contracts. For those clients who insist that we should take responsibility, we'll exercise the cancellation clause and terminate the outsourcing contract.

And another quote from Popek:

> We've found that a lot of our clients are in denial. We spoke to one CIO who just refused to deal with the problem, since he's going to retire next year.

But the problem is more subtle than just looking for date data fields. Timestamps are often buried inside encoding schemes. If the year-in-century is used for the high-order digits of a serial numbering system, then any program that depends on increasing serial numbers will fail. Those of you with magnetic tape libraries might want to look at your tape labels now. The five digits used in many mainframe shops for archive and tape management software also has the convention that if programmers want a tape to be kept indefinitely, they code the label with a retention date of 99365—that is, 1999-12-31—because the routine checks the last three digits to see that they are between 001 and 365. This method will fail at the start of the year 2000 when the retention label has 00001 in it.

9.5.4 Weird Dates

The phrase "weird dates" does not refer to situations you found yourself in when you were single. In the old days, when we lived in trees and did data processing on punch cards with early third-generation languages (read: Cobol), everyone wrote their own library routines to handle dates.

The results were not only that we had the infamous two-digit year fields, but very often some of the date fields were used to hold non-date values for other purposes. Even this is a sign of the changing times—what a structured programmer or a relational database designer would call an "overloaded" data item and regard as a bad thing, an object-oriented programmer would call "polymorphic" and regard as a good thing.

I used to work for the Georgia prison system, an institution whose one product is time. A file of inmate records had a field for the expected date of release. The original design used a four-digit year and, in general, we were pretty careful about avoiding two-digit years in most of the system.

However, we also had a year '9999-99-99', which was used to indicate that the inmate was doing a life sentence, and a year '8888-88-88', which was used to indicate that the inmate was under a death sentence.

In "Battle Plan for 2000" (*Datamation*, January 1, 1996), there was a suggestion that these special dates could be replaced with `NULL` values in SQL. Obviously, this would not have worked in my prison system example because these two expected release date codes are significantly different—especially to the inmate involved.

I refer to these special codes as "weird dates" for lack of a more technical term. There is an assumption that they will resolve themselves to a real date at some time in the future, but we just don't know what that date will be right now.

The most common weird dates in older file systems are

- '0000-00-00' or '00-00-00': A symbol for a missing date, assumed to be in the past. One of the reasons for the zeros is that in the old days, Fortran would automatically read blanks in a numeric field as a zero and Cobol could be set to do the same. Since most data entry work was done on punch cards, you got blanks when you skipped over a field. If you found out what the date should have been, then you could repunch the card.

- '9999-99-99' or '99-99-99': A symbol for a missing date, assumed to be in the future. One reason for all nines as a symbol for "eternity" in data fields is that this will sort to the bot-

tom of any printout, making these dates always appear at the end of a chronological ordering. You probably figured that out.

The other reason both these codes are all numeric has to do with the way that keypunch machines work. There is a control card inside the IBM series keypunch machine that controls the layout of the cards being punched. A series of columns that made up a data field could be set to be alphanumeric, numeric only, alphabetic only, skipped over, or duplicated from the previous card.

Since the date fields were set to be numeric only, you had to use a numeric code for a weird date. Allowing an alphabetic code like 'eternity' would have required allowing alphanumeric data in the field and would have increased the error rates drastically.

- '11-11-11' or '1911-11-11' or '2011-11-11': Used as a missing date, either in the past or in the future. This is another one that is hard to explain to younger programmers. Video terminal data entry systems often use a two-digit year in their displays and require that a valid date be put in a field even when the data entry clerk does not know it. The easiest way to get a valid date is to hold the "1" key down and let it repeat until it has filled the field. Internally, the system converts the first two digits of the string of 1s into the year 1911 or 2011, depending on how the program is set up.

- CURRENT_TIMESTAMP: Used as a missing date, either in the past or in the future. The data entry system has a function key or default value of the current system. The data entry clerk does not know the correct date, and the easiest way to get a valid date is to hit the function key or allow the default value to go into the system.

- Invalid dates: These are really errors, but they exist inside legacy systems, so you have to handle them. These dates are usually the result of a bad calculation or a poor edit routine:
  1. Nonexistent day is shown in a month, such as '1997-09-31'.
  2. Leap year day is shown in the wrong year.

3. Leap year day is not shown in a valid year. This means that when a program tries to insert leap year day, the edit routine will reject the valid date.
4. Just plain garbage in the field. There are so many ways that this can happen, I cannot begin to list them.

9.5.5 Solutions

First, become aware of the problem. A good place to start is to subscribe to an Internet newsgroup that deals with the topic. The best such newsgroup can be reached by sending an email to *listmanager @hookup.net* with *subscribe year2000* as the body of the text. You will get back a confirmation note if your subscription is successful.

This will get you up-to-date information on known problems with products; vendors that are marketing conversion tools aimed at the year 2000; and some general discussions on dates, times, and other temporal data problems.

Next, appoint a "Year 2000 Task Group" or "Year 2000 Coordinator" to inspect existing code and systems. The team can buy some tools, but even without tools, they will need to do the following tasks:

1. Check and validate the existing data files for improper date fields. In particular, if you are moving from Cobol and other legacy systems to SQL databases, look for special dates, such as "00/00/00" or "99/99/99", that were used for missing or unknown dates so you can replace them with `NULL` values.

2. Contact all your software and hardware vendors and ask them what they are doing to fix the problems.

3. Code, buy, or somehow get a "year 2000 compliant" subroutine library in all of the programming languages you use in your shop. Do not think that this is only a Cobol problem; you will see problems in C, C++, BASIC, Fortran, Powerbuilder, and any other 3GL or 4GL language that does not have a native temporal datatype and operators. If you can keep the subroutine names and functionality the same across languages, so much the better.

4. Get a report that tells you which programs access which databases and files. Correlate that with the appearance of date data in those files. You now know which programs you have to inspect. This might not be all the programs affected, but it is a good start.

5. There are three approaches to dealing with millennium problems, and you should pick one after you have an idea of the scope of the problem in your organization. The approaches are to change the data, to change the programs, or to change both.

6. The general solution for weird dates is to first allow such date fields to be `NULL` in an SQL database, and then add a non-`NULL` flag field attached to the date field to indicate the internal meaning or status of the date. Usually a small integer or single character can handle all of the special cases. These flag codes need to be standardized in the system and kept in a special table so that every programmer is using the same conventions in their programs. As a simple suggestion to get you started, consider this set of flag codes:

   0 = Valid date

   1 = Not applicable

   2 = Unknown past or future date; "missing date"

   3 = Unknown past date; "missing past date"

   4 = Unknown future date; "to be determined"

   8 = Indefinite past date; "minus eternity"

   9 = Indefinite future date; "eternity"

   The difference between a code 9 and a code 4 is that eternity never arrives. So I could use code 4 for a person's death date, and a code 9 for the date that a perpetual trust fund will run out of money.

   Likewise, the difference between a code 8 and a code 3 is that the minus eternity is never seen. So I could use code 3 for a person's birth date, and a code 8 for the date that air was invented.

In fairness, the minus eternity is mostly for sorting certain items to one end or the other of a report. The positive eternity, however, not only helps sort things chronologically, but it has real meaning for certain situations.

In a large company there might be no way to alter the data files with the staff and time available. You will have to replace your date routines with library calls that use some rule to determine the century and hope that they work in all cases. If you decide to change the data, then you can add the century digits explicitly to string fields, convert programs over to a 4GL or SQL database that has built-in temporal datatypes, or use a seven-digit date with one digit for century. This last approach will handle the next 800 years. The century digit is 1 for 1900, and 2 for 2000, so it sorts and compares correctly. Seven digits in packed decimal fit in the same space as six, so the conversion is often relatively easy.

The initial information gathering is quite hard. While it sounds a little silly, just scanning all the data declarations in the source code for the four-letter sequence "date", and other abbreviations for "date" such as "_dt", is a good way to start to locate the date fields. But it is not just source code that has problems.

Utility programs, such as sort packages, have parameters that assume a year-in-century date format. You cannot simply make the date fields four digits long. Many of the popular date formats did not have the day, month, and year fields in order, so the sort routine had to read the dates as three separate parameters and rearrange them internally. Dates in ISO format are already ordered properly for sorting.

Let's assume that you get the changes in place without any trouble. You now have to test the changes. Testing will cost you money, resources, and storage space. Can you perform a full regression test on any of your applications today? Does your company already have a testing method in place? Testing teams established? Automated testing tools?

7. When you finish with this, you then have to worry about changing all the paper forms, hardcopy reports, and screen

displays. Look for displays with a hard-coded century. It is usually in title lines, report headers, and other displays. You do not want to title a report "fiscal year ending 19__" in the year 2000 because you forgot to clean up a print statement or to change a preprinted form.

8. Oh yes, it is important that you get all of this done by 1999. This will give you a few days to try and figure out which of the systems that you connect to are going to blow up on you, so you can defend yourself. You might try talking to their "Year 2000 Coordinator," if they have one.

9.6 ISO Time of Day

In the ISO standards (as well as common usage), the time of day is based on the UTC (Universal Coordinated Time) and standard time zones. (Yes, I know that the initials and the words do not match. This occurs in many ISO standards because the French will not consent to having the English language name of a standard be the source of its abbreviation.)

The format for the time of day is *hh:mm:ss,* where *hh* is the number of complete hours that have passed since midnight (00–24), *mm* is the number of complete minutes that have passed since the start of the hour (00–59), and *ss* is the number of complete seconds since the start of the minute (00–59). The separator between the fields is a colon. The use of the colon will keep Americans happy, but Europeans will have to give up the periods used in their traditional time notations.

If the hour value is 24, then the minute and second values must be zero. That is, 24:00:00 on this day is really the first moment of the next day.

ISO 8601 does not mention the leap second. This is a correction to align the astronomical clock with a much more precise atomic clock standard. Thus, the *ss* field can officially have between 59 and 62 seconds in it. In practice, only one second has been added each year this standard has been in place. A single leap second 23:59:60 is inserted into the UTC time scale every few years as announced by the International Earth Rotation Service in Paris to keep UTC from wandering away more than 0.9 seconds from the less constant astronomical time scale UT1, defined by the actual rotation of the earth.

An example time is 23:59:59, which represents the time one second before midnight.

As with the date notation, the separating colons can also be omitted, as in 235959, and the precision can be reduced by omitting the seconds or both the seconds and minutes, as in 23:59, 2359, or 23.

It is also possible to add fractions of a second after a decimal dot or comma; for instance, the time 5.8 ms before midnight can be written as 23:59:59.9942 or 235959.9942.

As every day both starts and ends with midnight, the two notations 00:00 and 24:00 are available to distinguish the two midnights that can be associated with one date. This means that the following two notations refer to exactly the same point in time: 1995-02-04 24:00 = 1995-02-05 00:00. In case an unambiguous representation of time is required, 00:00 is usually the preferred notation for midnight and not 24:00. You might have noticed that digital clocks display 00:00 and not 24:00.

ISO 8601 does not specify whether this notation indicates an event (point in time) or a duration (time period).

If a date and a time are displayed on the same line, then always write the date in front of the time. If a date and a time value are stored together in a single data field, then ISO 8601 suggests that they should be separated by a Latin capital letter *T*, as in 19951231T235959.

The 24-hour time notation has been the de facto and de jure standard all over the world for decades, except in the United States (and some other English-speaking countries). We still use the notation that gives hours between 1 and 12 and adds a suffix of AM or PM to it. But shortly the United States will be the last holdout, much like our use of nonmetric measurements. Most other languages don't even have abbreviations that correspond to AM and PM in them.

Frankly, getting rid of the 12-hour notation will be a good thing. It uses more characters to write, and it is hard for a human being to quickly compare or calculate times with it. It is not clear just what you use to represent 00:00, 12:00, and 24:00 in the 12-hour notation. You will find conflicting advice in encyclopedias and style manuals. A

common kludge is to avoid "12:00 AM/PM" altogether and write "noon," "midnight," or "12:01 AM/PM" instead, although the word "midnight" still does not distinguish between 00:00 and 24:00. The *Chicago Manual of Style* now recommends using the ISO notation in publications.

9.6.1 Local Time, Lawful Time, and UTC

The SQL standard officially uses the Gregorian calendar as its basis and references several other ISO standards dealing with time. The most important standard is the UTC.

The most current information on the use of UTC can be found by subscribing to an email service at *tz-request@elsie.nci.nih.gov* in the usual manner.

People are sloppy about the distinctions between GMT, UT, and UTC. GMT (Greenwich Mean Time) was based on a standard set by the British Navy from the Greenwich Observatory, which was positioned at longitude zero but no longer exists. GMT was the official time base until the 1920s, when the term UT (Universal Time) took over; UTC is a UT variant that became codified as the basis for civil time around 1960.

Time zones were set up by railroads and ratified by 27 nations at a conference in Washington, DC, in 1884. Today, the International Air Transportation Association (IATA) has replaced the railroads as the industry most concerned about time zones. They publish a table of the time zones of the world (SSIM) twice a year, giving the dates that certain zones switch from regular to daylight saving time (DST).

Unfortunately, in recent years the breakup of the former Soviet Union and other political changes have caused very frequent changes in the names of the time zones as well as their DST schedules.

When a time is written as shown above, it is assumed to be in some local time zone. In order to indicate that a time is measured in UTC, you can append a capital letter Z to a time, as in 23:59:59Z or 2359Z.

The Z stands for the "zero meridian," which goes through Greenwich, England. There is a spoken alphabet code used in radio communication where Z is coded as "Zulu," so the ISO standard was also called "Zulu Time"; however, this term should no longer be used.

Since the introduction of an international atomic time scale, almost all existing civil time zones are now related to UTC, which is slightly different from the old and now unused GMT. On 1972 May 01, Liberia was the last country to switch from a UTC offset that was not a multiple of 15 minutes.

The suffixes *+hh:mm, +hhmm,* or *+hh* can be added to the time to indicate that the local time zone is *hh* hours and *mm* minutes ahead of UTC. For time zones west of the zero meridian, which are behind UTC, the notation uses a minus sign: *–hh:mm, –hhmm,* or *–hh.*

For example, Central European Time (CET) is +0100, and U.S./Canadian Eastern Standard Time (EST) is -0500. The following strings all indicate the same point of time: 12:00Z = 13:00+01:00 = 0700-0500. Strangely enough, there is no international standard that specifies abbreviations for civil time zones. However, the use of three-letter codes is common.

In addition, politicians enjoy modifying the rules for civil time zones, especially for daylight saving time, every few years, so the only really reliable way of describing a local time zone is to specify numerically the difference of local time to UTC. It is better to use UTC directly as your only time zone where this is possible; then you do not have to worry about time zones and daylight saving time changes at all.

The Web has several sources for time zone and daylight saving time data. Here are some links that may be of interest:

- *http://community.bellcore.com/mbr/gmt-explained.html*
- *http://www.energy.ca.gov/energy/daylightsaving.html*
- *http://www.dhl.com/dhl/dhlinfo/1bb.html*

The first two sites are government owned, but the last one belongs to the DHL package service. Given that DHL covers 217 countries and territories, they have been very concerned about local times.

9.7 Notes on SQL-92 and Temporal Data

SQL was the first language to have an explicit set of temporal datatypes, and it did a remarkable job of working the ISO standards

into the language. There are some peculiarities worth mentioning, however.

9.7.1 Time Zones in SQL-92

SQL-92 requires that all temporal data use ISO Standard 8601 formats for display and be stored as UTC. The local time displacement, a duration, for the UTC (or more properly, "lawful time") is kept in a schema information table. The addition of the AT TIME ZONE clause to temporal expressions lets the database do the conversions to and from UTC and local times for you. The syntax looks like this:

```
<datetime value expression> ::=
     <datetime term>
   | <interval value expression> <plus sign> <datetime term>
   | <datetime value expression> <plus sign> <interval term>
   | <datetime value expression> <minus sign> <interval term>

<datetime term> ::= <datetime factor>

<datetime factor> ::= <datetime primary> [<time zone>]

<datetime primary> ::=
     <value expression primary>
   | <datetime value function>

<time zone> ::=
   AT <time zone specifier>
<time zone specifier> ::=
      LOCAL | TIME ZONE <interval value expression>
```

9.7.2 The OVERLAPS Predicate

Fred Zemke of Oracle posted a request for an interpretation of <overlaps predicate> in December 1998 on the NCITS H2 Committee email list.

The <overlaps predicate> uses the operator OVERLAPS to determine whether or not two chronological periods overlap in time. A chronological period is specified either as a pair of datetimes (starting and ending) or as a starting datetime and an interval.

There are two possible intuitive notions of overlaps:

1. The periods have nonempty intersection.
2. The periods have nonempty intersection of more duration than a single point in time.

Let the first period start with time S1 and terminate with time T1, and the second period start with time S2 and terminate with time T2, and S1 ≤ T1 and S2 ≤ T2.

The final general rule for the `<overlaps predicate>` in the SQL-92 standard says that the predicate is equivalent to

```
(S1 > S2 AND NOT (S1 >= T2 AND T1 >= T2))
OR
(S2 > S1 AND NOT (S2 >= T1 AND T2 >= T1))
OR
(S1 = S2 AND (T1 <> T2 OR T1 = T2))
```

The problem comes when two periods abut, so that the upper bound of one equals the lower bound of the other. That is, S1 < T1 = S2 < T2, so their intersection of the periods is the single value {T1} = {S2}. If you evaluate the formula for this example, you get `FALSE`. So it seems that the general rule is not using interpretation 1 as its intuitive basis.

But look what happens when the interval is reduced to a single point (duration 0) and that point is between the bounds of the second period. That is, S2 < S1 = T1 < T2. In this case the intersection is a single point, but the `<overlaps predicate>` evaluates `TRUE`. So interpretation 2 is not the intuitive basis of the general rule.

Back to the drawing board. Perhaps the problem is the notion of a period of time. Interpretation 1 is correct if you think a period is closed at both ends (includes both endpoints). Interpretation 2 is correct if you think a period is open (excludes both endpoints). Neither interpretation 1 nor 2 works, so perhaps we need to find another notion of period.

Let's try half-open/half-closed periods; that is, a period that includes the starting time but excludes the termination time. Mathematicians denote this [S1, T1).

In that case we have trouble interpreting what a period of length 0 is. The lower bound is in, the upper bound is out, but they are the same, which is a contradiction. If we follow mathematics, we might resolve the contradiction by defining $[S1, T1) = \{x : S1 \leq x < T1\}$, which is empty if S1 = T1. Now an empty period must have an empty intersection with any other period, and so it cannot overlap with anything.

But the SQL-92 standard says that the case (S2 < S1 = T1 < T2) evaluates to TRUE. So we still have not found an interpretation that agrees with the rule.

One more try! Perhaps the problem is that we are equating datetime values with real numbers, which have no thickness. Perhaps we should be thinking that a DATE value represents a period of 1 day, from midnight to just before the next midnight. And similarly a TIMESTAMP(0) value represents a second, and a TIMESTAMP(6) represents a microsecond. Thus no period is ever of 0 length. The length of a period is actually one more than the difference of the termination time minus the starting time.

This interpretation founders too. For example, evaluate

```
(DATE'1998-01-01', DATE'1998-01-02') OVERLAPS
(DATE'1998-01-02', DATE'1998-01-03')
```

The first period is the time from the midnight that began 1998-01-01 through but not including the midnight that ends 1998-01-02. The second period is from midnight that began 1998-01-02 through but not including the midnight that ends 1998-01-03. The intersection is the period from the midnight that began 1998-01-02 through but not including the midnight that ends the same day. So the intersection is not empty. Nevertheless, the predicate evaluates FALSE.

The original temporal model in SQL-92 is supposed to be closed-open. But what about a closed-open period of duration 0? The point or granule D1 is both in and not in the period. We reach to mathematics to help here and think that $[D1, D1) = \{x : D1 \leq x < D1\}$, which is the empty set. In that case you would expect that a period of duration 0 could not overlap with anything, even itself, since it is an empty set. But the current rule makes the following TRUE:

```
[D1, D1) OVERLAPS [D0, D2)
[D1, D1) OVERLAPS [D1, D2)
[D1, D1) OVERLAPS [D1, D1)
```

but the following is FALSE:

```
[D1, D1) OVERLAPS [D0, D1)
```

We find the last two propositions hard to reconcile. The only way we can make sense of this is to say that a period of 0 duration is implicitly promoted to duration 1 granule. That is, [D1, D1) = [D1, D2).

The supposed advantage of the half-open intervals are that they are closed under concatenation and subtraction. That is, when you concatenate two such intervals, end to end, the result is a new half-open interval that does not count the common point in time twice. Likewise, when we remove a half-open interval from another half-open interval, the result is one or two new half-open intervals.

One choice that has been discussed is to promote the interval [a,a) to the point [a] as a special case, but as of this writing, no changes have been made to the standard.

Textual Data

THE MOST OBVIOUS nonrelational data in organizations is textual. Manuals, company rules, regulations, contracts, memos and a multitude of other documents actually run the organizations. In fact, most business rules are not in relational databases, but are in word processor files and vertical filing cabinets.

SQL and traditional records are based on a strict syntax and formal rules for extracting data and information. Natural language is a semantic system, and the syntax is not what carries the meaningful information. Unfortunately, while computers are good at formal syntax, they are lousy at semantics.

The result is that textbases use pattern matching operations instead of actually reading and understanding the documents they store. The textbase market is growing at the rate of 50% per year, according to a 1991 study by IDC and Delphi Consulting Group. Most of that growth is in centralized data centers.

10.1 Terminology and the Basics

There are two basic terms used in this field, *textbase* and *document base,* which are gradually being grouped under the term textbase. Strictly speaking, a textbase is just text. The documents

stored in a textbase are just blocks of text with a name. This name can be as simple as an accession number or a timestamp on a fax, or it can have some meaning. There is also no requirement that the documents have the same structure.

A document base is text that comes arranged in a structured format. Usually the documents have a header record, which gives some information about the document, and the body or actual text. Most documents are hierarchies of this header-body structure. Books break into chapters, chapters into paragraphs, paragraphs into sentences, and finally sentences into words. Manuals break into sections, subsections, and subsubsections.

There are two basic kinds of searches, on the headers or on the body of the documents. Much of the initial searching is done on the headers, so it is important that they all have the same format. A body or text search depends on pattern matching within the text itself.

A search has to return a result at a certain level of granularity within the body of the document. This level is usually adjustable. Obviously, searches that return all occurrences of a particular letter or word are useless. The smallest practical unit is a sentence (or enough characters that you will most likely see all of a sentence). The largest practical unit is the document—simply because the next level of this hierarchy is the whole document base itself.

The header is a record with fixed fields that apply to all the documents under consideration. It can be searched like a relational database, which is much faster than searching the text. The header information can include almost anything, but the most common fields are the title, author(s), publication date, classification codes, an abstract, or a keyword list.

An abstract is a short summary of the contents of the document to which it is attached. It must be created by a skilled reader, but there are attempts to automate this process.

A keyword list is a list of words or phrases drawn from a predefined set of words or phrases that have meaning to the searcher. For example, this chapter might have a keyword list with "textbase," "text retrieval," and "document retrieval" in it. A keyword does not have to appear in the body of the document itself. For example, not too many satires would include the word "satire." This is a powerful search tool, but it also requires a human being with knowledge of the field to design the vocabulary and make the choice of keywords. The vocabulary will have to be updated on a regular basis, adding and dropping terms.

Notice that the keyword list approach works for a single document, not for a collection of documents. Another version of this approach is a keyword-in-context (KWIC) system. A KWIC system uses a set of keywords and locates the words within phrases from the document. Usually the phrases are titles, but they can be short descriptive sentences from the original document. The old printed versions of KWIC indexes would print the phrases around a gutter to highlight the keyword; thus you might look up the keyword "domino" and see a listing like this:

	DOMINO Games for Children
Chinese	DOMINO Games
Internal queues in the	DOMINO Operating System
	DOMINOES and Other Stories

Another approach is to give each document a general classification code to narrow a search as soon as possible. The Dewey decimal system and the Library of Congress (LOC) classification scheme are ways of doing that for library books. There is at least one website using LOC, but most of the services have their own hierarchical schemes with the option to do a full search.

The subheaders become simpler in structure. For example, novels have chapters, which have only titles (or titles and synopsis if it is a 19th-century novel), and paragraphs have no headers. However, a technical manual might break this down further in section and subsection titles.

Semantic searching is more difficult because it has to understand the meaning of the documents and the search question. For example, an ideal semantic text search engine would have taken my query about "dominoes" and asked if I meant the Domino operating system or the game. When I said I mean the game, it would then look at the documents available and determine which ones deal with games.

Even better, the engine would have some machine intelligence to associate things that are not normally indexed together and tell someone looking at surgical techniques for damaged livers to consider a magazine article on underwater basket weaving because they use the same methods. Obviously, there are not many working semantic search systems, and they are expensive.

10.2 Indexing Text

Before text is searched, most systems usually index it. An index is a file of the location of each significant word in the document. The first step in the process is to determine which words are significant and which are noise words.

Noise words are words that are so common in English (or whatever language) that people would not search on them because every document will have them. They are usually linguistic structuring words such as articles, conjunctions, pronouns, and auxiliary verbs. But the noise word list can also include numerals, punctuation marks, spelled-out numbers, single letters, and words that are so common to a particular discipline that all documents would include them (for a list of the 1,000 most common words in English, see Gleason 1981). As a rule of thumb, removing the 150 most common words will reduce English text by 60% to 70% of the original word count.

Building a noise word list can be harder than you would think because of the homonym problem. For example, chemical abstracts need to use one- and two-letter chemical symbols, so you have to be sure to leave 'He' for helium in the documents. But most noise word lists ignore 'He', regarding it as the third-person singular pronoun. The best solution would be to tell the difference between the two words by parsing the text to see the context.

Some people feel that noise words are a bad idea in spite of the saving in index size and improved performance. In looking for quotations, the structure words can be important. The phrase 'To be or not to be, that is the question' has only 'question' as a possible search word. Likewise, 'Ask not what your country can do for you, ask what you can do for your country' has only 'country' as significant.

Once the noise words are pulled out, the index can be built. The index has a granularity, which is the level of the document to which it points. The index and retrieval granularity do not have to be the same. If the documents are short abstracts that can be shown on a screen, then the index can use word-level granularity, and the retrieval can return results at the document level. If you have used DIALOG information services, then you have seen this approach. Once you have read the abstracts, you have the option of getting the whole document in hardcopy offline or downloaded online.

If the documents are longer, then the retrieval level is usually the paragraph, but can be as fine as the sentence.

Index granularity can be as fine as the locations of each search word within the document (usually by byte position within the file) or as coarse as the name of the document in which it occurs.

Word-level granularity makes the index bigger, since each word is probably going to occur in many places. Another problem is that any changes to the document will change the location of all words that occur after the point where the change was made.

Document-level granularity returns the names of the documents very rapidly and is easy to update. However, once a list of candidate documents is found, they have to be searched in a linear fashion for text patterns. This can take quite some time for long documents.

In practice, most systems will keep one index for a set of documents that has the words, the file names, and their locations. This allows the search to find the document names and then look for word patterns afterwards.

A compromise between the whole document and individual word granularity is to break the document into pages. The pages can then be retrieved and searched in a linear fashion. The advantage of this compromise approach is that it is smaller than a full word index, but it has a slower search time. If text is removed from a document, the page can simply be padded with blanks, and there is no need to reindex. If text is added, then a new page can be created for the overflow, and all page numbers that follow the insertion are incremented. Search problems occur when a search needs to go over page boundaries—a search for "John Smith," where "John" is on one page and "Smith" is on the next page. However, such searches are exceptional and do not affect performance in most cases.

10.3 Text Searching

Once indexed, a document is ready for searching. All text query languages are based on matching character string patterns. Complex queries are composed by using operators such as AND, OR, and NOT to create expressions. The AND operator means that both patterns were found in the document, OR means that one or both patterns were found, and NOT means the term was absent. They are usually called Boolean operators, but they are actually set-oriented membership tests, not logical predicates.

Most products follow the rules that Boolean operators have the precedence NOT, AND, and finally OR, with the usual use of parentheses.

The simplest pattern matching operator is an equality test. We are looking for the documents that contain a word, such as "chocolate." The system will usually ignore the case and capitalization when it tests for equality. Most systems will also automatically look for plural forms by using a synonym list for irregular plurals and a small program for *-s* and *-es* plural forms.

The next most complicated operator is a pattern matcher that uses wildcards. Wildcard conventions vary greatly from product to product, but there is usually a single-character wildcard, like the '?' in DOS command lines or '_' in SQL's `LIKE` predicate, and a multi-character wildcard, like the '*' in DOS command lines or '%' in SQL's `LIKE` predicate.

The user must know if the wildcards match on one or zero characters in a word. For example, if a '?' stands for exactly one character, then the pattern 'chocolate?' will match the word 'chocolates', but not 'chocolate'.

Automatic synonyms for plurals have already been mentioned. A synonym can be thought of as a replacement of one word by a list separated by ORs. For example, the query ('chocolate' AND 'wife') might expand out in the system as (('chocolate' OR 'chocolates') AND ('wife' OR 'wives')).

There are three major types of synonyms. A grammatical synonym is a different form of the same word. For example, *be* has grammatical synonyms *am, is, are, been, was,* and *were.* Most textbases will have irregular plural forms in their thesaurus. Many automatically recognize grammatical postfixes, such as *-s, -es, -ing,* and *-ily,* and can store information about doubling the final consonant or dropping the final *e* in the index. This feature is also found in spell checkers in word processors.

The grammatical forms are often automatic and generated by a parsing program. User-controlled synonyms are kept in a thesaurus file, which again will differ from product to product.

True synonyms have a semantic equality to the word. For example, 'boat' has the true synonyms 'ship', 'craft', and 'vessel', and they can all be swapped around in place of each other.

Narrow synonyms are specific cases of the concept, such as 'Europe' narrowing down to countries such as 'France', 'Germany', and 'Italy'.

Synonyms for dates and numbers are a special problem. They are true synonyms, but their forms are very different and can be homonyms for other concepts. For example, 'one', '1', and 'I' are the English word, Hindu-Arabic numeral, and Roman numeral for the same concept. The Roman numeral is also a homonym for the first-person pronoun. But this list does not show 1.0, 1.00, 1.000, and so forth.

The English word 'pi', Greek letter π, and the numbers 3.14, 3.1415, and 3.14159 are all synonyms. But just how many decimal places should the thesaurus store? The trailing digits cannot be detected with a parsing program.

Proximity operators look for words within a certain distance of each other, where distance is measured by a word count, sentence count, paragraph count, or other structural unit. At least one version allows the user to set up the borders of the search to the text between a start word and a finish word (as in find the name 'Heathcliff' between 'Dear' and 'Sincerely' in a textbase of love letters).

The quorum operator looks for documents with *k* out of a list of *n* words or patterns, as in `2 OF [German, French, Spanish, Czech]`', for example. The quorum operator is often used to restrict a list of synonyms, but it is a shorthand for a Boolean expression.

Weighted searches assign a score that attempts to measure how well a document fits the query. This can be very useful when

searching a large textbase. It can also be a disaster if the weighting function is flawed.

There are several types of word scoring schemes. The simplest method is a tally of the presence or absence of query words in a document. No special weight is assigned to one term over another.

The second method is to report the number of occurrences of each word or pattern. It is assumed that the documents with the most hits are the best ones.

The third method is a mixed strategy. Each word or pattern gets a weight that is multiplied by the number of occurrences, to give a score. This is a little harder to do because you must assign weights somehow. The second method is really a special case of this, with a weight of one for each search term.

The fourth method is to have a semantic tree structure that assigns heavier weight to more specific synonyms. This means that the thesaurus has to know the difference between broader and narrower terms. A search for 'Southwest* Indian?' would give more points to documents containing names of particular tribes ('Hopi', 'Zuni', or 'Navaho'). A document with 'Amerind' or 'Native American' would get a few points, while a document on Slavic peoples would score nothing. Again, these term weights can be multiplied by the number of occurrences to give a final score.

More elaborate weighting schemes will give points for proximity, order of the search terms in the document, and statistical distribution within the document.

10.4 The grep() Search Tool

The most powerful pattern matching operator in general use is the `grep()` function in UNIX. The name `grep` is short for 'general regular expression parser' and refers to a class of formal languages that are called regular expressions. ANSI has a version of `grep()` pattern strings in its SQL3 working draft for use in the `SIMILAR TO` predicate. There are extended versions under various UNIX implementations with names like `xgrep()`.

The <pattern> is a regular expression, which is defined as one or more occurrences of the following characters optionally enclosed in quotes. The following symbols are treated specially:

^	start of line
.	match any single character
*	match zero or more occurrences of preceding character
$	end of line
\	next character is a literal, not a symbol
+	match one or more occurrences of preceding character
[]	match any character from the enclosed list
[^]	match any character not from the enclosed list
-	all characters between left and right characters in ASCII order (for example, [0-9] is short for [0123456789])

Regular expressions can match a great many character strings. Since grep() is used in UNIX systems and assumes that the C programming language is used, strings are enclosed in double quote marks, not single quote marks as in SQL. For example, any integer will match to "[0-9]+", any decimal number "[0-9]+.[0-9]*", any word to "[A-Z]*[a-z]+" (note that capitalization is allowed), and even patterns like "[^aeiou0-9]" to match anything but a vowel or a digit.

Grep() builds a table-driven automata from the pattern and very quickly parses words for a match. The patterns can even be optimized for faster parsing using algebraic reductions such as "aa*" = "a+" to improve performance.

However, there are some patterns that cannot be written as regular expressions. For example, there is no regular expression for *n* occurrences of "a", followed by the same number of occurrences of "b" in a string.

10.5 ANSI and ISO Search Languages

Both the ISO and ANSI text retrieval languages have about the same functionality, but the ANSI command set is more of a textbase language, and the ISO command set is more of a document base

language. Neither language deals with indexing, security, or inserting or deleting documents from the textbase. It is only in the last few years at all that information people (read "librarians") have started to develop computer-based standards. Even worse, editors in academic and commercial publishing are even further behind. Even today, the editors at many book publishers remove all the ISBN (International Standard Book Numbers) from the references and insist on putting the city in the citations.

10.5.1 ANSI Common Command Language

The ANSI Z39.58 "Common Command Language for Online Interactive Information Retrieval" was developed by the National Information Standards Organization (NISO). The syntax is designed to be entered one command at a time, much like BASIC. The first word on the line is the command, and it can be followed by zero or more parameters. Spaces and commas are equivalent and are significant. Semicolons separate multiple commands on a single line (this is useful in defining macros). The language is case insensitive and requires only the first three letters of a command.

The commands can be grouped as system related, session related, query related, I/O related, and macro related.

System-related commands include the following:

- `CHOOSE`: Select the textbase(s) to be searched
- `DELETE`: Delete macros, print requests, result sets
- `EXPLAIN`: Obtain information about the system
- `RELATE`: Display related terms from thesauri
- `SCAN`: Display sorted list of indexed terms

Notice that there is no logon or password command. `DELETE` can remove a wide range of user-defined system objects, but has no power over the documents and indexes themselves. We will see later that the `HELP` command is like the `EXPLAIN` command, but it applies only to a particular session.

The next class of commands modifies a session:

- SET: Change default parameters for the session
- SHOW: Display the default parameters for the session
- START: Begin a session, with default parameters
- STOP: End the session

The SET command has two parameters: the system parameter and its new value. Just what these are is system dependent and is not defined in the ANSI document. START begins a system-defined logon and may purge old results. Likewise, STOP begins a system-defined logout and may purge old results.

The following commands can be used in a session:

- BACK: Display preceding data or items in a list
- FIND: Search the textbase, indexes, or thesauri
- HELP: Obtain help in the context of the session
- REVIEW: Display a search history
- SORT: Arrange records in a result set

The FIND command serves the same purpose as the proximity operators in the ANSI language, but the wildcards are different. The "!" surrounded by spaces will match to exactly one word, not character. The "#" surrounded by spaces will match to zero or one word, not zero or one character.

Both word matching operators preserve the order of the words to either side. However, you can add a "%" to either side of them (%!, !%, %#, #%) and ordering is no longer required. This allows you to write patterns equivalent to the ANSI "Wn" and "Nn" proximity operators.

Boolean operators are the usual AND (union), OR (intersection), and NOT (set difference). Prior result sets can be mixed with search patterns in Boolean expressions. The precedence of operators is NOT, AND, and finally OR, which can be changed by the use of parentheses.

10.5.2 The ISO 8777 Language

The ISO language specifies a left-to-right order of evaluation; the ANSI language is silent on this. Character patterns are done first, then word patterns, and finally the Boolean operators.

Ranging or limiting operators are for use with numbers only. They are `GT` or > (greater than), `LT` or < (less than), `GE` or >= (greater than or equal to), `LE` or <= (less than or equal to), `NE` or <> (not equal to), and the hyphen or keyword `TO` for between.

Only a few products actually implement either the ANSI or ISO search languages. The good news is that most products resemble them, so you will not have much trouble moving from one product to another.

Exotic Data

DR. CODD DID more than just define the relational model so we could build SQL databases. He also gave us an idea as to how a persistent store of data should behave. SQL happens to use what would have been called "record-oriented" data in file systems, but the relational database model never spoke to the nature of the elements involved and dealt instead with general principles that can be applied to other forms of data, if they can be modeled with relations, logic, and sets.

This nontraditional data includes geographical data, still images, video and other moving images, two- and three-dimensional spatial data, audio, and other types of data that are now a part of the corporate landscape. Coined words such as "textbase," "imagebase," or "geobase" give a nod to the original databases.

This is not really new data in the sense that it never existed before, but it is data that we never thought we could store and manipulate before. The bad news for the author of this book is that the standards for these exotic "datatypes" are either in flux or do not exist yet. The other bad news is that technology is adding to the number of exotic datatypes available.

Let me discuss some of the more popular datatypes, but at a higher level than in the preceding chapters. I want to look for the common threads in all this diverse information.

11.1 The Nature of Data Manipulation

Part of the genius of the relational model is that it separates the logical from the physical representation of the data. This gives us a general approach to any data, not just the traditional record-oriented data that is the mainstay of data processing.

The "whatever-you-want-to-call-it" base is made up of

1. A single persistent schema for the data stores. This is a formal description of the logical—not the physical—storage of the data.

2. Persistent attributes and values within the data stores. This gets into the datatypes used and several other things; allow me to avoid the details at this point.

3. A formal language for data retrieval. Operators for the data are either open or closed. A closed operator returns a result of the same datatype as its inputs; an open operator does not. Very generally speaking, we like to have closure, but it is not always possible.

4. Data integrity maintained by the data stores rather than by the application programs or users. Files were very passive, but a "something-base" is more active about maintaining rules and relationships within itself.

5. Retrieval of the data in a format meaningful to the user. In the case of SQL, this meant that a result set is passed over to a host program, which then does some traditional data processing with it. In the case of an imagebase, the results might be pictures displayed on a screen along with some text component.

11.2 Physical versus Perceptual Data

As broad categories of nontraditional data, allow me to invent the terms *physical data* and *perceptual data*. Physical data has a measurable aspect to it, and that is what we want to capture. Perceptual data needs to have a human being to get any information from it; it is more sensory and semantic in nature.

11.2.1 Physical Data

Physical data can be divided into schematic or representative models. A schematic model tries to capture the relationships in the data; a representative model tries to capture the measurements.

For example, spatial data (either two- or three- dimensional) can be schematic or representative. Drafting systems are the most obvious type of spatial system and were probably the first. Input is usually done with some sort of mechanical cursor, then made more precise with actual values added to the dimensions on the drawings.

A plan for a house has to be very precise (representative), or you cannot build anything from it. A wiring diagram is usually done as a schematic, however.

GISs (geographical information systems) have become a special area in themselves, with several companies selling commercial products and services for them. The data they store and manipulate can be a topological model with information about the earth's crust—the representative data.

A subway map showing the stations, however, needs only be a schematic to serve its function. This type of map shows the connections but not the distances between the stations. The nice part about the schematic is that it adds the names or colors of the subway lines and the travel times between stations.

11.2.2 Perceptual Data

Perceptual data is aimed at giving a human being sensory information. Right now this means sight and sound, either separately or together, but if science fiction stories prove correct, we might hook into a virtual reality system.

Images can be either still or moving. Still images are usually photographs, but can be artwork. There are many different storage formats for the images, each one based on the idea of a pixel—a small dot of color and hue in a position within the image. Pixals are like the bytes that make up traditional data, and very often they are encoded as bytes. Broadly speaking, the different image formats use a different approach to color. The human eye does not see color exactly as it appears in the spectrum, so some adjustments have to be made.

Searching and indexing images are still new and not as precise as indexing traditional data. Image indexing consists of reducing the size and resolution of the image, instead of trying to overlay an exact match on a pixel-by-pixel basis. The most promising searching techniques match a known image against the imagebase records on color, texture, and general shape along with any identification you have. For example, IBM advertised a product by showing a match to a hand-drawn picture of a green bottle being used to search an imagebase of bottles.

However, the search can be fooled by an image shown at an odd angle or by a similar image. The classic story is an attempt to locate a banana in a photographic imagebase and retrieving a picture of a toucan with a large yellow beak.

The moral to the story is that today a human being is still better at making a final determination than a machine. However, the machine can do a nice job of pruning a candidate set to the size that a human being can handle.

Moving images are not widely stored yet. The usual indexing methods are based on scanning the video or film images and looking for scene changes. The first frame of the new scene is then indexed as if it were a still photograph.

This is usually good enough, but we need a query language that will search for motion, such as "Find me video clips with things running in horizontal circles," for example.

Audio data is usually displayed as a waveform over a time line. This waveform looks like the old sound track on a motion picture film. The advantage is that users can jump to any time point and begin playing the audio track at any speed they wish. Queries can be complex, such as matching abstract voice patterns to determine if the same person recorded two different sound tracks.

11.3 Stored versus Constructed Data

Data can be stored in a format that attempts to reproduce the original value directly. However, there is a trend to store "applets" or "scripts" (or whatever the current buzzword happens to be) that tell a virtual machine how to reconstruct the data item in the client machine.

The JPG-4 standard is a good example of this trend. Prior standards for still images attempt to directly record the original image in a binary format, using some version of the pixel concept. The JPG-4 standard is a "script language" that tells the client machine how to reconstruct the image. A high-powered video system will not build the same image as a desktop monitor with limited resolution and color palette, even though they are both displaying and processing the same JPG-4 data item.

The client gets a crude image and then requests more and more details to improve the resolution to the limit that its hardware can display.

In particular, fractals are proving to be most useful in reconstructing data. Without going into the technical details and mathematics of fractals, let me define them as "self-similar structures" and refer you to any of several popular books on them (see Briggs and Peat 1989; Briggs 1992; Mandelbrot 1977; Pickover 1996). The most common example given of fractals is the coastline of a country. It is irregular when viewed from a great height or on a large-scale map. As you "zoom in" or start using more detailed maps, it is still irregular and never straightens out. The details have the same defining formulas as the highest levels, so you can reconstruct the original data at any level with the formulas. The amount of data compression for images is impressive. The technique also applies to sounds (Pickover 1996 has a chapter on the uses of fractals for sound and music).

11.4 SQL/MM

As part of the SQL3 project in NCITS H2 (previously ANSI X3H2), a subcommittee for SQL/MM (multimedia) was formed to embed new datatypes into the SQL framework as part of object-oriented extensions. As of this writing, not much has come from this effort, and nothing has been made into a formal standard.

The most interesting proposal for an addition to the SQL-92 language came from Rick Snodgrass at the University of Arizona. He has been doing work with temporal databases and proposed extending SQL to handle periods of time at a primitive level. Although the proposal was later withdrawn, it was interesting nonetheless.

Scales and Measurements

BEFORE YOU CAN put data into a database, you actually need to think about how it will be represented and manipulated. This is true not just of SQL but of any record keeping system. If you don't believe that the representation is important, then try taking a square root in Roman numerals, in Mayan numerals, and in Hindu-Arabic numerals. The numbers are all the same, but the numerals are different, and it makes a world of difference in what you can do with the data.

This chapter deals with the representation of individual attributes of the entities we are trying to model in a database.

12.1 Measurement Theory

Measure all that is measurable and attempt to make measurable that which is not yet so.— Galileo

This is a short introduction to measurement theory and scales, so that you will have a good theoretical foundation to do any practical work. Besides, this is interesting stuff. Trust me. Measurement is not just assigning numbers to things or their attributes so much as it is assigning to things a structural property that can be expressed in numbers or other computable symbols. This structure is the scale

used to take the measurement; the numbers or symbols represent units of measure.

Scales are classified into types by the properties they do or do not have. The properties with which we are concerned are the following:

1. A natural origin point on the scale. This is sometimes called a "zero," but it does not have to be literally a numeric zero. For example, if the measurement is the distance between objects, the natural zero is zero meters—you cannot get any closer than that. If the measurement is the temperature of objects, the natural zero is zero degrees Kelvin—nothing can get any colder than absolute zero. However, consider time: it goes from an eternal past into an eternal future, so you cannot find a natural origin for it.

2. Meaningful operations that can be performed on the units. It makes sense to add weights together to get a new weight. However, adding names or shoe sizes together is absurd.

3. A natural ordering of the units. It makes sense to speak about an event's occurring before or after another, or a thing's being heavier, longer, or hotter than another.

   But the alphabetical order imposed on a list of names is arbitrary, not natural—a foreign language, with different names for the same objects, would impose another ordering.

4. A natural metric function on the units. A metric function has nothing to do with the "metric system" of measurements, which is more properly called SI (Système International d'Unités). Metric functions have the following three properties:
   a. The metric between an object and itself is the natural origin of the scale. We can write this in a semimathematical notation as $M(a, a) = 0$.
   b. The order of the objects in the metric function does not matter. Again in the notation, $M(a, b) = M(b, a)$.
   c. There is a natural additive function that obeys the rule that $M(a, b) + M(b, c) \geq M(a, c)$, which is also known as the triangular inequality.

This notation is meant to be more general than just arithmetic. The "zero" in the first property is the origin of the scale, not just a numeric zero. The third property, defined with a "plus" and a "greater than or equal" sign, is a symbolic way of expressing more general ordering relationships. The "greater than or equal" sign refers to a natural ordering on the attribute being measured. The "plus" sign refers to a meaningful operation in regard to that ordering, not just arithmetic addition.

The special case of the third property, where the "greater than or equal to" is always "greater than," is very desirable to people because it means that they can use numbers for units and do simple arithmetic with the scales. This is called a strong metric property. For example, human perceptions of sound and light intensity follow a cube root law—that is, if you double the intensity of light, the perception of the intensity increases by only 20% (Stevens 1957). The actual formula is "Physical intensity to the 0.3 power equals perceived intensity" in English. Knowing this, designers of stereo equipment use controls that work on a logarithmic scale internally, but that show evenly spaced marks on the control panel of the amplifier.

It is possible to have a scale that has any combination of the metric properties. For example, instead of measuring the distance between two places in meters, measure it in units of effort. Does it have the property that $M(a, a) = 0$? Yes, it takes no effort to get to where you already are located. Does it have the property that $M(a, b) = M(b, a)$? No, it takes less effort to go downhill than to go uphill. Does it have the property that $M(a, b) + M(b, c) \geq M(a, c)$? Yes, the amount of effort needed to go directly to a place will always be less than the effort of making another stop along the way.

12.2 Range and Granularity

Range and granularity are properties of the way the measurements are made. Since we have to store data in a database within certain limits, they are very important to a database designer.

12.2.1 Range

A scale also has other properties that are of interest to someone building a database. First, scales have a range—what are the highest and lowest values that can appear on the scale? It is possible to have a finite or an infinite limit on either the lower or the upper bound. Overflow and underflow errors are the result of range violations inside the database.

Database designers do not have infinite storage, so we have to pick a subrange to use in the database when we have no upper or lower bound. For example, very few computer calendar routines will handle geological time periods. But then very few companies have bills that have been outstanding for that long either, so we do not mind.

12.2.2 Granularity and Precision

Look at a ruler and a micrometer. They both measure length, using the same scale, but there is a difference. A micrometer is more precise because it has a finer granularity of units. *Granularity* is a static property of the scale itself—how many notches there are on your ruler. In Europe, all industrial drawings are done in millimeters; the United States has been using $\frac{1}{32}$ of an inch.

Precision is how close the measurements are to the actual value. *Accuracy* is a measure of how repeatable a measurement is. Both depend on granularity, but they are not the same thing. Human nature says that a number impresses according to the square of the number of decimal places. Hence, some people will use a computer system to express things to as many decimal places as possible, even when it makes no sense. For example, civil engineering in the United States uses decimal feet for road design. Nobody can build a road any more precise than that, but you will see civil engineering students turning in work that is expressed in ten-thousandths of a foot. You don't use a micrometer on asphalt! A database often does not give the user a choice of precision for many calculations. In fact, the SQL standards leave the number of decimal places in the results of many arithmetic operations to be implementor-defined.

The ideas are easier to explain with handgun targets, which are scales to measure the ability of the shooter to put bullets in the center of a target. A bigger target has a wider range than a smaller target. A target with more rings has a higher granularity.

Once you start shooting, a group of shots that is closer together is more precise because the shots were more repeatable. A shot group that is closer to the center is more accurate because the shots were closer to the goal. Notice that precision and accuracy are not the same thing! If I have a good gun whose sights are off, I can get a very tight cluster that is not near the bull's-eye (see Fig. 12.1).

Fig. 12.1

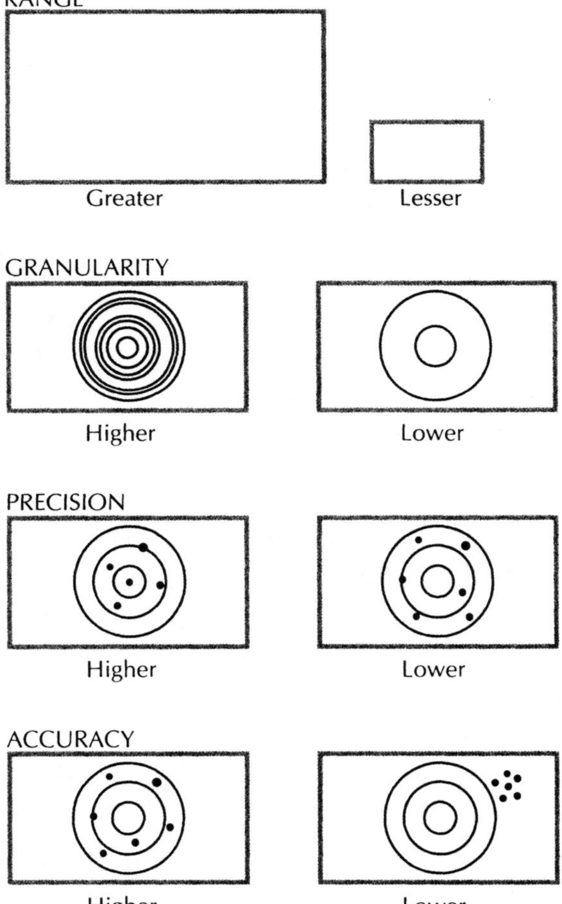

12.3 Types of Scales

The lack or presence of precision and accuracy determines the kind of scale you should choose. Scales are either quantitative or qualitative. The quantitative scales are what most people mean when they think of measurements because these scales can be manipulated and are usually represented as numbers. Qualitative scales attempt to impose an order on an attribute, but they do not allow for computations—just comparisons.

12.3.1 Nominal Scales

The simplest scales are the nominal scales. They simply assign a unique symbol, usually a number or a name, to each member of the set that they attempt to measure. For example, a list of city names is a nominal scale.

Right away we are into philosophical differences, because many people do not consider listing to be measurement. Since there is no clear property being measured, that school of thought would tell us this cannot be a scale.

There is no natural origin point for a set, and likewise there is no ordering. We tend to use alphabetical ordering for names, but it makes just as much sense to use frequency of occurrence or increasing size or almost any other attribute that does have a natural ordering.

The only meaningful operation that can be done with such a list is a test for equality—"Is this city New York or not?"—which will test either TRUE, FALSE, or UNKNOWN.

Nominal scales are very common in databases because they are used for unique identifiers, such as names and descriptions.

12.3.2 Categorical Scales

The next simplest scales are the categorical scales. They place an entity into a category that is assigned a unique symbol, usually a number or a name. For example, the class of animals might be categorized as reptiles, mammals, and so forth. The categories have to be within the same class of things to make sense.

Again, many people do not consider categorizing to be measurement. The categories are probably defined by a large number of properties, but there are two potential problems with them.

The first problem is that an entity might fall in one or more categories. For example, a platypus is a furry, warm-blooded, egg-laying animal. Mammals are warm blooded, but give live birth and optionally have fur. The second problem is that an entity might not fall into any of the categories at all. If we find a creature with chlorophyll and fur on Mars, we do not have a category of animal in which to place it.

The two common solutions are either to create a new category of animal (monotremes for the platypus and echidna), or to allow an entity to be a member of more than one category.

There is no natural origin point for a collection of subsets, and likewise there is no ordering of the subsets. The only meaningful operation that can be done with such a scale is a test for membership—"Is this animal a mammal or not?"—which will test either TRUE, FALSE, or UNKNOWN.

12.3.3 Absolute Scales

An absolute scale is a count of the elements in a set. Its natural origin is zero, or the empty set. The count is the ordering (a set of five elements is bigger than a set of three elements, and so on). Addition and subtraction are metric functions. Each element is taken to be identical and interchangeable. For example, when you buy a dozen Grade A eggs, you assume that for your purposes any Grade A egg will do the same job as any other Grade A egg.

Again, absolute scales are very common in databases because they are used for quantities.

12.3.4 Ordinal Scales

Ordinal scales put things in order, but have no origin and no operations. For example, geologists use Mohs' scale to measure the hardness of minerals. It is based on a set of standard minerals, which are ordered by relative hardness (talc = 1, gypsum = 2, calcite = 3, fluorite = 4, apatite = 5, feldspar = 6, quartz = 7, topaz = 8, sapphire = 9, diamond = 10). To measure an unknown mineral, you try to scratch

the polished surface of one of the standard minerals with it; if it scratches the surface, the unknown is harder. Notice that I can get two different unknown minerals with the same measurement that are not equal to each other, and that I can get minerals that are softer than my lower bound or harder than my upper bound. There is no origin point and operations on the measurements make no sense (e.g., if I add 10 talc units I do not get a diamond).

Perhaps the most common use we see of ordinal scales today is to measure preferences or opinions. You are given a product or a situation and asked to decide how much you like or dislike it, how much you agree or disagree with a statement, and so forth. The scale is usually given a set of labels such as "strongly agree" through "strongly disagree," or the labels are ordered from 1 to 5.

Consider pairwise choices between ice cream flavors. Saying that vanilla is preferred over wet leather in our taste test might well be expressing a universal truth, but there is no objective unit of "likability" to apply. The lack of a unit means that such things as opinion polls that try to average such scales are meaningless; the best you can do is a bar graph of the number of respondents in each category.

Another problem is that an ordinal scale may not be transitive. Transitivity is the property of a relationship in which if $R(a, b)$ and $R(b, c)$ then $R(a, c)$. We like this property and expect it in the real world, where we have relationships like "heavier than," "older than," and so forth. This is the result of a strong metric property.

But an ice cream taster, who has just found out that the shop is out of vanilla, might prefer squid over wet leather, prefer wet leather over wood, and yet prefer wood over squid, so there is no metric function or linear ordering at all. Again, we are into philosophical differences, since many people do not consider a nontransitive relationship to be a scale.

If you are interested in the problems of nontransitive relationships, look at the book *Wheels, Life, and Other Mathematical Amusements* (Gardner 1983), which has a chapter on nontransitive relationships. Voting theory is a branch of political science that shows that there are still problems even when an individual's preferences are well ordered (Hively 1996; Murakami 1968; Taylor 1995).

12.3.5 Rank Scales

Rank scales have an origin and an ordering, but no natural operations. The most common example of this would be military ranks. Nobody is lower than a private, and that rank is a starting point in your military career, but it makes no sense to somehow combine three privates to get a sergeant.

Rank scales have to be transitive: a sergeant gives orders to a private, and since a major gives orders to a sergeant, he can also give orders to a private. You will see ordinal and rank scales grouped together in some of the literature if the author does not allow nontransitive ordinal scales. You will also see the same fallacies committed when people try to do statistical summaries of such scales.

12.3.6 Quantitative Scales and Sets

There are some subtle differences among different quantitative scales. To make the point, we will use four army buddies and try to measure them on different quantitative scales. Let's start with their military ranks:

Tom = sergeant

Dick = corporal

Richard = corporal

Harry = private

Clearly, Tom has the highest rank and Harry has the lowest. Dick and Richard have the same rank. If Tom or Harry were to get shot in combat, Dick and Richard would still have the rank of corporal. Likewise, the rank of corporal would still be on the scale even if there were no members at that level. A ranking can have zero or more elements in each unit of the scale.

The boys now get out of the army and go to school. The grades on their first report card are

Tom = A

Dick = B

Richard = B

Harry = C

Clearly, Tom is the top student. But note that Harry is fourth in his class because there are three students with better grades than his. If Richard drops out of school, Harry moves up to third in the class. Class standing is not a ranking; it is a positioning. Each position must have one or more members, so there has to be a promotion rule when an element is taken from the data set. The convention in schools has been to give both Dick and Richard the honor of being second in their class, with Harry as third. That is, we fill all the gaps from first to *n*th standing with one or more data items.

Now the boys go to work for the same company as salesmen. Their boss has a sales contest, in which they perform like this:

Tom = $100,000

Dick = $90,000

Richard = $90,000

Harry = $80,000

Nobody beats Tom, and he is the Salesman of the Month. Harry is fourth because there are three other people who sold more than he did. Again, the promotion rule applies if one of the boys should get hit by a beer truck. But what is the contest standing for Dick and Richard? The convention here is to allow gaps and say that they are both third and nobody is second.

These last two situations, class standing and contest placement, are not scales. Their values depend on a rule that needs the rest of the set, whereas a scale is external to the data set. If you try to put a standing or a placement in a database, then you have to recalculate it every time you change anything in the database. These last two situations are statistics and can be useful.

12.3.7 Interval Scales

Interval scales have a metric function, ordering, and meaningful operations among the units, but no natural origin. Calendars are the best example; some arbitrary historical event is the starting point for the scale, and all measurements are related to it using identical units or intervals. Time extends from a past eternity to a future eternity.

The metric function is the number of days between two dates. Looking at the three properties: (1) $M(a, a) = 0$: there are zero days between today and today. (2) $M(a, b) = M(b, a)$: there are just as many days from today to next Monday as there are from next Monday to today. (3) $M(a, b) + M(b, c) \geq M(a, c)$: the number of days from today to next Monday plus the number of days from next Monday to Christmas is the same as the number of days from today until Christmas.

Ordering is very natural and strong: 1900-July-1 occurs before 1993-July-1.

Aggregations of the basic unit (days) into other units (weeks, months, and years) are also arbitrary. (For a good discussion of the history of these aggregated units, see Zerubavel 1985.)

12.3.8 Ratio Scales

Ratio scales are what people think of when they think about a measurement. Ratio scales have an origin (usually zero units), an ordering, and a set of operations that can be expressed in arithmetic. They are called ratio scales because all measurements are expressed as multiples or fractions of a certain unit or interval.

Length, mass, and volume are examples of this type of scale. The unit is what is arbitrary; mass is still mass whether it is measured in kilograms or in pounds. Another nice property is that the units are identical; a kilogram is still a kilogram whether it is measuring feathers or bricks.

Absolute and ratio scales are also called *extensive scales* because they deal with quantities, as opposed to the remaining scales, which are intensive because they measure qualities. Quantities can be added and manipulated together; qualities cannot.

type of scale	natural ordering	natural origin	natural functions	example
Nominal	no	no	no	city names ('Atlanta')
Categorical	no	no	no	animals (dogs, cats)
Absolute	yes	yes	yes	egg cartons (dozen)
Ordinal	yes	no	no	preferences (better than)
Rank	yes	yes	no	contests (win, place, show)
Interval	yes	no	yes	time (hour, minute)
Ratio	yes	yes	yes	length, weight (meter, kilogram)

The origin for the absolute scale is numeric zero, and the natural functions are simple arithmetic. However, things are not always this simple. Temperature has an origin point at absolute zero, and its natural functions average heat over mass. This is why you cannot defrost a refrigerator that is at 0°C by putting a chicken whose body temperature is 35°C inside it. The decibel scale for sound and the Richter scale for earthquakes are exponential, so their functions involve logarithms.

12.4 Scale Conversion

The important principle of measurement theory is that you can convert from one scale to another only if they are of the same type and measure the same attribute.

Absolute scales do not convert, which is why they are called absolute scales. Five apples are five apples, no matter how many times you count them or how you arrange them on the table.

Nominal scales are converted to other nominal scales by a mapping between the scales. That means you look things up in a table. For example, I can convert my English city names to Polish city names with a dictionary. The problem comes when there is not a one-to-one mapping between the two nominal scales. For example,

English uses the word "cousin" to identify the offspring of your parents' siblings, and tradition treats them all pretty much alike. Chinese language and culture have separate words for the same relations based on the genders of your parents' siblings and the age relationships among them (e.g., the oldest son of your father's oldest brother is a particular type of cousin, and you have different social obligations to him). Something is lost in translation.

Ordinal scales are converted to ordinal scales by a monotonic function. That means you preserve the ordering when you convert. Looking at the Mohs' scale for geologists, I can pick another set of minerals, plastics, or metals to scratch, but rock samples that were definitely softer than others will still be softer. Again, there are problems when there is not a one-to-one mapping between the two scales. My new scale may be able to tell the difference between rocks where the Mohs' scale could not.

Rank scales are converted to rank scales by a monotonic function that preserves the ordering, like ordinal scales. Again, there are problems when there is not a one-to-one mapping between the two scales. For example, different military branches have slightly different ranks that don't quite correspond to each other.

In both the nominal and the ordinal scales, the problem was that things that looked equal on one scale were different on another. This has to do with range and granularity, discussed in section 12.2.

Interval scales are converted to interval scales by a linear function; that is, a function of the form $y = ax + b$. This preserves the ordering, but shifts the origin point when you convert. For example, I can convert temperature from degrees Celsius to degrees Fahrenheit using the formula F = (9/5 * C) + 32.

Ratio scales are converted to ratio scales by a constant multiplier, since both scales have the same ordering and origin point. For example, I can convert from pounds to kilograms using the formula $p = 0.4536 * k$. This is why people like to use ratio scales.

12.5 Derived Units

Many of the scales that we use are not primary units, but derived units—measures that are constructed from primary units, such as miles per hour (time and distance) or square miles (distance and

distance). You can use only ratio and interval scales to construct derived units.

If you use an absolute scale with a ratio or interval scale, you are dealing with statistics, not measurements. For example, using weight (ratio scale) and the number of people in New York (absolute scale), we can compute the average weight of a New Yorker, which is a statistic, not a unit of measurement.

The SI measurements use a basic set of seven units (meter for length, kilogram for mass, second for time, ampere for electrical current, degree Kelvin for temperature, mole for molecules, and candela for light) and construct derived units. ISO standard 2955 ("Information Processing—Representation of SI and Other Units for Use in Systems with Limited Character Sets"), for expressing derived units as formulas, has a notation for expressing SI units in ASCII character strings. The notation uses parentheses, spaces, multiplication (shown by a period), division (shown by a solidus, or slash), and exponents (shown by numerals immediately after the unit abbreviation). There are also names for most of the standard derived units. For example, "100 kg.m/s2" converts to 10 newtons (the unit of force), written as "10 N" instead.

12.6 Punctuation and Standard Units

A database stores measurements as numeric data represented in a binary format, but when the data is input or output, a human being wants readable characters and punctuation.

Punctuation serves to identify the units being used and can be used for prefix, postfix, or infix symbols. It can also be implicit or explicit.

If I write "$25.15", you know that the unit of measure is the dollar because of the explicit prefix dollar sign. If I write "160 lbs.", you know that the unit of measure is pounds because of the explicit postfix abbreviation for the unit. If I write "1989 MAR 12", you know that this is a date because of the implicit infix separation among month, day, and year, achieved by changing from numerals to letters, and the optional spaces. The ISO and SQL defaults represent the same date, using explicit infix punctuation, with 1989-03-12 instead. Likewise, a column header on a report that gives the units used is explicit punctuation.

Databases do not generally store punctuation. The sole exception might be the `MONEY` or `CURRENCY` datatype found in many SQL implementations as a vendor extension.

Punctuation wastes storage space, and the units can be represented in some internal format that can be used in calculations. Punctuation is only for display.

It is possible to put the units in a column next to a numeric column that holds their quantities. This is awkward and wastes storage space. If everything is expressed in the same unit, the units column is redundant. If things are expressed in different units, you have to convert them to a common unit to do any calculations, so why not store them in a common unit in the first place? The DBA has to be sure that all data in a column of a table is expressed in the same units before it is stored. There are some horror stories about multinational companies sending the same input programs used in the United States to their European offices, where SI and English measurements were mixed into the same database without conversion.

Ideally, the DBA should be sure that data is kept in the same units in all the tables in the database. If different units are needed, they can be provided in a `VIEW` that hides the conversions (thus the office in the United States sees English measurements and the European offices see SI units and date formats; neither is aware of the conversions being done for it).

12.7 General Guidelines for Using Scales in a Database

The following are general guidelines for using measurements and scales in a database, and not firm, hard rules. You will find exceptions to all of them.

1. Use `CHECK()` clauses on table declarations to make sure that only the allowed values appear in the database. If you have the `CREATE DOMAIN` feature of SQL-92, use it to build your scales. Nominal scales would have a list of possible values; other scales would have range checking.

   Likewise, use the `DEFAULT()` clauses to be sure that each scale starts with its origin value, a `NULL`, or a default value that makes sense.

2. Declare at least one more decimal place than you think you will need for units that can be expressed as fractions. In most SQL implementations, rounding and truncation will improve with more decimal places.

   The downside of SQL is that precision and the rules for truncation and rounding are implementation-dependent, so a query with calculations might not give the same results on another product. However, SQL is more merciful than older file systems, since the DBA can `ALTER` a numeric column so it will have more precision and a greater range without destroying existing data or queries. Host programs may have to be changed to display the extra characters in the results, however.

3. Try to store primary units rather than derived units. This is not always possible, since you might not be able to measure anything but the derived unit. Look at your new tire gauge; it is set for pascals (newtons per square meter) and will not tell you how many square meters you have on the surface of the tire or the force exerted by the air.

   And you simply cannot figure these things out from the pascals given. A set of primary units can be arranged in many different ways to construct any possible derived unit desired.

   Never store both the derived and the primary units in the same table. Not only is this redundant, but it opens the door to possible errors when a primary unit column is changed and the derived units based on it are not updated. Also, most computers can recalculate the derived units much faster than they can read a value from a disk drive.

4. Use the same punctuation whenever a unit is displayed. For example, do not mix ISO and ANSI date formats, or express weight in pounds and kilograms on the same report. Ideally, everything should be displayed the same way in the entire application system.

Missing Data

IN A PERFECT mathematical model, we know everything. However, the real world is not a perfect mathematical model. There will be values of attributes that are missing from our database.

The Interim Report 75-02-08 to the ANSI X3 (SPARC Study Group 1975) had 14 different kinds of incomplete data that could appear as the result of queries or as attribute values. These types included overflows, underflows, errors, and other problems in trying to represent the real world within the limits of a database.

People have trouble with things that are not there. It took centuries for Hindu-Arabic numerals (with the new concept of zero) to surpass the zeroless Roman numerals in popularity in Europe. In fact, many early Renaissance accounting firms advertised that they did not use the fancy, newfangled notation and kept records in well-understood Roman numerals instead.

Many of the conceptual problems with zero arose from not knowing the difference between ordinal and cardinal numbers. Ordinal numbers measure position; cardinal numbers measure quantity or magnitude. The argument against the zero was this: If there is no quantity or magnitude there, how can you count or measure it? What does it mean to multiply or divide a number by zero?

Likewise, it was a long time before the idea of an empty set found its way into mathematics. The argument was that if there are no elements, how can you have a set of them? Is the empty set a subset of itself? Is the empty set a subset of all other sets? Is there only one universal empty set, or one empty set for each type of set?

Many programmers who are used to file systems have a hard time understanding that an empty table in SQL still has a structure of columns and constraints, but no rows. In a file system, an empty file was simply a name in a directory with a pointer to zero bytes of storage. These same programmers are also bothered by the idea that an empty table can be a valid result from a query and can trigger the same actions as a table with rows.

13.1 Types of Missing Data

Let us use the notation E(A) = V to represent the idea that an entity, E, has an attribute, A, which has a value, V. For example, I could write "John(hair) = black" to say that John has black hair. This model assumes that the values can be drawn only from a domain that makes sense for the attribute. That is, "John(hair) = 3.14159" makes no sense because the entity is a person and the attribute is hair color, so the value must be a color, not a number.

Let us extend this notation to use the word `NULL` to represent missing values, attributes, and entities. The missing value, regardless of the reason it is missing, would be shown in our notation as E(A) = `NULL`. This means that we know the entity, we know the attribute, but we do not know the value.

Another flavor of `NULL` is "not applicable"—shown as N/A on forms and spreadsheets and called "I-marks" by Dr. E. F. Codd (1990) in the second version of his relational model—which we have been using on paper forms and in some spreadsheets for years. For example, a bald man's hair color attribute is a missing-value `NULL` drawn from the hair color domain, but his feather color attribute is a "not applicable" `NULL`. The attribute itself is missing, not just the value. This missing-attribute `NULL` could be written as E(`NULL`) = `NULL` in the formula notation.

How could an attribute not belonging to an entity show up in a table? Suppose you consolidate medical records and put everyone together for statistical purposes. You should not find any male pregnancies in the result table. You have a choice as to how to handle pregnancies. You could have a column in the consolidated table for "number of pregnancies," put a zero or a NULL in the rows where sex = 'male', and then add some CHECK( ) clauses to make sure that this integrity rule is enforced.

The other way is to have a column for "medical condition" and one for "number of occurrences" beside it. Another CHECK( ) clause would make sure male pregnancies don't appear. But what happens when the sex is unknown and all we have is a name like 'Alex Morgan', which could belong to either gender? Can we use the presence of one or more pregnancies to determine that Alex is a woman? What if Alex is a woman without children?

The case where we have NULL(A) = V is a bit strange. It means that we do not know the entity, but we are looking for a known attribute, A, which has a value of V. This is like asking, "What things are colored red?"—a perfectly good question but very hard to ask in an SQL database.

For completeness, we could play with all eight possible combinations of known and unknown values in the basic E(A) = V formula. But such combinations are of little use or meaning. For example, NULL(NULL) = V would mean that we know a value, but not the entity or the attribute. This is like the running joke from Douglas Adams's *Hitchhiker's Guide to the Galaxy,* in which the answer to the question "What is the meaning of life, the universe, and everything?" is 42. Likewise, "total ignorance" NULL, shown as NULL(NULL) = NULL, means that we have no information about the entity, even about its existence, its attributes, or their values.

Getting back to missing values, let us look at the most common reasons that the values might be missing by following a scenario at a hospital.

13.1.1 Unknown

In this situation we know that an entity exists and that it has attributes, but we do not know the value of an attribute. As a real-world example of this, consider a hospital admission form. A patient arrives

in a coma, so we cannot get their name. We know that they have one, so we might assign a dummy value ('John Doe', 'Jane Roe', or an admission tag number) to the patient to act as a placeholder. This is also how we would classify their condition upon arrival at the emergency room.

13.1.2 Not Applicable

Continuing down the admission form, we can see that our comatose patient is a man, so the question about the number of pregnancies he has had does not apply. In this situation, the attribute itself, rather than the value, is missing, and the entity never could have had this attribute.

13.1.3 Missing

A quick triage reveals that this patient has no money because he has no wallet. The section of the form for "cash on hand" can be filled out with a zero. But this is not quite the situation. A zero is more often used as a quantity rather than a missing-value token. A patient with an empty wallet is slightly different from our walletless guy. In this situation, the attribute, and therefore the value, is missing, but the entity could have or should have had the attribute.

13.1.4 Not Classified

We now continue to diagnose the patient, and we see that he is a bright shade of green with purple spots. When we try to enter a code for the disease, we cannot find any such disease. In this situation, the attribute and a value exist, but we do not have a way to express it in the database.

This is very often handled with a special code. In the case of the ICDA-9 (International Classification of Diseases, version 9) the code is 999.999, in contrast to ICDA code 000.000 for undiagnosed conditions.

13.1.5 Erroneous Data

We now take our patient's temperature and we get a reading of 100°C on our digital thermometer. The entity has the attribute, and we have a measured value for the attribute. But we know that the value is in error.

Errors, error detection, and error correction are topics in themselves. In this case, the error is confined to one attribute, and it can be detected by inspection of the column itself. However, knowing that a human being cannot have boiling hot blood does not tell us what his temperature really is.

If we had shown a male patient with a prior pregnancy, then we have two attributes, at least one of which is in error. This generalizes to the situation in which you have *n* attributes and several possible subsets of errors.

Error correcting codes are a formal mathematical model of this problem, in which the errors are incorrect digits in a number of length *n*. By adding extra digits to the number, it is possible to correct up to *k* errors, where $k < n$.

Illegal Results

Here a calculation is illegal (division by zero) or absurd (dividing shoe size by body weight to determine age). While the value is not usable, you at least know that some attempt was made to obtain it.

Error in Representation

In this situation, the calculation is valid, but the the database lacks the ability to represent the results. Numeric overflow and underflow are common examples in computers. Dates outside the range of the temporal datatypes are another source of such errors.

Limited Values

In this case, if you know that all of a certain set of values must appear in the data, and you know which of those values have already been used, then you know which of those values are remaining.

Imagine that you are playing a game of dominoes. You do not know where the double blank tile is because you do not see it on the

tableau or in your hand. But you know that it must be in your opponent's hand or in the boneyard. As the game progresses and more tiles are played or come into your hand, you gain more and more knowledge of the location of the double blank. When your opponent is down to one tile in his hand, you should have perfect knowledge of the location of the double blank—it is either on the table, in your own hand, or it is the last tile in your opponent's hand. You do not have to actually see the tile to know the location.

The limited value approach to data is not relational because each attribute is a subset of values. The goal is to reduce the subset down to a single value and thus make it a scalar.

13.2 The NULL in SQL

SQL has had a `NULL` in it since the first version of the language. Don Chamberlin once described the development of SQL at IBM's laboratories as a fight over `NULL`s and not over the relational model.

One camp feels that `NULL`s are a bad idea and wants to have none. This viewpoint is best represented by Chris Date, and I strongly recommend reading his writings for a strong defense of this position (see Date and Darwen 1992, chapter 18).

Dr. E. F. Codd, creator of the relational model, now favors two types of missing-value tokens, one for "unknown" (the eye color of a man wearing sunglasses) and one for "not applicable" (the eye color of an automobile). The idea is that the attribute exists in the first case, but not the value; at some time in the future we find a value for this attribute. In the second case, the attribute itself is missing, so no value is ever possible.

The `NULL` is not supposed to have a datatype, but a compiler must know how to allocate space in a real database so it can hold data if or when the `NULL` is replaced by a value in the column of the table. Therefore, SQL-92 has the expression `CAST (NULL AS <datatype>)` for the compiler.

There are three basic rules for `NULL`s in SQL.

First, `NULL`s are not equal to each other or to any value. Because of this, any comparison with a `NULL` has to return an `UNKNOWN` value. To test for a `NULL`, you must use the `<row value constructor> IS [NOT] NULL` predicate. It is the only way to test to see if an expression is

NULL or not, and it has been in SQL-86 and all later versions of the standard. The SQL-92 standard extended it to accept `<row value constructor>` instead of a single column or scalar expression. This extended version will start showing up in implementations when other row expressions are allowed. If all the values in row R are the NULL value, then R IS NULL is TRUE; otherwise, it is FALSE. If none of the values in R are the NULL value, R IS NOT NULL is TRUE; otherwise, it is FALSE. The case where the row is a mix of NULL and non-NULL values is defined by the following table, where "degree" means the number of columns in the row expression.

expression	R IS NULL	R IS NOT NULL	NOT R IS NULL	NOT R IS NOT NULL
Degree = 1				
NULL	TRUE	FALSE	FALSE	TRUE
No NULL	FALSE	TRUE	TRUE	FALSE
Degree > 1				
All NULLs	TRUE	FALSE	FALSE	TRUE
Some NULLs	FALSE	FALSE	TRUE	TRUE
No NULLs	FALSE	TRUE	TRUE	FALSE

Note that R IS NOT NULL has the same result as NOT R IS NULL if and only if R is of degree 1. This is a break in the usual pattern of predicates with a NOT option in them. Here are some examples:

```
(1, 2, 3) IS NULL = FALSE
(1, NULL, 3) IS NULL = FALSE
(1, NULL, 3) IS NOT NULL = FALSE
(NULL, NULL, NULL) IS NULL = TRUE
(NULL, NULL, NULL) IS NOT NULL = FALSE
NOT (1, 2, 3) IS NULL = TRUE
NOT (1, NULL, 3) IS NULL = TRUE
NOT (1, NULL, 3) IS NOT NULL = TRUE
NOT (NULL, NULL, NULL) IS NULL = TRUE
NOT (NULL, NULL, NULL) IS NOT NULL = FALSE
```

The second rule is that NULLs propagate in operations and functions. A NULL as an input to an operation or function will produce a NULL as the result. The exceptions to this rule are those functions that convert NULLs into values. The NULLIF( ) and COALESCE( ) functions replace expressions with NULL and vice versa. These functions are not yet present in most SQL implementations, but you will often find something like them. The NULLIF(V1, V2) function has two parameters. It is equivalent to the following CASE expression:

```
NULLIF(V1, V2) := CASE
                  WHEN (V1 = V2)
                  THEN NULL
                  ELSE V1 END;
```

That is, when the first parameter is equal to the second, the function returns a NULL; otherwise, it returns the first parameter's value.

The COALESCE(<value expression>, . . . , <value expression>) function scans the list of <value expression>s from left to right and returns the first non-NULL value in the list. If all the <value expression>s are NULL, the result is NULL. This is the same function, under a new name, as the VALUE(<value expression>, . . . , <value expression>) in DB2 and other SQL implementations based on DB2.

The third rule is that NULLs are treated as if they are equal to each other when forming groups. This was a decision made by the ANSI X3H2 committee early in the development of the language. The decision was based largely on the fact that almost all existing SQL products had implemented this convention.

However, a good theoretical argument can be made that a grouped table is a set of a different kind of elements than the set from which it was constructed. Each of the rows of a grouped table is made up of group characteristics, either grouping columns, summary functions, constants, system variables, or expressions built from these. Therefore, we have simply made a group from NULLs, using a rule that is not the same as equality comparisons between pairs of values.

Data Encoding Schemes

YOU DO NOT put data directly into a database. You convert it into an encoding scheme first, then put the encoding into the rows of the tables. Words have to be written in an alphabet and belong to a language; measurements are expressed as numbers. We are so used to seeing words and numbers that we no longer think of them as encoding schemes. We also often fail to distinguish among the possible ways to identify (and therefore to encode) an entity or property. Do we encode the person receiving medical services or the policy that is paying for them? That might depend on whether the database is for the doctor or for the insurance company. Do we encode the first title of a song or the alternate title or both? Or should we include the music itself in a multimedia database? And should it be as an image of the sheet music or as an audio recording? Nobody teaches people how to design these encoding schemes, so they are all too often done on the fly. Where standardized encoding schemes exist, they are too often ignored in favor of some ad hoc scheme. Beginning programmers have the attitude that encoding schemes do not really matter because the computer will take care of it, so they don't have to spend time on the design of their encoding schemes. This attitude has probably gotten worse with SQL than it was before.

Database designers think that an ALTER statement can fix any bad things they did at the start of the project.

Yes, the computer can take care of a lot of problems. But the data entry and validation programs become very complex and hard to maintain. Database queries that have to follow the same convoluted encodings will cost both computer time and money. And a human being still has to use the code at some point. Bad schemes give rise to errors in data entry and misreadings of outputs, and can lead to incorrect data models.

14.1 Bad Encoding Schemes

To use an actual example, the automobile license plate system for a certain southern state started as a punch card system written in Cobol. Many readers are too young to remember card punching (keypunch) machines. A punch card is a piece of stiff paper in which a character is represented as one or more rectangular holes made into one of 80 vertical columns on the card. Contiguous groups of columns make up fixed-length fields of data. The keypunch machine has a typewriter-like keyboard; it automatically feeds cards into the punch as fast as a human being can type. The position, length, and alphabetical or numeric shift for each field on the card can be set by a control card in the keypunch machine to save the operator keystrokes. This is a very fixed format and a very fast input method, and making changes to a program once it is in place is very hard.

The license plate system had a single card column for a single-position numeric code to indicate the type of plate: private car, chauffeured car, taxi, truck, public bus, and so forth. As time went on, more plate types were added for veterans of assorted wars, for university alumni, and for whatever other pressure group happened to have the political power to pass a bill allowing it a special license plate.

Soon there were more than 10 types, so a single digit could not represent them all. There was room on the punch card to change the length of the field to two digits. But Cobol uses fixed-length fields, so changing the card layout would require changes in the programs and in the keypunch procedures.

The first new license plate code was handled by letting the data entry clerk press a punctuation mark key instead of changing from numeric lock to manual shift mode. Once that decision was made, it was followed for each new code thereafter, until the scheme looked like everything on the upper row of keys on a typewriter.

Unfortunately, different makes and models of keypunch machines have different punctuation marks in the same keyboard position, so each deck of cards had to have a special program to convert its punches to the original model IBM 026 keypunch codes before the master file was updated. This practice continued even after all the original machines had been retired to used-equipment heaven.

The edit programs could not check for a simple numeric range to validate input, but had to use a small lookup routine with over 20 values in it. That does not sound like much until you realize that the system had to handle over three million records in the first quarter of the year. The error rate was quite high, and each batch needed to know which machine had punched the cards before it could use a lookup table.

If the encoding scheme had been designed with two digits (00 to 99) at the beginning, all of the problems would have been avoided. If I were to put this system into a database today, using video terminals for data entry, the plate type could be INTEGER and it could hold as many plate types as I would ever need. This is part of the legacy database problem.

The second example was reported in *Information Systems Week* (Roman 1987). The first sentence told the whole story: "The chaos and rampant error rates in New York City's new Welfare Management System appear to be due to a tremendous increase in the number of codes it requires in data entry and the subsequent difficulty for users in learning to use it." The rest of the article explained how the new system attempted to merge several old existing systems. In the merger, the error rates increased from 2% to over 20% because the encoding schemes used could not be matched up and consolidated.

14.1.1 Characteristics of a Bad Encoding Scheme

How do you know a bad encoding scheme when you see one? One bad feature is the failure to allow for growth. Talk to anyone who had to reconfigure a fixed-length record system to allow for the change

from the old ZIP codes to the current ZIP + 4 codes. SQL does not have this as a physical problem, but it can show up as a logical problem.

Another bad property is ambiguous encodings in the scheme. Perhaps the funniest example of this problem was the Italian telephone system's attempt at a "time of day" service. They used a special three-digit number, like the 411 information number in the United States. But the three digits they picked were also those of a telephone exchange in Milan, so nobody could call into that exchange without getting the time signal before they completed their call.

This happens more often than you would think, but the form that it usually takes is that of a "miscellaneous" code that is too general. Very different cases are then encoded as identical, and users are given incorrect or misleading information when they do a query.

A bad encoding scheme lacks codes for missing, unknown, not applicable, or miscellaneous values. The classic story is the man in California who bought a vanity license plate reading "NONE" and got thousands of traffic tickets as a result. The police had no special provision for a missing license plate on the tickets, so when a car had no license plate, they wrote "none" in the field for the license plate number. The database simply matched his name and address to every unpaid missing-plate ticket on file at the time.

Before you say that the `NULL` in SQL is a quick solution to this problem, think about how `NULL` is ignored in many SQL functions. The SQL query `SELECT plateno, SUM(fine) FROM tickets GROUP BY plateno;` will give the total fines on each car. But it also puts all the missing tags into one group (i.e., one car) although we want to see each one as a separate case, since it is very unlikely that there is only one car without a license plate in all of California.

There are also differences among "missing," "unknown," "not applicable," and "miscellaneous" values. They are subtle but important. For example, the International Classification of Disease uses 999.999 for miscellaneous illness. It means that we have diagnosed the patient, know that he or she has an illness, and cannot classify it—a very scary condition for the patient, but not quite the same thing as a missing disease code (just admitted, might not be sick), an

inapplicable disease code (pregnancy complications in a male), or an unknown disease code (sick and awaiting lab results).

14.2 Encoding Scheme Types

The following is my classification system for encoding schemes and suggestions for using each of them. You will find some of these same ideas in library science and other fields, but I have never seen anyone else attempt a classification system for data processing.

14.2.1 Enumeration Encoding

An enumeration encoding arranges the attribute values in some order and assigns a number or a letter to each value. Numbers are usually a better choice than letters because they can be increased without limit as more values are added. Enumeration schemes are a good choice for a short list of values, but a bad choice for a long list. It is too hard to remember a long list of codes, and very soon any natural ordering principle is violated as new values are tacked on the end.

A good heuristic is to order the values in some natural manner, if one exists in the data, so that table lookup will be easier. Chronological order (1 occurs before 2) or procedural order (1 must be done before 2) is often a good choice. Another good heuristic is to order the values from most common to least common. That way you will have shorter codes for the most common cases. Other orderings could be based on physical characteristics such as largest to smallest, rainbow color order, and so on.

After arguing for a natural order in the list, I must admit that the most common scheme is alphabetical order because it is simple to implement on a computer and makes it easy for a person to look up values in a table. ANSI standard X3.31 ("Structure for the Identification of Counties of the United States for Information Interchange") encodes county names within a state by first alphabetizing the names, then numbering them from 1 to whatever is needed.

14.2.2 Scale Encoding

A scale encoding is given in some unit of measure, such as pounds, meters, volts, or liters.

This can be done in one of two ways:

1. The column contains an implied unit of measure, and the numbers represent the quantity in that unit.
2. The column explicitly contains the unit. The most common example of this case would be money fields where a dollar sign is used in the column; you know that the unit is dollars, not pounds or yen, by the sign.

Scales and measurement theory are a whole separate topic and are discussed in detail in chapter 12.

14.2.3 Abbreviation Encoding

Abbreviation codes shorten the attribute values to fit into less storage space, but they are easily understood by the reader on sight. The codes can be either of fixed length or of variable length, but computer people tend to prefer fixed length. The most common example is the two-letter postal state abbreviations ("CA" for California, "AL" for Alabama), which replaced the old variable-length abbreviations ("Calif." for California, "Ala." for Alabama).

A good abbreviation scheme is very handy, but as the set of values becomes larger, the possibility for misunderstanding increases. The three-letter codes for airport baggage are pretty obvious for major cities: "LAX" for Los Angeles, "SFO" for San Francisco, "BOS" for Boston, "ATL" for Atlanta. But nobody can figure out the abbreviations for the really small airports.

Rounding numbers before they are stored in the database is actually a special case of abbreviation. But people usually think of rounding as a range or granularity problem, not as an encoding choice.

14.2.4 Algorithmic Encoding

Algorithmic encoding takes the value to be encoded and puts it through an algorithm to obtain the encodings. The algorithm should be reversible, so that the original value can be recovered. Though it is not required, the encoding is usually shorter (or at least of known maximum size) and more uniform in some useful way than the original value.

Computer people are used to using Julianized dates, which convert a date into an integer. As an aside, please note that astronomers used the *Julian date,* which is a large number that represents the number of days since a particular heavenly event. The *Julianized date* is a number between 1 and 365 or 366, which represents the ordinal position of the day within the year.

Algorithms take up computer time in both data input and output, but the encoding is useful in itself because it allows searching or calculations to be done that would be hard using the original data. Julianized dates can be used for computations; Soundex names give a phonetic matching that would not be possible with the original text. Another example is hashing functions, which convert numeric values into other numeric values for placing them in storage and retrieving them.

The difference between an abbreviation and an algorithm is not that clear. An abbreviation can be considered a special case of an algorithm, which tells you how to remove or replace letters. The tests to tell them apart are

1. when a human can read it without effort, it is an abbreviation, and
2. an algorithmic encoding can return the same code for more than one value, but an abbreviation is always one-to-one.

14.2.5 Hierarchical Encoding

A hierarchy partitions the set of values into disjoint categories, then partitions those categories into subcategories, and so forth until some final level is reached. Such schemes are shown either as nested sets or as tree charts. Each category has some meaning in itself, and the subcategories refine the meaning further.

The most common example is the ZIP code, which partitions the United States geographically. Each digit, as you read from left to right, further isolates the location of the address, first by postal region, then by state, then by city, and finally by the post office that has to make the delivery. For example, given the ZIP code 30310, we know that the 30000–39999 range means the southeastern United States. Within the southeastern codes, we know that the 30000–30399 range is

Georgia, and that 30300–30399 is metropolitan Atlanta. Finally, the whole code, 30310, identifies substation A in the West End section of the city. The ZIP code can be parsed by reading it from left to right, reading first one digit, then two, and then the last two digits.

Another example is the Dewey decimal system, used in public libraries in the United States. The 500 number series covers "Natural Sciences." Within that, the 510s cover "Mathematics." Finally, 512 deals with "Algebra" in particular. The scheme could be carried further, with decimal fractions for kinds of algebra.

Hierarchical encoding schemes are great for large data domains that have a natural hierarchy. They organize the data for searching and reporting along that natural hierarchy and make it very easy. But there can be problems in designing these schemes.

First, the tree structure does not have to be neatly balanced, so some categories may need more codes than others and hence more breakdowns. Eastern and ancient religions are shortchanged in the Dewey decimal system, reflecting a prejudice toward Christian and Jewish writings. Asian religions were pushed into a very small set of codes, although today the Library of Congress has more books on Buddhist thought than on any other religion.

Second, you might not have made the right choices as to where to place certain values in the tree. For example, in the Dewey decimal system, books on logic are encoded as 164, in the philosophy section, and not under the 510s, mathematics. In the 19th century, there was no mathematical logic. Today, nobody would think of looking for logic under philosophy. Dewey was simply following the conventions of his day. And like today's programmers, he found that the system specifications changed while he was working.

14.2.6 Vector Encoding

A vector is made up of a fixed number of components. These components can be ordered or unordered, but are almost always ordered; they can be of fixed or variable length. The components can be dependent on or independent of each other, but the code applies to a single entity. The components of the vector can be determined by punctuation, symbol set changes, or position within the code.

The most common example is a date, whose components are year, month, and day. The parts have some meaning by themselves, but the real meaning is in the vector—the date—as a whole. The different date formats used in computer systems give examples of all the options. The three components can be written in year-month-day order, month-day-year order, or just about any other way you wish.

The limits on the values for the day are dependent on the year (is it leap year or not?) and the month (28, 29, 30, or 31 days?). The components can be separated by punctuation (12/1/1990, using slashes and American date format), symbol set changes (1990 DEC 01, using digits-letters-digits), or position (19901201, using positions 1–4, 5–6, and 7–8 for year, month, and day, respectively).

Another example is the ISO code for tire sizes, which is made up of a wheel diameter (scaled in inches), a tire type (abbreviation code), and a width (scaled in centimeters).

Thus, 15R155 means a 15-inch radial tire that is 155 centimeters wide; 15SR155 is a steel-belted radial tire with the same dimensions. In spite of the mixed American and ISO units, this is a general physical description of a tire in a single code.

Vector schemes are very informative and allow you to pick the best scheme for each component. But they have to be disassembled to get to the components (many database products provide special functions to do this for dates, street addresses, and people's names). Sorting by components is hard unless you want them in the order given; try to sort the tire sizes by construction, width, and diameter instead of by diameter, construction, and width.

Another disadvantage is that a bad choice in one component can destroy the usefulness of the whole scheme. Another problem is extending the code. For example, if the standard tire number had to be expanded to include thickness in millimeters, where would that measurement go? Another number would have to be separated by a punctuation mark. It could not be inserted into a position inside the code without giving ambiguous codes. The code cannot be easily converted to a fixed-position vector encoding without changing many of the database routines.

Social Security Numbers

The Social Security number (SSN) is composed of three parts, XXX-XX-XXXX, called the Area, Group, and Serial. For the most part (there are exceptions), the Area is determined by where the individual *applied* for the SSN (before 1972) or *resided* at the time of application (after 1972). The areas are assigned as follows:

000	unused	303–317	IN	516–517	MT
001–003	NH	318–361	IL	518–519	ID
004–007	ME	362–386	MI	520	WY
008–009	VT	387–399	WI	521–524	CO
010–034	MA	400–407	KY	525	NM
035–039	RI	408–415	TN	526–527	AZ
040–049	CT	416–424	AL	528–529	UT
050–134	NY	425–428	MS	530	NV
135–158	NJ	429–432	AR	531–539	WA
159–211	PA	433–439	LA	540–544	OR
212–220	MD	440–448	OK	545–573	CA
221–222	DE	449–467	TX	574	AK
223–231	VA	468–477	MN	575–576	HI
232–236	WV	478–485	IA	577–579	DC
237–246	NC	486–500	MO	580	VI Virgin Islands
247–251	SC	501–502	ND	581–584	PR Puerto Rico
252–260	GA	503–504	SD	585	NM
261–267	FL	505–508	NE		
268–302	OH	509–515	KS		

586	PI Pacific Islands (Northern Mariana Islands,Guam, American Samoa, Philippine Islands)
587–588	MS
589–595	FL
596–599	PR Puerto Rico
600–601	AZ
602–626	CA
627–699	unassigned, for future use
700–728	Railroad workers through 1963, then discontinued
729–899	unassigned, for future use
900–999	not valid SSNs, but were used for program purposes when state aid to the aged, blind, and disabled was converted to a federal program administered by SSA

As the Areas assigned to a locality are exhausted, new areas from the pool are assigned. This is why some states have noncontiguous groups of Areas.

The Group portion of the SSN has no meaning other than to determine whether or not a number has been assigned. The Social Security Administration publishes a list every month of the highest group assigned for each SSN Area. The order of assignment for the Groups is odd numbers under 10, even numbers over 9, even numbers under 9 (except for 00, which is never used), and odd numbers over 10. For example, if the highest group assigned for area 999 is 72, then we know that the number 999-04-1234 is an invalid number because even Groups under 9 have not yet been assigned.

The Serial portion of the SSN has no meaning. The Serial is not assigned in strictly numerical order. The Serial 0000 is never assigned.

Before 1973, Social Security cards with preprinted numbers were issued to each local SSA office. The numbers were assigned by the local office. In 1973, SSN assignment was automated and outstanding

stocks of preprinted cards were destroyed. All SSNs are now assigned by computer from headquarters. There are rare cases in which the computer system can be forced to accept a manual assignment, such as a person refusing a number with 666 in it.

A pamphlet entitled "The Social Security Number" (Pub. No. 05-10633) provides an explanation of the SSN's structure and the method of assigning and validating Social Security numbers.

I have used the GO TRACE service on CompuServe for looking up death records from Social Security. The first five digits of the Social Security number are displayed, along with where issued and the approximate year of issue.

The U.S. government ancestry website has a Social Security death search that gives the full nine-digit number of the deceased individual. It does not supply the year or location of issue.

This information is from 1988, and there may be changes in the particulars since then. However, the Social Security Administration (SSA) actively resists giving information to citizens on their number system. There are commercial firms such as Security Software Solutions (Box 30125, Tucson, AZ 85751-0125; phone 800-681-8933; *http://www.veris-ssn.com*), which will verify SSNs for living and deceased persons.

14.2.7 Concatenation Encoding

A concatenation code is made up of a variable number of components that are concatenated together. As in a vector encoding, the components can be ordered or unordered, dependent on or independent of each other, and determined by punctuation, symbol set changes, or position.

A concatenation code is often a hierarchy that is refined by additions to the right. These are also known as facet codes in Europe. Or the code can be a list of features, any of which can be present or missing. The order of the components may or may not be important.

Concatenation codes were popular in machine shops at the turn of the century: a paper tag was attached to a piece of work, and workers at different stations would sign off on their parts of the manufacturing process. Concatenation codes are still used in parts of the airplane industry, where longer codes represent subassemblies of the assembly in the head (also called the root or parent) of the code.

Another type of concatenation code is a quorum code, which is not ordered. These codes say that *n* out of *k* marks must be present for the code to have meaning. For example, three out of five inspectors must approve a part before it passes.

The most common use of concatenation codes is in keyword lists in the header records of documents in textbases. The author or librarian assigns each article in the system a list of keywords that describe the material covered by the article. The keywords are picked from a limited, specialized vocabulary that belongs to a particular discipline.

Concatenation codes fell out of general use because their variable length made them harder to store in older computer systems, which used fixed-length records (think of a punch card). The codes had to be ordered and stored as left-justified strings to sort correctly.

These codes could also be ambiguous if they were poorly designed. For example, is the head of 1234 the 1 or the 12 substring? When concatenation codes are used in databases, they usually become a set of "yes/no" check boxes, represented as adjacent columns in the file. This makes them Boolean vector codes, instead of true concatenation codes.

14.3 General Guidelines for Designing Encoding Schemes

These are general guidelines for designing encoding schemes in a database, not firm, hard rules. You will find exceptions to all of them.

14.3.1 Use Existing Encoding Standards

The use of existing standard encoding schemes is always recommended. You can get quite a lot of help from your local government printing office and even obtain schemes on magnetic media. Commonly used schemes are supposed to be registered with and available through the Federal Information Processing Standards (FIPS) program. The idea is that if everyone uses the same codes, data will be easy to transfer and collect in a uniform manner. Also, someone who sat down and did nothing else but work on this scheme probably

did a better job than you could while trying to get a database up and running.

The U.S. government is a good source for such encoding schemes. The Bureau of Labor Statistics published the Dictionary of Occupational Titles (DOT), which encodes job descriptions, and the Standard Industrial Classification (SIC), which encodes businesses by type. The Bureau of the Census has lots of encoding schemes for demographic data. ZIP code tapes can be had from the U.S. Postal Service.

Unfortunately, not all government agencies are that eager to help the public. In the 1970s, the Social Security Administration provided programs and files to validate Social Security numbers under the name "Project Clean Data," but later discontinued the practice.

The FBI administers the National Crime Information Center (NCIC), which logs stolen automobiles. The automobile codes are a good, complete system for describing a car and would be useful for dealers, companies, and other institutions that deal with a large number of automobiles. But the FBI no longer shares its encoding scheme, on the grounds that this is confidential information. The only other standard way to identify a vehicle is by the VIN (vehicle identification number) on the engine block, which contains the manufacturer, make, model, and year, as well as a unique identifier for that vehicle. But it is a complicated task to get that information out of the VIN. The FBI has deliberately made reporting a stolen car take longer and be less accurate than it should be.

Industry groups often have standard encoding schemes. The insurance industry is a good source for medical and dental codes, which are used to process claims.

14.3.2 Allow for Expansion

Allow for expansion of the codes. The `ALTER` statement can create more storage when a single-character code becomes a two-character code, but it will not change the spacing on the printed reports and screens. Start with at least one more decimal place or position than you think you will need. Visual psychology makes "01" look like an encoding, whereas "1" looks like a quantity.

14.3.3 Use Explicit Missing Values to Avoid NULLs

Avoid the SQL general NULL as much as possible by putting special values in the encoding scheme instead. SQL handles NULLs differently from values, and NULLs don't tell you what kind of missing value you are dealing with.

All zeros are often used for missing values; all nines, for miscellaneous values. For example, the ISO gender codes are 0 = Unknown, 1 = Male, 2 = Female, and 9 = Not Applicable. "Not Applicable" means a legal entity, such as a corporation, which has no gender.

This is another holdover from the days of punch cards. Versions of Fortran before the 1977 standard read blank (unpunched) columns as zeros, so if you did not know a value, you skipped those columns and punched them later, when you did know. Likewise, using encoding schemes with leading zeros was a security trick to prevent blanks in a punch card from being altered. The Fortran 77 standard fixed this problem.

The use of all nines or all Zs for miscellaneous values will make those values sort to the end of the screen or report. NULLs sort either always to the front or always to the rear, but which way they sort is implementation-defined.

Read chapter 12 on missing data, then determine which meanings of NULL you wish to capture in your encoding scheme.

14.3.4 Translate Codes for the User

As much as possible, avoid displaying pure codes to the user, but try to provide a translation. For some things, however, this is not possible or reasonable. For example, most people do not need to see the two-letter state abbreviation written out in full or the parts of the ISO tire size vector code explained. At the other extreme, however, nobody could read the billing codes used by several long-distance telephone companies.

A part of translation is formatting the display so that it can be read. Punctuation marks, such as dashes, commas, currency signs, and so forth, are important.

14.3.5 Keep the Codes in the Database

There should be a part of the database that has all of the codes stored in tables. These tables can be used to validate input, to translate codes in displays, and as part of the system documentation.

I was amazed to go to a major hospital in Los Angeles in mid-1993 and see the clerk still looking up codes in a dog-eared looseleaf notebook instead of bringing them up on her terminal screen. The hospital was still using a very old IBM mainframe system, which had "dumb" 3270 terminals, rather than a client/server system with workstations. There was not even a help screen available to the clerk.

The translation tables can be downloaded to the workstations in a client/server system to reduce network traffic. They can also be used to build picklists on interactive screens and thereby reduce typographical errors. Changes to the codes are propagated in the system without the need to rewrite application code. If the codes change over time, the table for a code should include a pair of "date effective" fields. This will allow a data warehouse to correctly read and translate old data.

Check Digits

CHARLES BABBAGE, THE father of the computer, observed in the mid-1800s that an inseparable part of the cost of obtaining data is the cost of verifying its accuracy. He was concerned with errors because he conceived of his "difference engine" as a way to calculate accurate mathematical tables for the British navy. The manual calculations done by clerks were filled with errors; no chart or table then in use was regarded as accurate when it was issued. Dionysus Lardner, a well-known popular science writer, wrote in 1834 that a random selection of 40 books of mathematical tables had a total of 3,700 known errata, some of which had their own errors.

The best situation is to exclude bad data on entry so that it is never in the system. If the data itself can contain its own verification, then we do not have to rely on another program or database to check what we are putting into the system. That is the idea of a check digit.

Just consider the problem of entering data at a supermarket checkout. The scanner reads the UCC (Universal Container Code) bar code (formerly called the UPC, for Universal Product Code) on the package, looks up the code in the database, displays the description on the cash register for the clerk, and prints the description

and price on the receipt. But the scanner does not read the code correctly every time.

Statistics classifies errors as either Type I or Type II. A Type I error rejects truth, and a Type II error accepts falsehood. If the bar code reader cannot scan the package, the clerk can read the code, printed in numerals under the bars, enter it manually, and verify the description shown on the cash register display against the actual package to avoid Type I errors—in this case, rejecting a valid purchase. But what about Type II errors?

The Type II errors are handled in the bar code itself. The UCC is 10 digits long, 5 for the manufacturer and 5 for the product, but the bar code also includes extra digits, which are not usually printed in numerals on the package. One of these digits is a check digit, as opposed to the 10 information digits that do the work. By applying a formula to the information digits, the scanner should get the check digit as a result. If it does, it assumes that it has read the code correctly; if it does not, it assumes it has made a read error and asks for a rescan.

Before you can design a formula, you have to know something about the keying errors that you can expect to have in the data. Banks, insurance companies, the U.S. Army, and other organizations that are interested in keeping statistics and reducing errors have already done that work for us. F. J. Damerau (1964) reported that four common input errors cause 80% of the total spelling errors:

1. A single missing character
2. A single extra character
3. A single erroneous character
4. Pairwise-transposed characters

Verhoeff gave more details in his study, "Error-Detecting Decimal Codes" (Verhoeff 1969). The single erroneous, missing, or extra character explained 60% to 95% of all errors in his sample of 12,000 errors; pairwise transposes accounted for 10% to 20% of the total.

The first three categories can be expanded to more than a single character, but the single-character cases are by far the most common. In the last category, pairwise transposes ("ab" becomes "ba") are far more common than jump transposes (transposes of pairs with one or more characters between them, as when "abc" becomes "cba"). If a human is doing the data entry from verbal input, you might wish to include a special case for phonetic errors, which are language-dependent (e.g., "thirty" and "thirteen" sound alike in English, but the corresponding words in other languages do not).

15.1 Error Detection versus Error Correction

The distinction between error-detecting and error-correcting codes is worth mentioning. The error-detecting code will find that an encoding is wrong, but gives no help in finding the error itself. An error-correcting code will try to repair the problem. Error-correcting schemes for binary numbers play an important part in highly reliable computers, but require several extra digits on each computer word to work. If you would like to do research on error-correction codes, some of the algorithms are

- Hamming codes
- Fire codes
- Bose-Chandhuri-Hocquenghem (BCH) codes
- Reed-Solomon (RS) codes
- Goppa codes

On the other hand, error detection can be done with only one extra digit. It is important to people who design codes for a database because they keep the data clean without triggers or procedures by simply excluding bad data. The algorithms can often be written in `CHECK()` clauses, too.

15.2 MOD Functions and Casting Functions

Check digit algorithms usually involve either the modulo (MOD) function or casting functions to reduce the calculations to a single digit. Both functions have a fixed base, or modulus, which is applied against the other argument to produce a result.

15.2.1 MOD Function

The MOD function, also called "remainder arithmetic" in elementary algebra books, is very common in programming languages. It returns the remainder of integer division of the argument by the modulus. For example, MOD(4123, 23) = 6 because (179 * 23) + 6 = 4123.

Different programming languages handle a negative argument or a negative modulus differently, but this is usually not a programming problem for check digit work, since all the numbers are positive. Notice that a MOD function can always produce a zero result if the argument is a multiple of the modulus.

The arithmetic laws of the MOD function make it useful for quickly checking calculations. Here are some of the rules:

- Addition:

  (MOD(*a*, *m*) = MOD(*b*, *m*)) AND (MOD(*c*, *m*) = MOD(*d*, *m*))
  implies that (MOD(*a* + *c*, *m*) = MOD(*b* + *d*, *m*))

- Multiplication:

  (MOD(*a*, *m*) = MOD(*b*, *m*)) AND (MOD(*c*, *m*) = MOD(*d*, *m*))
  implies that (MOD(*a* * *c*, *m*) = MOD(*b* * *d*, *m*))

- Exponentiation:

  (MOD(*a*, *m*) = MOD(*b*, *m*))
  implies that (MOD(*an*, *m*) = MOD(*bn*, *m*))

As an example of how this can be useful, let *m* = 10, so that the result of MOD(*x*, 10) is the last digit of the number. Let *a* = 7 and *b* = 117. Is the last digit of 1175 = 21,924,480,357 correct or not? It has to be the same as the last digit of 75 = 16,807, so we know that at least the last digit is right.

15.2.2 Casting Functions

Casting functions were first used as a way of checking arithmetic results. The most popular system was casting nines; it was taught in the U.S. public schools until the early 1960s.

Though other bases are possible, casting usually means casting nines unless otherwise stated. The easiest way to define casting nines is to think of it as repeatedly summing the digits of a number until you are left with a single-digit answer. Using the previous example, cast9(4123) = (4 + 1 + 2 + 3) = 10, and then cast9(10) = (1 + 0) = 1.

The cast function has an arithmetic property of being invariant over addition, subtraction, multiplication, and division, which is why it could be used to check results. For example, to check 785 * 456 = 357,860, we would do the following:

cast9(cast9(785) * cast9(456)) = cast9(357,860)

cast9(cast9(20) * cast9(15)) = cast9(29)

cast9(2 * 6) = cast9(11)

cast9(12) = 2

3 = 2 (Error!)

Sure enough, the correct answer was 357,960. The reason this was a popular method before computers and calculators is that it can be done manually by scanning a digit at a time across the number and remembering the final result.

The casting function can also be done with a simple program using MOD and integer division (DIV) operators; however, the multiplication and division operations hidden in those operators are expensive in terms of computer time, and faster algorithms exist. Given single digits x and y and digit strings a and b, we know that

1. cast9(x) = x
2. cast9(xy) = (($x + y$) DIV 10) + (($x + y$) MOD 10)
3. cast9(ab) = cast9(cast9(a) + cast9(b))

The only way that a casting function can produce a zero result is with a zero input. Casting is considered weak because any permutation of the same digits will cast to the same result, so this method cannot find any transposes.

This is also a method for obtaining check digits. The ability to test arithmetic operations can be a bonus in some situations. The problem is that this is one of the worst methods for finding input errors. It will not detect transposes, extra zeros, missing zeros, or a host of other errors. The SKU (stock control unit) code used in the garment

industry is always seven digits. The rightmost digit is the check digit; it is calculated by a cast function with base 9.

A slightly better version of the same idea is called casting 11s: you alternate adding and subtracting the digits in the number from right to left. This is a weighted sum, with the weights alternating from 1 to –1 and 11 as the divisor. Although this fixes the problem with pair-wise transposes, it still suffers from the other weaknesses of any simple modulus scheme. The problem above, done by casting 11s, looks like this:

cast11(cast11(785) * cast11(456)) = cast11(357,960)

cast11((+ 7 – 8 + 5) * (+ 4 – 5 + 6)) = (– 3 + 5 – 7 + 9 – 6 + 0)

cast11(4 * 5) = – 2

cast11(20) = – 2

cast11(– 2 + 0) = – 2

– 2 = – 2

15.3 Classes of Algorithms

The most common check digit procedures come in a few broad classes. One class takes the individual digits, multiplies them by a constant value (called a *weight*) for each position, sums the results, divides the sum by another constant, and uses the remainder as the check digit. These are called *weighted-sum algorithms.*

Another approach is to use functions based on group theory, a branch of abstract algebra; these are called *algebraic algorithms*. A discussion of group theory is a little too complex to take up here, so I will do a little hand-waving when I get to the mathematics. Finally, you can use lookup tables for check digit functions that cannot be easily calculated.

The lookup tables can be almost anything, including functions that are tuned for the data in a particular application.

15.3.1 Weighted-Sum Algorithms

Weighted-sum algorithms are probably the most common class of check digit. They have the advantage of being easy to compute by hand, since they require no tables or complex arithmetic, so they were first used in manual systems. Casting 11s, which we discussed in this chapter, is an example of these algorithms.

To calculate the check digit for a UCC bar code, you first need to know that the UCC code is comprised of 12 digits, but you only see 10 of the digits printed in human-readable numerals under the bar code on the label of the products you buy. The first digit (the leftmost) is commonly called the system code; most retail UCC codes have a system code of 0 or 1. The next five digits (the left group) are the manufacturer code, which is assigned by the Uniform Code Council. The next five digits (the right group) are assigned by the manufacturer to the specific product. The last (rightmost) is the check digit. The check digit is calculated as follows:

1. Multiply each of the 11 digits by a weight. The weights are alternating 1s and 3s. In other words, multiply the first digit by 1, the second by 3, the third by 1, the fourth by 3, and so forth.
2. Add the products of the above multiplications.
3. Take the number MOD 10 (this is the same as using the digit in the unit's position).
4. Subtract this result from 10. If the result is 10, set it to zero. This is your check digit.

Here's an example using the UCC code from a box of KAO diskettes:

UCC: 0 92785 32099

Weight: 1 31313 13131

0 + 27 + 2 + 21 + 8 + 15 + 3 + 6 + 0 + 27 + 9 = 118

118 MOD 10 = 8

10 – 8 = 2

The toll-free number for the Uniform Code Council is 1-800-548-8137. You will have to join them to receive a valid manufacturer code, which is the first 6 digits of the 11-digit code (includes the system

code). In case you're interested in UCC specifications and technical literature, you can reach the UCC at

Uniform Code Council
8163 Old Yankee Road #J
Dayton, OH 45459
phone: 513-435-3870
fax: 513-435-4749

You may also want to get in touch with AIM USA, the bar code equipment vendors' trade association. Ask for their "ADC Advantage" paper, which serves as a very brief primer on the technologies and has listings of their member companies.

AIM USA
634 Alpha Drive
Pittsburgh, PA 15238
phone: 412-963-8588
fax: 412-963-8753
Internet: *adc@aimusa.org*

A better method using modulus 11 is the International Standard Book Number (ISBN) check digit. Look on the back cover or the copyright page of any book. You will see the ISBN. It consists of 10 digits, broken into four groupings by dashes. The first grouping is the language of the book (zero is English), the second is the publisher (the bigger the publisher, the smaller the group), the third group is the title code, and the last digit is the check digit. There are always 10 digits.

Starting at the left side, multiply each digit by its position. Sum the products and divide the result by 11. The remainder is the check digit. For example, given the ISBN 1-55860-576-2, you would check it by this calculation:

1 * 1 = 1

2 * 5 = 10

3 * 5 = 15

4 * 8 = 32

5 * 6 = 30

6 * 0 = 0

7 * 5 = 35

8 * 7 = 56

9 * 6 = 54

total 233

233 MOD 11 = 2

You can verify this result by looking on the back cover of the American edition of *SQL for Smarties* (2nd ed.). To use this scheme with a number longer than 10 positions, weight the positions as 1 through 10 repeatedly. That is, each weight is the position MOD 11; a position with a weight of 11 is useless because of the division by 11.

This is one of the most popular check digit procedures because it will detect most of the four types of errors we discussed earlier for single characters and pairwise transposes.

However, it is not perfect. The first thing you will see is that you could have a remainder of 10, which would require two positions, not one. The ISBN uses an *X* for 10, like the Roman numeral; other implementations use a zero for both zero and 10. This second method will lose many of the advantages of the algorithm in exchange for an all-decimal encoding.

It is also possible for a pairwise transpose to be accepted if the digits 5 and 6 appear in positions five and six, as in the case of ISBN 0-201-56235-9 and ISBN 0-201-65235-9. One way around this problem is to disallow the use of certain digits in certain positions by checking for them.

Another common weighted sum that uses MOD 10 is the Bank Check Digit, whose weights are 3, 7, and 1, repeated as needed. This is used in the United States on personal checks, where the bank processing numbers have eight information digits. Look at the lower-left corner of your checkbook in the MICR (Magnetic Ink Character Recognition) numbers for your bank's code. The formula uses the check digit itself in the formula, so that the result should be a constant zero for correct numbers. Otherwise, you could use "10 – (total MOD 10) = check digit" for your formula.

This scheme fails when the digits of a pairwise transpose differ by 5. For example, imagine that we wanted to validate the number 1621, but we typed 6121 instead, swapping the first two digits. Since 6 – 1 = 5, this algorithm cannot detect the problem. Here is the arithmetic:

```
  1 * 3 =  3
+ 6 * 7 = 42
+ 2 * 1 =  2
+ 1 * 3 =  3
------------
total     50

50 MOD 10 = 0

  6 * 3 = 18
+ 1 * 7 =  7
+ 2 * 1 =  2
+ 1 * 3 =  3
------------
total     30
MOD(30, 10) = 0
```

A better scheme is the IBM Check, whose weights alternate between 1 and $f(x)$, where $f(x)$ is defined by the lookup table given below or by the formula $f(x)$ = IF ($x < 9$) THEN MOD(($x + x$), 9) ELSE 9, where x is the position of the digit in the code.

f(1) = 2

f(2) = 4

f(3) = 6

f(4) = 8

f(5) = 1

f(6) = 3

f(7) = 5

f(8) = 7

f(9) = 9

The reason for mentioning the lookup table as well as the formula is that a lookup table is usually faster than doing the arithmetic, and the tables for these schemes are usually not too big.

15.3.2 Power-Sum Check Digits

The weights can be defined as variable powers of a fixed base number and then a modulus applied to get the remainder. Prime numbers are the best modulus, but 10 is very common. The most common schemes use a base of 2 or 3 with a modulus of 7, 10, or 11. The combination of 2 and 11 with a separate symbol for a remainder of 10 is one example of this type of check digit. For example, we could check the code 2350 with these calculations:

$$(2^2) + (2^3) + (2^5) = 44$$

$$44 \text{ MOD } 11 = 0$$

15.3.3 Bull Check Digits

Another popular version of the weighted-sum check digit is the Bull codes, which use the sum of two alternating sums, each with a modulus less than 10. The modulus pair has to be relatively prime. The most popular pairs, in order of increasing error-detection ability, are (4, 5), (4, 7), (3, 7), (3, 5), (5, 6), and (3, 8).

For example, using the pair (4, 5) and modulus 7, we could check the code 2345-1 with these calculations:

$$((2 * 4) + (3 * 5) + (4 * 4) + (5 * 5)) = 6464 \text{ MOD } 7 = 1$$

15.3.4 Dihedral Five Check Digit

A very good, but somewhat complicated, scheme was proposed by J. Verhoeff in a tract from the Mathematical Centre in Amsterdam, Netherlands (Verhoeff 1969). It is based on the properties of multiplication in an algebraic structure known as the dihedral five group.

Though some of the calculations could be done with arithmetic formulas, the easiest and fastest way is to build lookup tables into the functions. The lookup tables involved are a multiplication lookup table, an inverse lookup table, and a permutation table. This makes

the programs look larger, but the superior ability of this scheme to detect errors more than makes up for the very slight increase in size.

The following (partial) table is reproduced from Burch and Strater (1974). Columns include

mod:	check digit modulus
a:	range of weights that may be used
b:	maximum length of number without repeating weight
v:	transcription errors
w:	single transposition errors
x:	double transposition errors
y:	other transposition errors
z:	random errors

				—percentage of errors detected—				
mod	**a**	**b**	**weights used**	**v**	**w**	**x**	**y**	**z**
10	1-9	8	1-2-1-2-1	100.0	98.8	0.0	48.9	90.0
			1-3-1-3-1	100.0	88.9	0.0	44.5	90.0
			7-6-4-3-2	87.0	100.0	88.9	88.9	90.0
			9-8-7-4-3-2	94.4	100.0	88.9	74.1	90.0
			1-3-7-1-3-7	100.0	88.9	88.9	74.4	90.0
11	1-10	9	10-9-8...2	100.0	100.0	100.0	100.0	90.9
			1-2-4-8-16...	100.0	100.0	100.0	100.0	90.9

Burch and Strater also say that "using modulus 11 with prime number weighting, a method developed by Friden, Inc., detects the highest number of possible transposition and transcription errors." No statistics on that method are given.

15.4 Check Digit Algorithms

The following Pascal functions will compute the different check digits given in this chapter. They assume that the program has the following global declarations:

```
CONST
   N = 10; { size of information digits string }
TYPE
   InfoDigits = ARRAY [1..N] OF INTEGER;
```

`N` is replaced by a literal value in all of the programs for a particular application, so these are more templates than programs. The `InfoDigits` datatype assumes that the number to be given a check digit is stored in an array of integers, with the leftmost digit in position 1.

15.4.1 Casting Nines

The iterative algorithm is based on the idea that you keep repeating the casting operation as a scan from right to left, over and over, until the result is less than 10. This means two nested loops, an inner one to do the summing and an outer one to control it.

```
FUNCTION IterativeCast9 (inputnumber : INTEGER) : INTEGER;
{ Loops from right to left, totaling as it goes.
   Keeps looping until the total is less than 10. }
VAR
   total : INTEGER;
BEGIN
WHILE (inputnumber >= 10)
DO BEGIN
   total := 0;
   WHILE (inputnumber > 0)
   DO BEGIN
      { cut off the rightmost digit }
      total := total + (inputnumber MOD 10);
      inputnumber := inputnumber DIV 10;
      END;
   inputnumber := total;
   END;
IterativeCast9 := inputnumber;
END;
```

The preceding algorithm is not the fastest. The following table lookup algorithm requires a constant table stored as an array of 100 integers. This one scans from right to left, but uses the table to find the running total and cast the answer "on the fly." By inspection, *n* digits require *n* iterations. You can generalize this approach by cutting off the rightmost *n*-tuple of digits, and using a huge table (10*n* by 10*n* elements) and tricky logic. This is a good choice for speed at the expense of space.

```
FUNCTION LookupCast9 (inputnumber : INTEGER) : INTEGER;
{ Scans from right to left, keeping inputnumber running. Casting is
done via the lookup table during the scan. }
VAR check : INTEGER;
CONST
CastTable : ARRAY [0..9, 0..9] OF INTEGER =
   ((0, 1, 2, 3, 4, 5, 6, 7, 8, 9),
    (1, 2, 3, 4, 5, 6, 7, 8, 9, 1),
    (2, 3, 4, 5, 6, 7, 8, 9, 1, 2),
    (3, 4, 5, 6, 7, 8, 9, 1, 2, 3),
    (4, 5, 6, 7, 8, 9, 1, 2, 3, 4),
    (5, 6, 7, 8, 9, 1, 2, 3, 4, 5),
    (6, 7, 8, 9, 1, 2, 3, 4, 5, 6),
    (7, 8, 9, 1, 2, 3, 4, 5, 6, 7),
    (8, 9, 1, 2, 3, 4, 5, 6, 7, 8),
    (9, 1, 2, 3, 4, 5, 6, 7, 8, 9));
BEGIN check := 0;
WHILE (inputnumber > 0)
DO BEGIN
   { cut off the rightmost digit and use for table lookup }
   check := CastTable [check, (inputnumber MOD 10)];
   inputnumber := inputnumber DIV 10;
   END;
LookupCast9 := check;
END;
```

The following routine was submitted by J. R. Yozallinas of Chicago, Illinois (Yozallinas 1981). He claims better performance than the array lookup method because the simple arithmetic involved uses only increment and decrement operations, which are usually built into the computer hardware.

```
FUNCTION Cast9(a : inputnumber) : INTEGER;
VAR
   total : INTEGER;
BEGIN
IF (inputnumber > 9)
THEN BEGIN
   total := 0;
   WHILE (inputnumber > 0)
   DO BEGIN
      total := total + (inputnumber MOD 10);
      IF (total > 9) THEN total := total - 9;
      inputnumber := inputnumber DIV 10;
      END;
   END
ELSE total := inputnumber;
Cast9 := total
END;
```

As an exercise, try to write a recursive routine for casting nines. Would it be an improvement over the preceding algorithms?

15.4.2 Dihedral Five Check Digits

Remember that this method is based on a mathematical group known as the dihedral five group. It could be defined with complex arithmetic, but the easiest way is to use a table lookup.

```
FUNCTION MakeCheck(a : InfoDigits; n : INTEGER) : INTEGER;
{ This will generate Verhoeff's dihedral five check digit. }
CONST
MultTable : ARRAY [0..9, 0..9] OF INTEGER =
   ((0, 1, 2, 3, 4, 5, 6, 7, 8, 9),
    (1, 2, 3, 4, 0, 6, 7, 8, 9, 5),
    (2, 3, 4, 0, 1, 7, 8, 9, 5, 6),
    (3, 4, 0, 1, 2, 8, 9, 5, 6, 7),
```

```
    (4, 0, 1, 2, 3, 9, 5, 6, 7, 8),
    (5, 9, 8, 7, 6, 0, 4, 3, 2, 1),
    (6, 5, 9, 8, 7, 1, 0, 4, 3, 2),
    (7, 6, 5, 9, 8, 2, 1, 0, 4, 3),
    (8, 7, 6, 5, 9, 3, 2, 1, 0, 4),
    (9, 8, 7, 6, 5, 4, 3, 2, 1, 0));

PermTable : ARRAY [0..9, 0..9] OF INTEGER =
   ((0, 1, 2, 3, 4, 5, 6, 7, 8, 9),
    (1, 5, 7, 6, 2, 8, 3, 0, 9, 4),
    (5, 8, 0, 3, 7, 9, 6, 1, 4, 2),
    (8, 9, 1, 6, 0, 4, 3, 5, 2, 7),
    (9, 4, 5, 3, 1, 2, 6, 8, 7, 0),
    (4, 2, 8, 6, 5, 7, 3, 9, 0, 1),
    (2, 7, 9, 3, 8, 0, 6, 4, 1, 5),
    (7, 0, 4, 6, 9, 1, 3, 2, 5, 8),
    (8, 1, 2, 3, 4, 5, 6, 7, 8, 9),
    (9, 5, 7, 6, 2, 8, 3, 0, 9, 4));

InverseTable : ARRAY [0..9] OF INTEGER =
   (0, 4, 3, 2, 1, 5, 6, 7, 8, 9);
VAR
   Check, i : INTEGER;
BEGIN
Check := 0;
FOR i := 1 TO n
DO Check := MultTable[Check, PermTable[(i MOD 8), a[i]]];
MakeCheck := InverseTable[Check];

END;

FUNCTION VerifyCheck(a : InfoDigits; n : INTEGER) : BOOLEAN;
{ This will verify Verhoeff's dihedral five check digit. Note that
it is different from the generator. }
CONST
MultTable : ARRAY [0..9, 0..9] OF INTEGER =
   ((0, 1, 2, 3, 4, 5, 6, 7, 8, 9),
    (1, 2, 3, 4, 0, 6, 7, 8, 9, 5),
```

```
    (2, 3, 4, 0, 1, 7, 8, 9, 5, 6),
    (3, 4, 0, 1, 2, 8, 9, 5, 6, 7),
    (4, 0, 1, 2, 3, 9, 5, 6, 7, 8),
    (5, 9, 8, 7, 6, 0, 4, 3, 2, 1),
    (6, 5, 9, 8, 7, 1, 0, 4, 3, 2),
    (7, 6, 5, 9, 8, 2, 1, 0, 4, 3),
    (8, 7, 6, 5, 9, 3, 2, 1, 0, 4),
    (9, 8, 7, 6, 5, 4, 3, 2, 1, 0));

PermTable : ARRAY [0..9, 0..9] OF INTEGER =
   ((0, 1, 2, 3, 4, 5, 6, 7, 8, 9),
    (1, 5, 7, 6, 2, 8, 3, 0, 9, 4),
    (5, 8, 0, 3, 7, 9, 6, 1, 4, 2),
    (8, 9, 1, 6, 0, 4, 3, 5, 2, 7),
    (9, 4, 5, 3, 1, 2, 6, 8, 7, 0),
    (4, 2, 8, 6, 5, 7, 3, 9, 0, 1),
    (2, 7, 9, 3, 8, 0, 6, 4, 1, 5),
    (7, 0, 4, 6, 9, 1, 3, 2, 5, 8),
    (8, 1, 2, 3, 4, 5, 6, 7, 8, 9),
    (9, 5, 7, 6, 2, 8, 3, 0, 9, 4));
VAR
   Check, i : INTEGER;
BEGIN
Check := 0;
FOR i := 1 TO n
DO Check := MultTable[Check, PermTable[(i MOD 8), a[i]]];
VerifyCheck := (Check = 0);
END;
```

15.4.3 Bull Function

```
FUNCTION BullCheck(a : InfoDigits; n, x, y : INTEGER) : INTEGER;
{ The most popular pairs (x, y), in order of increasing error
detection ability, are (4, 5), (4, 7), (3, 7), (3, 5), (5, 6), and
(3, 8). }
VAR
   CheckX, CheckY, i : INTEGER;
```

```
BEGIN
CheckX := 0;
CheckY := 0;
FOR i := 1 TO n
DO IF (Odd(i))
      THEN CheckX := CheckX + a[i]
      ELSE CheckY := CheckY + a[i];
BullCheck := (CheckX MOD X)+ (CheckY MOD Y)
END;
```

15.4.4 Power Function

```
FUNCTION PowerCheck(a : InfoDigits; base, x : INTEGER) : INTEGER;
{ Base is usually 2 or 3.  x is usually 7, 10, or 11. }
VAR
   Check, i, Term : INTEGER;
BEGIN
Check := 0;
Term := 1;
FOR i := 1 TO n
DO BEGIN
      Check := Check + (Term * a[i]);
      Term := Term * base;
      END;
PowerCheck := (Check MOD x)
END;
```

15.4.5 ISBN Function

This check digit function is used for other purposes besides the International Standard Book Number, but since that is the most common place where people will see it, I have given it that name. It should be called the "MOD 11" algorithm, but there are other algorithms that also use that divisor but different weights.

```
FUNCTION ISBNCheck(a : InfoDigits) : INTEGER;
VAR
   Check, i : INTEGER;
```

```
BEGIN
Check := 0;
FOR i := 1 TO n
DO Check := Check + (i * a[i]);
ISBNCheck := (Check MOD 11)
{ Let calling program handle a value of 10 as X as it wishes. }
END;
```

15.4.6 SKU Code Algorithm

The SKU code is a weighted-sum code used in the garment industry and in other retail industries. Though not as sophisticated as other check digit schemes, it is very easy to implement in simple cash register hardware.

```
FUNCTION GarmentChk (a : INTEGER) : BOOLEAN;
{ returns TRUE if the item code is valid }
VAR
   total, i, workdigit : INTEGER;
BEGIN
total := 0;
FOR i := 1 TO 7
DO BEGIN
      workdigit := a MOD 10;
{ double even digits }
      IF NOT (Odd(i))
      THEN workdigit := workdigit + workdigit;
{ cast nines }
      total := total + ((workdigit MOD 10) + (workdigit DIV 10));
{ get next digit from rightmost side }
      a := a DIV 10;
{ return a Boolean result }
GarmentChk := ((total MOD 10) = 0)
END;
```

15.4.7 Code 39 Algorithm

Code 39 is used by many bar code systems. The advantage it has is that it handles digits, letters, and a small set of special characters.

Sum the values of the characters:

Numerics = their own value

Alpha values = 10–35 (A–Z)

– = 36

SPACE = 38

$ = 39

/ = 40

+ = 41

% = 42

Divide by 43. Take the remainder and find the character with that value. That's the check character.

Note that the check character can be the SPACE character, so that's why many people print the * as a start/stop indicator in the event a worker has to key the check character. Using the * helps ensure (but doesn't guarantee) that they'll see the space.

The Basic Relational Model

LIKE MOST NEW ideas, the hard part of understanding what the relational model is comes in unlearning what you know about file systems. Artemus Ward (William Graham Sumner, 1840–1910) put it very nicely: "It ain't what you don't know that kills you; it's what you know that ain't so that kills you."

If you already have a background in data processing with traditional file systems, the first things to unlearn are

1. Databases are not file sets.
2. Tables are not files.
3. Rows are not records.
4. Columns are not fields.

Do not feel ashamed of getting stuck in a conceptual rut; every new technology has this problem.

The U.S. standard railroad gauge (distance between the rails) is 4 feet, 8.5 inches. This gauge is used because the English built railroads to that gauge, and U.S. railroads were built by English expatriates.

Why did the English build railroads to that gauge? Because the first rail lines were built by the same people who built the prerailroad tramways, and that's the gauge they used. Why did those wheelwrights use that gauge then? Because the people who built the horse-drawn trams used the same jigs and tools that they used for building wagons, which used that wheel spacing.

Why did the wagons use that odd wheel spacing? For the practical reason that any other spacing would break an axle on some of the old, long-distance roads, because this is the measure of the old wheel ruts.

So who built these old rutted roads? The first long-distance roads in Europe were built by Imperial Rome for their legions and have been used ever since. The initial ruts were first made by Roman war chariots, which were of uniform military issue. The Imperial Roman chariots were made to be just wide enough to accommodate the back ends of two war horses. (This example is originally due to Professor Tom O'Hare, Germanic Languages, University of Texas at Austin.)

16.1 Databases versus File Sets

In a similar fashion, modern data processing began with punch cards, or Hollerith cards, used by the Bureau of the Census. Their original size was that of a U.S. dollar bill. This size was set by their inventor, Herman Hollerith, because he could get furniture to store the cards from the U.S. Treasury Department, just across the street. Likewise, physical constraints limited each card to 80 columns of holes in which to record a symbol.

The influence of the punch card lingered on long after the invention of magnetic tapes and disk for data storage. This is why early video display terminals were 80 columns across. Even today, files that were migrated from cards to magnetic tape files or disk storage still use 80 column records.

But the influence was not just on the physical side of data processing. The methods for handling data from the prior media were imitated in the new media.

Data processing first consisted of sorting and merging decks of punch cards (later, magnetic tape files) in a series of distinct steps. The result of each step feeds into the next step in the process.

Relational databases do not work that way. Each user connects to the entire database all at once, not to one file at a time in a sequence of steps. The users might not all have the same access rights once they are connected, however. Magnetic tapes could not be shared among users at the same time, but shared data is the point of a database.

16.2 Tables versus Files

A file is closely related to its physical storage media. A table may or may not be a physical file. DB2 from IBM uses one file per table, while Sybase puts several entire databases inside one file. A table is a *set* of rows of the same kind of thing. A set has no ordering, and it makes no sense to ask for the first or last row.

A deck of punch cards is sequential, and so are magnetic tapes. Therefore, a file of sequential records also became the *mental* model for all file processing, and it is still hard to shake. Anytime you look at data, it is in some physical ordering.

Yes, I know about the various indexing and hashing access methods on disk storage systems. But even with these access methods, the goal of using them is very often to impose a physical ordering on the data.

And yes, I know that SQL is really based on a multiset (or "bag") model and not a pure set theoretical model. However, in actual practice, duplicates are avoided in the tables by declaring a `PRIMARY KEY`, and they are only a problem in query results.

Another conceptual difference is that a file is usually data that deals with a whole business process. A file has to have enough data in itself to support applications for that business process. Files tend to be "mixed" data that can be described by the name of the business process, such as the "payroll file," or something like that.

Tables can be either entities or relationships within a business process. This means that the data that was held in one file is often put into several tables. Tables tend to be "pure" data that can be described by single words. The payroll would now have separate tables for timecards, employees, projects, and so forth.

16.2.1 Tables as Entities

An entity is a physical or conceptual "thing" that has meaning by itself. A person, a sale, or a product would be an example. In a relational database, an entity is defined by its attributes, which are shown as values in columns in rows in a table.

To remind users that tables are sets of entities, I like to use plural or collective nouns that describe the function of the entities within the system for the names of tables. Thus "Employee" is a bad name because it is singular; "Employees" is a better name because it is plural. "Personnel" is best because it is collective and does not summon up a mental picture of individual persons.

16.2.2 Tables as Relationships

A relationship is shown in a table by columns that reference one or more entity tables. Without the entities, the relationship has no meaning, but the relationship can have attributes of its own. For example, a show business contract might have an agent, an employer, and a talent. The method of payment is an attribute of the contract itself, and not of any of the three parties.

16.3 Rows versus Records

Rows are not records. A record is defined in the application program that reads it; rows are defined in the database schema and not by a program at all. The name of the field is given in the `READ` or `INPUT` statements of the application program; a column is named in the database schema.

All empty files look alike; they are a directory entry in the operating system with a name and a length of zero bytes of storage. Empty tables still have columns, constraints, security privileges, and other structures, even though they have no rows.

This is in keeping with the set theoretical model, in which the empty set is a perfectly good set. The difference between SQL's set model and standard mathematical set theory is that set theory has only one empty set, but in SQL each table has a different structure, so they cannot be used in places where nonempty versions of themselves could not be used.

Another characteristic of rows in a table is that they are all alike in structure and they are all the "same kind of thing" in the model. In a file system, records can vary in structure—Pascal's variant record, C's `struc` syntax, and Cobol's `OCCURS` clause are common examples of this. Furthermore, records in the same file can represent different kinds of things. The use of flags in Cobol and the union syntax in C are two examples. But even more than that, files often contained records that were summaries of subsets of the other records—so-called control break reports.

16.4 Columns versus Fields

A field within a record is defined by the application program that reads it. A column in a row in a table is defined by the database schema. The datatypes in a column are always scalar.

The order of the application program variables in the `READ` or `INPUT` statements is important because the values are read into the program variables in that order. In SQL, columns are referenced only by their names. Yes, there are shorthands, like the `SELECT *` clause and `INSERT INTO <table name>` statements, that expand into a list of column names in the physical order in which the column names appear within their table declaration, but these are shorthands that resolve to named lists.

The use of `NULL`s in SQL is also unique to the language. Fields do not support a missing data marker as part of the field, record, or file itself. Nor do fields have constraints that can be added to them in the record, like the `DEFAULT` and `CHECK()` clauses in SQL.

16.5 Relationships among Tables within a Database

Files are pretty passive creatures and will take whatever an application program throws at them without much objection. Files are also independent of each other simply because they are connected to one application program at a time and therefore have no idea what other files look like.

A database actively seeks to maintain the correctness of all its data. The methods used are triggers, constraints, and declarative referential integrity (DRI).

DRI says, in effect, that data in one table has a particular relationship with data in a second (possibly the same) table. It is also possible to have the database change itself via referential actions associated with the DRI.

For example, a business rule might be that we do not sell products that are not in inventory. This rule would be enforced by a REFERENCES clause on the Orders table that references the Inventory table and a referential action of ON DELETE CASCADE.

Triggers are a more general way of doing much the same thing as DRI. A trigger is a block of procedural code that is executed before, after, or instead of an INSERT INTO or UPDATE statement. You can do anything with a trigger that you can do with DRI, and more.

However, there are problems with triggers. First, although there is a standard syntax for them in the SQL-92 standard, most vendors have not implemented it. What they have is very proprietary syntax instead. Second, a trigger cannot pass information to the optimizer like DRI. In the example in this section, I know that for every product number in the Orders table, I have that same product number in the Inventory table. The optimizer can use that information in setting up EXISTS() predicates and JOINs in the queries. There is no reasonable way to parse procedural trigger code to determine this relationship.

The CREATE ASSERTION statement in SQL-92 will allow the database to enforce conditions on the entire database as a whole. An ASSERTION is not like a CHECK() clause, but the difference is subtle. A CHECK() clause is executed when there are rows in the table to which it is attached. If the table is empty, then all CHECK() clauses are effectively TRUE. Thus, if we wanted to be sure that the Inventory table is never empty, and we wrote

```
CREATE TABLE Inventory
( . . .
  CONSTRAINT inventory_not_empty
   CHECK ((SELECT COUNT(*) FROM Inventory) > 0),
   . . . );
```

it would not work. However, we could write

```
CREATE ASSERTION Inventory_not_empty
  CHECK ((SELECT COUNT(*) FROM Inventory) > 0);
```

and we would get the desired results. The assertion is checked at the schema level and not at the table level.

16.6 Codd's Rules for a Relational Database

The relational model and the normal forms of the relational model were first defined by Dr. E. F. Codd (1970), then extended by other writers after him. He invented the term "normalized relations" by borrowing from the political jargon of the day. A branch of mathematics called "relations" deals with mappings among sets defined by predicate calculus from formal logic. Just as in an algebraic equation, there are many forms of the same relational statement, but the "normal forms" of relations are certain formally defined desirable constructions.

Dr. Codd gave 12 rules that defined how a database can conform to the relational model:

0. (Yes, there is a rule zero.) For a system to qualify as a relational database management system, that system must use its relational facilities (exclusively) to manage the database. SQL is not so pure on this rule, since you can often do procedural things to the data.

1. The information rule: This simply requires all information in the database to be represented in one and only one way, namely, by values in column positions within rows of tables. SQL is good here.

2. The guaranteed access rule: This rule is essentially a restatement of the fundamental requirement for primary keys. It states that every individual scalar value in the database must be logically addressable by specifying the name of the containing table, the name of the containing column, and the primary key value of the containing row. SQL follows this rule for tables that have a primary key, but does not require a table to have a key at all.

3. Systematic treatment of NULL values: The DBMS is required to support a representation of missing information and inapplicable information that is systematic, distinct from all regular values, and independent of datatype. It is also implied that such representations must be manipulated by the DBMS in a systematic way. SQL has a NULL that is used for both missing information and inapplicable information, rather than having two separate tokens as Dr. Codd wished.

4. Dynamic online catalog based on the relational model: The system is required to support an online, in-line, relational catalog that is accessible to authorized users by means of their regular query language. SQL does this.

5. The comprehensive data sublanguage rule: The system must support at least one relational language that (a) has a linear syntax; (b) can be used both interactively and within application programs; and (c) supports data definition operations (including view definitions), data manipulation operations (update as well as retrieval), security and integrity constraints, and transaction management operations (begin, commit, and rollback). SQL is pretty good on this point, since all of the operations Codd defined can be written in the DML (Data Manipulation Language).

6. The view updating rule: All views that are theoretically updatable must be updatable by the system. SQL is weak here and has elected to standardize on the safest case. View updatability is a very complex problem.

7. High-level insert, update, and delete: The system must support set-at-a-time INSERT, UPDATE, and DELETE operators. SQL does this.

8. Physical data independence: This is self-explanatory. Any real product is going to have some physical dependence, but SQL is better than most programming languages on this point.

9. Logical data independence: This is self-explanatory. SQL is quite good about this point.

10. Integrity independence: Integrity constraints must be specified separately from application programs and stored in the catalog. It must be possible to change such constraints as and when appropriate without unnecessarily affecting existing applications. SQL-92 has this.

11. Distribution independence: Existing applications should continue to operate successfully (a) when a distributed version of the DBMS is first introduced and (b) when existing distributed data is redistributed around the system. We are just starting to get distributed versions of SQL, so it is a little early to say whether SQL will meet this criterion or not.

12. The nonsubversion rule: If the system provides a low-level (record-at-a-time) interface, that interface cannot be used to subvert the system (e.g., bypassing a relational security or integrity constraint). SQL-92 is good about this one.

Codd also specified 9 structural features, 3 integrity features, and 18 manipulative features, all of which are required as well. He later extended the list from 12 rules to 333 in the second version of the relational model. I am not going to go into those features because that would take too long and you can look them up for yourself in his book.

Is Your DBMS Really Relational?

By E. F. Codd

In recent years, the data base management system market has undergone a very rapid swing in favor of products that take the relational approach to data base management. It is hard to find a vendor that does not claim its DBMS is relational. This swing has been so extensive that some vendors of nonrelational DBMS have quickly (and recently) added a few relational features—in some cases, very few features—in order to be able to claim their systems are relational, even though they may not meet the simple requirements for being rated "minimally relational." We shall refer to this kind of DBMS as "born again."

It is a safe bet that these Johnny-come-lately vendors have not taken the time or manpower to investigate optimization techniques needed in relational DBMS to yield good performance. This is the principal reason they continue to proclaim the "performance myth"—namely, that relational DBMS must perform poorly because they are relational!

One consequence of this rapid swing of the market to the relational approach is that products that are claimed by their vendors to be relational DBMS range from those that support the relational model with substantial fidelity to those that definitely do not deserve the label "relational," because their support is only token.

Some vendors claim that fourth-generation languages will provide all the productivity advantages. This claim conveniently overlooks the fact that most of these languages do little or nothing for shared data (the programming language fraternity still does not appear to realize that support for the dynamic sharing of data is an absolute requirement). In addition, there is no accepted theoretical foundation for fourth-generation languages and not even an accepted, precise definition.

This article outlines a technique that should help users determine how relational a DBMS really is. . . .

I shall not attempt a complete description of the relational model here—a relatively brief and concise definition appears in the article "RM/T: Extending the Relational Model to Capture More Meaning," (Chapter 2, "The Basic Relational Model") in the Association for Computing Machinery's "Transactions on Data Base Systems" (December 1979). It is, however, vitally important to remember that the relational model includes three major parts: the structural part, the manipulative part and the integrity part—a fact that is frequently and conveniently forgotten.

In this paper, I supply a set of rules with which a DBMS should comply if it is claimed to be fully relational. **No existing DBMS product that I know of can honestly claim to be fully relational**, at this time.

The proposed Ansi standard does not fully comply with the relational model, because it is based heavily on that nucleus of SQL that is supported in common by numerous vendors. Moreover, it takes a static, schema-based approach to data base description—reminiscent of Codasyl—instead of specifying a comprehensive, dual-mode data sublanguage that provides the powerful yet easy access to relational data bases and that is unique to the relational approach. Thus, the fidelity of the proposed Ansi standard to the relational model is even less than that of some relational DBMS products.

However, the standard could be readily modified to be more faithful to the model, and pressure should be brought on Ansi to do so. In fact, vendors are advised to extend their products soon in these respects so that they support customers' DBMS needs more fully and avoid possibly large customer expenses in application program maintenance at the time of the improvement.

The 12 rules

Twelve rules are cited below as part of a test to determine whether a product that is claimed to be fully relational is actually so. Use of the term "fully relational" in this report is slightly more stringent than in my Turing paper (written in 1981). This is partly because vendors in their ads and manuals have translated the term "minimally relational" to "fully relational" and partly because in this report, we are dealing with relational DBMS and not relational systems in general, which would include mere query-reporting systems.

However, the 12 rules tend to explain why full support of the relational model is in the users' interest. No new requirements are added to the relational model. A grading scheme is later defined and used to measure the degree of fidelity to the relational model.

First, I define these rules. Although I have defined each rule in earlier papers, I believe this to be the first occurrence of all 12 of them together.

In rules eight through 11, I specify and require four different types of independence aimed at protecting customers' investments in application programs, terminal activities and training. Rules eight and nine—physical and logical data independence—have been heavily discussed for many years.

Rules 10 and 11—integrity independence and distribution independence—are aspects of the relational approach that have received inadequate attention to date but are likely to become as important as eight and nine.

These rules are based on a single foundation rule, which I shall call Rule Zero:

For any system that is advertised as, or claimed to be, a relational data base management system, that system must be able to manage data bases entirely through its relational capabilities.

This rule must hold whether or not the system supports any nonrelational capabilities of managing data. Any DBMS that does not satisfy this Rule Zero is not worth rating as a relational DBMS.

One consequence of this rule: Any system claimed to be a relational DBMS must support data base insert, update and delete at the relational level (multiple-record-at-a-time). Another consequence is the necessity of supporting the information rule and the guaranteed access rule.

"Multiple-record-at-a-time" includes as special cases those situations in which zero or one record is retrieved, inserted, updated or deleted. In other words, a relation (table) may have either zero tuples (rows) or one tuple and still be a valid relation.

Any statement in the manuals of a system claimed to be a relational DBMS that advises users to revert to some nonrelational capabilities "to achieve acceptable performance"—or for any reason other than compatibility with programs written in the past on nonrelational data base systems—should be interpreted as an apology by the vendor. Such a statement indicates the vendor has not done the work necessary for achieving good performance with the relational approach.

What is the danger to buyers and users of a system that is claimed to be a relational DBMS and that fails on Rule Zero? Buyers and users will expect all the advantages of a truly relational DBMS, and they will fail to get these advantages.

Now I shall describe the 12 rules that, together with the nine structural, 18 manipulative and three integrity features of the relational model, determine in specific detail the extent of validity of a vendor's claim to have a "fully relational DBMS."

All 12 rules are motivated by Rule Zero defined above, but a DBMS can be more readily checked for compliance with these 12 than with Rule Zero.

The information rule.

Rule 1: *All information in a relational data base is represented explicitly at the logical level and in exactly one way—by values in tables. . . .*

Guaranteed access rule.

Rule 2: *Each and every datum (atomic value) in a relational data base is guaranteed to be logically accessible by resorting to a combination of table name, primary key value and column name. . . .*

Systematic treatment of null values.

Rule 3: *Null values (distinct from the empty character string or a string of blank characters*

and distinct from zero or any other number) are supported in fully relational DBMS for representing missing information and inapplicable information in a systematic way, independent of data type. . . .

Dynamic on-line catalog based on the relational model.

Rule 4: *The data base description is represented at the logical level in the same way as ordinary data, so that authorized users can apply the same relational language to its interrogation as they apply to the regular data. . . .*

Comprehensive data sublanguage rule.

Rule 5: *A relational system may support several languages and various modes of terminal use (for example, the fill-in-the-blanks mode). However, there must be at least one language whose statements are expressible, per some well-defined syntax, as character strings and that is comprehensive in supporting all of the following items:*

- *Data definition.*
- *View definition.*
- *Data manipulation (interactive and by program).*
- *Integrity constraints.*
- *Authorization.*
- *Transaction boundaries (begin, commit and rollback). . . .*

View updating rule.

Rule 6: *All views that are theoretically updatable are also updatable by the system. . . .*

High-level insert, update and delete.

Rule 7: *The capability of handling a base relation or a derived relation as a single operand applies not only to the retrieval of data but also to the insertion, update and deletion of data. . . .*

Physical data independence.

Rule 8: *Application programs and terminal activities remain logically unimpared* [sic] *whenever any changes are made in either storage representations or access methods. . . .*

Logical data independence.

Rule 9: *Application programs and terminal activities remain logically unimpared* [sic] *when information-preserving changes of any kind that theoretically permit unimpairment are made to the base tables. . . .*

Integrity independence.

Rule 10: *Integrity constraints specific to a particular relational data base must be definable in the relational data sublanguage and storable in the catalog, not in the application programs. . . .*

Distribution independence.

Rule 11: *A relational DBMS has distribution independence. . . .*

Nonsubversion rule.

Rule 12: *If a relational system has a low-level (single-record-at-a-time) language, that low level cannot be used to subvert or bypass the integrity rules and constraints expressed in the higher level relational language (multiple-records-at-a-time). . . .*

Excerpts from E. F. Codd, "Is Your DMBS Really Relational?" *Computerworld*, Oct. 14, 1985, pgs. ID/1–ID/9.

Keys

A KEY IS A combination of one or more columns in a table that uniquely identify each row of the table. In a relational database, you cannot access the data by its physical location, so you need a logical description of it for the engine to find it. There are four desirable properties of any key:

1. *Familiarity:* Key values should be meaningful to users.
2. *Stability:* Key values should not be volatile.
3. *Minimality:* Columns should be included in a key only if they are necessary for uniqueness.
4. *Simplicity:* Short, simple keys are preferable over long, conceptually complex keys.

These criteria may conflict in certain circumstances, and you may have to make trade-offs. For example, the longitude and latitude of a building are very stable, minimal, and simple in structure, but they are not familiar to most postal carriers; therefore, we will use the street address to locate the building when we address mail. However, the longitude and latitude of the building can be important in a database of deeds and titles.

Implementations of keys will vary from product to product, but they usually involve an index or other access method that includes an operation for assuring uniqueness. You might want to look at chapter 5 for details.

17.1 Types of Keys

Here is a simple list of terminology that we will use for the rest of the chapter:

- *Primary key:* A key that has been chosen by the DBA to represent the table. In Codd's original relational model, a table had to have a primary key. However, most relational theorists recognize the fact that a key is a key, and that logically there is nothing special about a primary key.

  In SQL engines, however, the `PRIMARY KEY` constraint may have special properties. The database engines often create predefined joins in special indexing structures for the `PRIMARY KEY`. The `PRIMARY KEY` is also the default used by the `REFERENCES` constraint, so there may be other special indexing structures that maintain the constraint between the referenced and referencing tables.

- *Secondary or candidate key:* A combination of columns different from the primary key that also makes a key. The keys are shown with the `UNIQUE` and `NOT NULL` constraints in SQL. However, there is a difference in SQL between a `UNIQUE` constraint and a `PRIMARY KEY` constraint: the `PRIMARY KEY` constraint is always `NOT NULL` on all its columns, while the `UNIQUE` constraint allows one and only one `NULL` in each column unless it is otherwise constrained.

- *Simple key:* A key consisting of just one attribute. Ideally, we would like the shortest, simplest datatype possible, so that joins can be done quickly. That means we really like to see `INTEGER` or other numeric datatypes that have hardware support for their operations and comparisons.

- *Compound or composite key:* A key consisting of more than one attribute.

- *Surrogate key:* Also called a "meaningless key" or "artificial key"; a key constructed inside the database that contains no information in itself. A surrogate key is often used in place of a meaningful compound key that is too unwieldy to use in an actual database.
- *Intelligent key:* Also called a "meaningful key" or "natural key"; a key that also has the values of an attribute(s) embedded in it and thus contains information.
- *Natural key:* A special case of the intelligent key that is in some way natural and immutable to the application; for example, identifying a location by its physical coordinates or a person by their DNA or fingerprints. The main characteristic is that when you have the entity, you can find the key from the entity itself.

  Mike Packard described the difference between intelligent and natural keys by observing that an intelligent key contains overloaded meanings, while a natural key contains singular meaning.
- *Super key:* A compound key with more columns than it needs to be a unique identifier. This is not always a bad thing, since the redundancy might be useful to a user.
- *Overlapping keys:* Compound keys that have one or more columns in common. We will discuss this in more detail later.

17.2 Intelligent Keys versus Surrogate Keys

A database table can have two kinds of keys. If the key has a meaning in itself, it is an intelligent key. If the key has no meaning other than to identify the entity represented in a row of the table, it is a surrogate key.

Object-oriented programmers would call this an object identifier, but that is not quite right. Consider the old story about the man showing off an axe that has been in his family for 500 years. Oh sure, they have had to replace the head and the handle a few times, but it is still the same axe.

This "sameness" is used in the object-oriented model where it becomes the object identifier, but not in the relational model of the

world. The relational model agrees more with Leibniz that a thing is the sum of all of its attributes; change the attributes and the thing is different. But SQL says that if you change the key attributes, the entity is then different.

17.2.1 Arguments against Intelligent Keys

Chris Date and other relational database proponents argue for surrogate keys over intelligent keys on the grounds that changes in the data encoded in an intelligent key will disrupt the database (see Date and Darwen 1992, chapter 30). To use one of Date's examples, the Zitzi Automobile Company uses part numbers 0000–4999 for parts that are bought from outside suppliers, and 5000–9999 for parts made in-house. One day, the company buys its 5001st part from an outside supplier and, to quote Date, "Any program that relied on the fact that purchased parts have numbers less than 5000 will now fail."

I do not think that this is a good example of his point, however. The Zitzi Automobile Company has put a nonkey attribute in its intelligent key. Suppliers can clearly change, so the source of the part should not be encoded in this key. Perhaps the part number should relate to the assembly or subassembly to which the part belongs. This is done with the industry standard codes for aircraft parts, a concatenation code that gets longer and longer as you go down the parts explosion. Ideally, when the same physical item is used in more than one subassembly, the key ends the same way in both cases. For example, xxxxxx-005 and yyyyyy-005 might mean "the number five machine screw used in the Frammistat" and "the number five machine screw used in the Freppometer," which are separate part numbers, but the same physical item.

Autoincremented Surrogate Keys

Most SQL and other database products have some sort of autoincrement function used to generate surrogate keys. These are not relational functions because they work on the data one row at a time, giving each row a different value usually based on some physical position within the storage or a global counter variable. The usual forms of this feature are

1. A column property that adds one to a counter maintained by the database engine for that column for each individual row as it is inserted. For example, the Sybase T-SQL language has the `IDENTITY` column constraint with the implication that it is exact numeric and `NOT NULL`.
2. A function that increments a counter (starting at one) maintained by the database engine for the rows of the result set in the statement. The Sybase SQL Anywhere function `NUMBER(*)` is an example, and again the datatype returned is exact numeric and `NOT NULL`.

The serial datatype vendor extensions to SQL have several problems. The autoincremented key column constraint can be assumed to be monotonic over time; that is, lower numbers were created earlier than later numbers. There is also a possibility that the counter will run out of numbers, but since most integers are 32 or 64 bytes long, it takes a long time in actual practice.

Assume I have a table called Foobar1 with a serial datatype column that is defined as `NOT NULL`, `UNIQUE`, and a positive `INTEGER` handled by the system instead of the user and a second table of names like this:

Foobar1

increment	name
1	'Larry'
2	'Moe'
3	'Curly'

SomeJunk

name
'Tom'
'Dick'
'Harry'

What is the meaning of the expression

```
INSERT INTO Foobar1(name)
SELECT name FROM SomeJunk;
```

The rules are that a missing column in such an expression would get the default value. So which rows in the table SomeJunk are associated with the default values (4, 5, 6)? Remember that the results of a SELECT are not in any particular order.

Should I require an ORDER BY clause on the SELECT or some other vendor syntax extension that destroys the relational model? The ORDER BY clause is allowed only on cursors now.

Next, given this table:

Foobar2

increment	name
6	'Huey'
7	'Louey'
8	'Dewey'

what is the meaning of

```
INSERT INTO Foobar1
SELECT * FROM Foobar2
```

The serial datatype column in both tables Foobar and SomeJunk already had values, but we are missing increments of 4 and 5. Is that a problem? If I then ran the first query on this result, would the missing values be created by the system?

I will not even deal with the multiuser problems, where one user deletes the last row and a second user creates a new row at the same time. The problem is that serial datatypes destroy the basic set property of an SQL table that says that row orderings have no meaning to the database.

(MAX() + 1) surrogate key generators

If the database is updated one row at a time, the simple SQL-92 statement

```
INSERT INTO Foobar (keycol, ..)
 VALUES ((SELECT MAX(keycol) FROM Foobar) + 1, ..);
```

will provide a valid next value to use. The reason that the increment is done outside the scalar subquery expression is that many SQL products have shortcuts for finding the MAX( ) of a column, but would have to do a full table scan if the MAX( ) is in an expression. Also, since this is one statement, we are guaranteed that it will be atomic.

However, if more than one user can update the database, this technique does not guarantee that there will not be gaps in the values used in keycol. Users A, B, and C all attempt to INSERT INTO Foobar, and what happens next depends on their transaction levels.

Let's assume that users A and B can both see the uncommitted work, and at the start of their sessions, keycol = 1.

1. User A executes his statement first and builds a row where keycol = 2.
2. User B executes her statement next and builds a row where keycol = 3.
3. User C executes his statement last and builds a row where keycol = 2.

Several things can now happen:

4a. User A does a COMMIT, and user B does a COMMIT. Everything is fine for them, but user C gets an error message about duplicate key values when he tries his COMMIT.

4b. User A does a ROLLBACK, and user B does a COMMIT. The value keycol = 2 is still free at this point, so user C can COMMIT his work.

If you want to know if a table has gaps, you can find out with the simple query:

```
SELECT DISTINCT 'We got gaps!'
  FROM Foobar
HAVING COUNT(*) <> MAX(keycol);
```

A HAVING clause without a GROUP BY clause will treat the entire table as one group and compute aggregate functions on it.

Surrogate Key Tables

Another approach is to build an auxiliary table of surrogate keys to hold the next value for each surrogate primary key in the database, and a stored procedure to return new key values and update the surrogate key table. This table has a column for the value of the keys and a column for the name of the key itself.

This looks simple: the stored procedure will SELECT the next value and then update it for later use. But this approach has the same gapping problems of the (MAX() + 1) approach because it would still allow two users to SELECT the same next value in a multiuser scenario unless you can give an exclusive lock on the surrogate key table to the user who is currently executing the stored procedure.

However, an exclusive lock prevents other users from accessing the key value (even with row-level granularity in your particular SQL product) and can slow down transaction processing.

Random Number Surrogate Keys

Another version of the procedural surrogate key generator uses a pseudorandom number generator that does not repeat for millions of numbers. The procedure will hide the last seed (key value) internally, and if your procedural language does not allow multiple copies of the same procedure to exist at the same time (i.e., reentrant code), the system will protect you from duplicate keys.

The advantages of random surrogate keys include

1. *Security:* Predicting the next value in the series is very difficult, which can be a security advantage. In a sequentially allocated key system, you know that if k is a key, then $k - 1$ is also a valid key. This is not true with a random key.

2. *Uniform distribution of keys:* Many of the pseudorandom number generators will give a uniform statistical distribution of values. Indexes with tree structures have to rebalance themselves when their updates are all skewed toward one value, as they are in a sequential key generator. Rebalancing

is an expensive process both in terms of time and resources, and can be avoided with pseudorandom numbers.

3. *Physical disk pages:* If the gap between the pseudorandom numbers is, on average, large enough, the next number will tend to be put on another page of physical storage. This avoids unwanted physical clustering of the most recent records, which can be a good thing if the most recent records are the most likely to be accessed.

The disadvantages of random surrogate keys include

1. *Size:* Because the pseudorandom number can be in the millions, you need to allow for the largest possible key from the start. This can lead to some very large keys for some very small sets of entities.
2. *Complexity:* The pseudorandom functions can be complex and hard for personnel to understand and maintain. The stored procedure needs to have a way to retry when it runs into duplicate numbers. This can mean keeping track of a chain of seeds in local variables in a multiuser situation.
3. *Cyclicity:* Pseudorandom numbers run in cycles; that is, when you generate a number that has already been used in the sequence, the sequence will repeat itself and give you duplicates. Certain seeds can lead to shorter or longer cycles in the pseudorandom numbers.

Picking the initial set of seed values is not a trivial exercise. But if you use a known seed, you can lose the security advantages of a random number. In fact, this has already happened in a Canadian lottery. One contestant realized that the lottery was using a particular pseudorandom number generator and simply "guessed" the next numbers in the series for several weeks in a row.

17.2.2 Arguments for Intelligent Keys

While many of the SQL experts argue for surrogate keys, I would like to point out some of the useful features of intelligent keys—partly

because I just like to be contrary, but I also feel that there are advantages to a natural intelligent key when they exist.

Saving Space in the Database

The first obvious advantage is that intelligent keys save space because the information they provide must be represented somewhere in the columns of tables. In fairness, saving the space required for extra columns because of surrogate keys is a minor advantage, considering the cheap storage that is available today and that a surrogate key is most often an `INTEGER` requiring only 2, 4, or 8 bytes.

There is further space savings in not having extra indexes and integrity rules needed to maintain the extra columns holding information that would have been in an intelligent key. In the case of Zitzi's automobile parts, you would need a column to identify parts made in-house and those provided by a supplier. This column would have to be indexed if it was used heavily in reports.

Verification of the Data

A major advantage is that you can construct and verify an intelligent key by inspection or a procedure, but you cannot do this with a surrogate key. An employee can tell you what his Social Security number is, but he will probably not know what his randomly generated surrogate employee identifier is. In fact, he will not have any existence in the system until he is assigned such a random number, and there is no way he could guess what it will be.

Even better, a machine that creates an employee identification number from the employee's fingerprints, retina prints, or DNA code would produce a verifiable identifier that the employer would have a very hard time misplacing.

You are more likely to have a rule for generating an intelligent key than a biometric or physical device. If you're lucky enough to use a full implementation of SQL-92 with a `CREATE DOMAIN` statement, you can define a "part number" or "employee number" domain that has a `CHECK()` clause with this rule to validate the code to a certain level of authenticity at every insert or update—something that is difficult or impossible with a surrogate key.

Chris Date and Hugh Darwen (1992, chapter 30, section 3) have used the ISBN as an example of a bad intelligent key. As discussed in chapter 15, the ISBN is made up of four subcomponents. The leftmost one or two digits is the group code (basically, the language in which the book is written). The next few digits are the publisher code (the bigger the publisher, the shorter the code number). The next set of digits is the book title within that publisher. There is also a single MOD 11 check digit on the right to ensure that the entire code is correct. An ISBN is always 10 digits long, but the final position can be an *X*, like the Roman numeral, if the check digit was 10.

Although not a perfect system, all this extra information makes ordering a book much easier than the old system, in which every publisher had a different internal stock code for each book. I think that one problem Date and Darwen have is that they do not see a difference between a book (the physical product of the publisher) and a title (the semantic content of the book). They are bothered that each of several versions of the same book (book club edition, hardback, paperback, and so forth) has a different ISBN.

Difficulty of Changing Surrogate Keys

Proponents of surrogate keys claim that surrogate keys make it easier to change the structure of a relational database. Things were even worse in the real world before SQL, as was pointed out to me by Gerald Whyte via CompuServe. Let's assume that you invent a new part-numbering scheme to replace the old one at Zitzi Automobile Company. This change might not be a matter of choice if the industry suddenly starts using a standard such as EDI and you must conform to it to talk to your suppliers.

In older navigational (network and hierarchical) databases, such as IDMS, the value of the primary key was often used to control the physical location of the records. This meant that you could not issue an in-place update of the keys as you could with nonkey fields. The physical position of each record was the result of a hashing algorithm within a preallocated file structure based on the primary key. The update of the key would require an unload and reload of all the data, even before you started to rewrite all of your application code.

In this case, changing the keys on a few thousand master records to a new part number scheme was a bad enough problem to shut you down for a day. The real work involved changing the millions of transaction records that also had to use the new part numbers. Changing the transaction records also required an unload and reload of all the data after you changed the old parent record key to the new key. Keep in mind that all access was based on physical pointers in those products.

However, it is not clear that a relational database and a surrogate key are going to protect you from problems with changing a primary key. Relational database theory deals with an ideal model; SQL databases exist in the real world, where they have to worry about performance. This means dealing with indexes, hashing, and sequential access methods to get to the data.

A primary key in an SQL database usually has a unique index on it, which must be reorganized if the key is changed. What you actually do is alter the table and add a column for the new key to one table. Then, insert the new key values in the new column and spend some time verifying that you got things right.

In the Zitzi Automobile Company example, too much of the programming logic would depend on having the source of the part within the part number to factor it into a separate nonkey column. In the real world, they would probably expand the size of the part number from four to five or six digits by multiplying the old numbers by 10 or 100 to extend the existing pattern. Yes, this is a bad idea, but this is the way of the world.

In the case of a new industry standard code, you would probably have to build or buy a conversion file and write a program to run the file against the database.

The real problem with a change in an intelligent key is that the paper forms and reports must also change. You can sometimes hide surrogate keys from the user on reports; for example, a surrogate employee number might never print out on reports organized by last name. However, preprinted paper forms are dying out, and they do not really cost that much anyway. More and more forms are laser printed as needed. A good report writer will recompile and resize a report with no trouble at all.

Because the new column is a key, you must check for uniqueness and coverage. This task is easy. Allow NULLs in the new column when you are inserting data, and then attempt to add a NOT NULL constraint after the data is in place. When all rows have a new value, add a unique index and see if it fails.

Once you have modified one table, you can alter other tables by adding a new column and using a join in an UPDATE statement to insert the new foreign key values. Again, you must check to see that every row gets a new key. You will probably find errors at this point, so fix them while you have the chance.

When all the tables have their new primary and foreign keys, you can drop the old key columns (which will also drop their indexes), rename the new columns to the old names, and reindex them. Response time is terrible during this process, and the other users will probably hate you for it, but the database is never completely shut down. I am going to ignore the issues of old codes and data warehouse problems.

Getting New Keys

You can run out of surrogate keys as easily as you can run out of intelligent keys. If you use a five-digit surrogate key and get to 100,000 items in the table, you have pretty much the same problems as with a five-digit intelligent key.

Going to the Zitzi Automobile Company parts example again, there is no way to tell the origin of a part if you use a surrogate key, so you need a column for the part's origin (in-house or outside supplier). Assume that you make a part and also buy it from a supplier when you cannot meet your own internal demand. Should those two identical parts have the same surrogate key and be differentiated by the origin code? Or should they have different surrogate keys?

You can make good arguments either way. The original problem implies that you are very concerned with the origin of the parts, so that is probably more important than what the part actually is. On the other hand, you would report inventory levels on parts without regard to their origin, so an identical internal identifier would help.

I have a rule of thumb about reports and intelligent keys. DBAs should create a VIEW that looks as if it were a table designed for a

specific report alone. The VIEW will perform all calculations, decoding, and joins on the database side of the system. A corollary to this rule is that the report's VIEW should present the information contained in an intelligent key as if it were in a separate column. In this case, the VIEW and not the base table would have the origin flag as a column.

The rules for defining those VIEWs would be very simple at the start—part numbers 0000–4999 are flagged as in-house, and 5000–9999 are flagged as outside suppliers. As that simple rule breaks down with the addition of new part numbers, you could change the two VIEWs and the reports would run the same as before.

While adding an origin column to the table is one approach, a better alternative is to flag the origin by adding a subfield to the part number. This would imply that the same part could come from inside or outside the company. You could then change the VIEWs to use the new column or look for the flag in the code. Either way, the reports would never show that anything had happened to the base tables.

Clustering versus Random Distribution

Surrogate keys tend to be randomly distributed, while intelligent keys tend to cluster in a useful fashion. In fact, surrogate keys are often created by random number generators. The clustering of an intelligent key can speed up searches if you have a clustered index on the column. Using the ISBN example again, books by the same publisher will tend to be on the same page of physical storage because the publisher code appears in the high-order digits (which is how they sort in the index).

A clustered index on a surrogate key would be useless because you would have to create a unique index for the surrogate key and a clustered index on the publisher's name, which increases the cost of updating the database by a column and an index.

You must now decide how to encode the publishers' names. A text column will be large and subject to errors: "John Wiley & Sons," "John Wiley and Sons," and "John Wiley" are all possible spellings of the same publisher, and one publisher could do business under several different names. You should probably go with a numeric code, which means another table in the schema to decode the numbers into publisher names.

Standards versus "Roll Your Own"

Intelligent keys tend to be standardized and have support from outside sources that surrogate keys do not. Consider a bookstore database in which you build your own codes for the books and publishers. You need an integrity rule that will keep the publisher and its books properly aligned. If you change the publisher code, you do not have the same book anymore. It might be the same title, but it is not the same book. Of course, all this work and research was done for you by the ISBN people.

Even if you come up with a better scheme for encoding books, you would still have to order them from the publisher using the ISBN because the ISBN is the industry standard. What would happen if you bought out another book dealer who also has his own surrogate keys? How would you merge his publisher codes with your publisher codes when neither of you has standardized? Merging the databases becomes a major task with surrogates—you will find duplicate keys, different-sized fields on screens and forms, and a whole host of problems.

Data Warehousing

Another point in favor of intelligent keys is that they tend to stay unique over time, but surrogate keys may not. Using the automobile parts database again, assume that you have been adding and deleting parts from the database over the years. You have just removed all of the Yugo parts, and must now add the Kia parts to the table. A lot of surrogate key generators will repeat an old number because all random number generators cycle. When you attempt to see if an old Yugo code number value is available, you will find that it is and will probably reuse it. This is fine for daily operations.

However, Jeff Winchell, a writer for *DBMS* magazine, pointed out via a CompuServe message that this is a problem because DBMSs do not support spanning primary keys between live data and archival data. To quote Jeff, "Med AI told me that one hospital was on HCFA's high mortality list. [It was] obviously concerned about the bad publicity and contracted Med AI to help it. The culprit turned

out to be reusing surrogate key values so that some patients 'died' many times."

The problem is that the duplicated number means that you cannot use a data warehouse. Your historical data does not have unique surrogate keys over time. If you had used an intelligent key such as the vehicle identification number (VIN), which has the manufacturer, make, model, and year encoded into it, you would not have the duplication problem.

Replicated and Distributed Databases

A *distributed database* is a logical database that resides on several different physical units connected by a network of some kind. Each unit is more or less independent operationally, but not logically. *Replication* is the general term for techniques that keep the units in a distributed database "in synch" with each other over the network.

In our examples, the Zitzi Automobile Company might put a computer in each of its dealerships and connect them to the company mainframe via a leased telephone line. If the local databases are creating their own local surrogate invoice numbers, you are going to have problems with duplicates in the logical database. If the mainframe database is creating all the surrogate invoice numbers, you are going to have problems with performance.

The solution is to have local databases create their own local intelligent invoice numbers, which include a code or component that is unique to that database.

17.3 Simple versus Compound Keys

When the relational model was first proposed, one of the requirements was that every table had to have a primary key to identify each row. SQL did not pick this up as a requirement and allows a table to have no keys (i.e., columns with `UNIQUE` constraints) at all. However, SQL standards and implementations made the `PRIMARY KEY` constraint something special. The standard says that this declaration automatically implies that all the columns are `NOT NULL` and the collection is `UNIQUE`. The `PRIMARY KEY` is also the default used by `REFERENCES` clauses in other tables.

Many, if not most, implementations assume that the PRIMARY KEY columns will be the most common way that this table is accessed in queries, since it was designated from all possible candidate keys. Therefore, this key might get some special treatment in the underlying storage structure. Graphic notations and CASE tools often use special symbols and icons for primary keys, thus furthering the idea that they are in some way required, fundamentally different from other keys, or special.

Furthermore, implementations will often create special indexing structures that "prejoin" the referenced and referencing tables together. This leads to the question as to how your particular SQL engine will create an index for the keys. The SQL-92 standard requires that the number, datatypes, and position of the columns given in the REFERENCES clause match the number, datatypes, and position of the columns in the referenced table's uniquely constrained column set.

It was only a few years ago that relational theory experts dropped the requirement of having a primary key on a table in favor of having at least one key per table.

17.3.1 Super Keys and Overlapping Keys

Two special cases of a compound key are worth mentioning. A compound key with more columns than it needs to be a unique identifier is called a super key. The most obvious case is using the entire set of columns in the table as the key, since any key contained within it will make it into a key in its own right.

Super keys are of two basic types. Their extra columns can be nonkey attributes in addition to key attributes, or the key might be made up of two or more candidate keys combined together.

In the first case, you would like to drop the nonkey attributes, but perhaps still show them in a query. For example, the employee number and the employee's name are a super key because the employee number should be unique in itself, while common names like "John Smith" will be duplicated within a large database. However, this sort of super key might be useful to a user in a real-life situation because the user can get some confirmation of the correctness of the employee number by asking the employee's name.

Overlapping keys are compound keys that have one or more columns in common. As an example, consider this table, with all the candidate keys shown as `UNIQUE()` constraints:

```
CREATE TABLE Schedule
(teacher CHAR(20) NOT NULL,
 period INTEGER NOT NULL CHECK (period BETWEEN 1 AND 6),
 classroom INTEGER NOT NULL,
 UNIQUE (teacher, period),              – candidate key
 UNIQUE (teacher, classroom),           – candidate key
 UNIQUE (period, classroom),            – candidate key
 UNIQUE (teacher, period, classroom)    – super key
 );
```

One teacher can only be in one classroom (assume no team teaching) during any given period. Additionally, there is a super key of all three columns in the table. You can obviously extend this pattern of key formation to any *k* out of *n* columns.

17.3.2 Queries with Compound Keys

Compound keys can lead to somewhat awkward queries. For instance, consider the following education database of courses, offerings, and enrollments taken from Date and Darwen(1992, chapter 31):

```
CREATE TABLE Courses
(course_no INTEGER NOT NULL PRIMARY KEY,
 title CHAR(15) NOT NULL);

CREATE TABLE Offerings
(course_no CHAR(5) NOT NULL,
 off_no CHAR(5) NOT NULL,
 loc CHAR(15) NOT NULL,
 PRIMARY KEY (course_no, off_no),
 FOREIGN KEY (course_no) REFERENCES Courses(course_no));

CREATE TABLE Enrollments
(course_no CHAR(5) NOT NULL,
 off_no CHAR(5) NOT NULL,
```

```
 emp_no CHAR(5) NOT NULL,
 grade CHAR(1) NOT NULL
      CHECK (grade IN ('A', 'B', 'C', 'D', 'F')),
 PRIMARY KEY (course_no, emp_no),
 FOREIGN KEY (course_no, off_no)
   REFERENCES Offerings (course_no, off_no));
```

A query to find the courses and offerings numbers for all New York offerings in which employee 'Celko' is enrolled might look like this in SQL-89:

```
SELECT E1.course_no, E1.off_no
  FROM Enrollments AS E1, Offerings AS O1
 WHERE E1.emp_no = 'Celko'
   AND E1.course_no = O1.course_no
   AND E1.off_no = O1.off_no
   AND O1.loc = 'New York';
```

The pair (course_no, off_no) is mentioned three times in this query. However, in SQL-92, we can use row constructors to write the query several different ways:

Version #1:

```
SELECT E1.course_no, E1.off_no
  FROM Enrollments AS E1,
       Offerings AS O1
 WHERE (E1.course_no, E1.off_no) = (O1.course_no, O1.off_no)
   AND E1.emp_no = 'Celko'
   AND O1.loc = 'New York';
```

Or to really use the new SQL-92 syntax:

Version #2:

```
SELECT E1.course_no, E1.off_no
  FROM Enrollments AS E1
       INNER JOIN
       Offerings AS O1
       ON (E1.course_no, E1.off_no) = (O1.course_no, O1.off_no)
          AND (E1.emp_no, O1.loc) = ('Celko', 'New York');
```

This lets us regard the combination of course_no and off_no as a single thing, but without giving the pair a name of its own. This is not a problem with a two-column compound key, but if the key gets to be very long, a shorthand might be nice.

The quick way to do this with CHAR( ) and VARCHAR( ) columns would be to create a VIEW in which the concatenation of the columns has a single name. For example:

```
CREATE VIEW OV (co_no, loc)
AS SELECT (course_no || ' ' || off_no), loc
     FROM Offerings;

CREATE VIEW EV (co_no, emp_no, grade)
AS SELECT (course_no || ' ' || off_no), emp_no, grade
     FROM Enrollments;

SELECT EV.co_no
  FROM OV, EV
 WHERE EV.co_no = OV.co_no
   AND EV.emp_no = 'Celko'
   AND OV.loc = 'New York';
```

The derived column co_no can also be useful in an ORDER BY clause. Another consideration is that the compound key can be used to optimize code. Consider the query:

```
SELECT *
  FROM Enrollments
 WHERE course_no
       IN (SELECT O1.course_no
             FROM Offerings AS O1
            WHERE )1.loc = 'New York')
   AND off_no
       IN (SELECT O2.off_no
             FROM Offerings AS O2
            WHERE O2.loc = 'New York');
```

which can be replaced by the more efficient single subquery expression:

```
SELECT *
  FROM Enrollments
 WHERE course_no || '=' || off_no
       IN (SELECT course_no || '=' || off_no
             FROM Offerings
            WHERE loc = 'New York');
```

This trick requires that the columns involved be character data or cast as character data, which is a limitation because type conversions can be expensive. But using the SQL-92 syntax, you could also write

```
SELECT *
  FROM Enrollments
 WHERE (course_no, off_no)
       IN (SELECT course_no, off_no
             FROM Offerings
            WHERE loc = 'New York');
```

and there is no restriction on the datatypes used.

The idea of giving a compound key a name as part of the table or schema declaration, then using that name in queries, sounds simple, but turns out to be surprisingly complex. Chris Date (1995) has made an argument against allowing such a shorthand construction for compound keys in queries. He demonstrates that this would lead to problems where the pair is regarded as if it were a column in its own right. The problems result from the destruction of scalar properties in the compound column.

Different Relational Models

THERE IS NO such thing as *the* relational model for databases anymore than there is just one geometry.

In the 19th century, Bolyai, Gauss, and Lobachevski all realized that the parallel postulate of Euclidean geometry could be changed and whole new geometries developed. For example, if I draw a triangle on a plane, it always has 180 degrees; if I draw it on the surface of a sphere, it always has more than 180 degrees; and if I draw it on the surface of a trumpet, it always has less than 180 degrees.

Which geometry is true? Well, it depends where I am. My backyard is roughly a plane, the surface of the earth is roughly a sphere, and the gravity well of a star is roughly a trumpet.

Models are consistent and constructible. Consistent means that you cannot prove something to be both true and false using the rules of the model. Constructible means that I can build a finite version of it in the real world.

18.1 Chris Date = No Duplicates, No NULLs

Although Chris Date was not the first person to work with the relational model, his version is the simplest and closest to the "usual file model" of data, so it is where we will start this chapter.

Date's relational model allows no duplicate rows in tables and has no NULL. Missing values are shown either by special values in the encoding schemes or by an indicator column that is paired with the original column.

Date is also a vocal opponent of the ANSI/ISO SQL standard efforts, although he has never attended a committee meeting or submitted a paper for consideration.

Date has also added other operators and proposed special notations for extensions to an unimplemented language based on the relational algebra. These proposals include the MAYBE postfixed unary logical operator that returns TRUE when its operand is TRUE or UNKNOWN. His EXTEND operator adds a column with a computation in it to a table. His SUMMARIZE operator is a generalized columnar function constructor. These are discussed in [Date 1995]. He also came up with an EXPLODE operator for doing parts explosions from hierarchies stored in an adjacency list table.

18.2 E. F. Codd, RM Version I

Dr. Codd's original model of the relational database has been given the name "RM version I" to differentiate it from the revised version that came years later. This classic model allowed no duplicate rows and has one NULL to show missing values.

Dr. Codd developed a mathematical notation that is still used in academic textbooks.

18.3 E. F Codd, RM Version II

In 1990, Dr. Codd released a second version of his relational model, which was greatly expanded from the original paper. He still does not allow duplicate rows in a table, but he added two types of NULL markers. One represents data for which there is an attribute but a value is missing. The other NULL represents data for which there is not an attribute, which is why the value is missing.

A working SQL product with both types of NULLs is available from FirstSQL.

18.4 SQL-92 = Duplicates, One NULL

The SQL language was developed by IBM's Santa Teresa labs. Both Chris Date and Dr. Codd were employees of IBM during this time, but the actual language and implementation were done by a team directed by Don Chamberlin. The big debate during development was not over the relational model, but over how NULLs should be handled.

The result was System R and Sequel (Structured English-like Query Language) as their first product. The word "structured" was the buzzword of the day because "structured programming" had just been invented. The nesting of queries within each other was seen as a version of modularization used in block-structured procedural languages. Actually, this is not quite proper because modularization referred to the flow of control within a program, and a nonprocedural language has no such concept. The language was later extended a bit and became the first version of SQL.

SQL was based on Dr. Codd's RM version I model, but just as Fortran was supposed to be based on algebra, there were some changes made in the actual implementation.

Removing redundant duplicates was considered too expensive and too strange for programmers, so SQL uses a multiset model instead of a pure set model.

18.5 Duplicates, One NULL, Non-1NF Tables

In a first normal form (1NF) database, all the columns in the rows of a table contain only scalar values. We will discuss normal forms and define scalar values in detail a bit later, but for now, let's just say that a scalar value is simple and has no structure of its own.

Roth and Korth (1998) developed a model that extends the SQL model by allowing a table to contain another table within a column. For example, a table of employees might include a column for dependents; in that column we could insert a table for the dependents of each employee.

They added operators for nesting and unnesting these tables and extended some of the existing operators. They documented their ideas in a series of papers available from the Computer Science Department of the University of Texas at Austin.

18.6 Rick Snodgrass = Temporal SQL

Rick Snodgrass (1995) at the University of Arizona has a series of papers that add temporal operations to standard SQL. He is not the only researcher in this area, but his work is the only project that has been brought to the attention of the NCITS H2 Committee for SQL3.

The set models used in all of the data models discussed so far are state oriented and lack a temporal dimension. That is, when a fact is entered or changed in the database, the database engine makes no note of when this event occurred. Instead, the database is a model of the current state of the real world as of a moment in time. The real worry is that the model be consistent with logical constraints on the data.

Temporal SQL adds extra clauses to the usual `SELECT` statement that match rows based on when they occurred relative to each other.

Basic Relational Operations

DR. E. F. CODD defined a simple set of operators for relational tables in his original work. The goal for the set of operators was to be both complete and minimal; mathematicians like those properties. These original operators were the basis for SQL statements and expressions, but SQL has extended this set to include operators that are useful to programmers.

You can classify the operators as

1. operating on a whole table without regard to the nature of the rows
2. operating on the rows of a table
3. operating on the columns within the rows of a table

19.1 Projection

A *projection* operates on a single table to produce a new table by removing columns in the original table. The term was originally used in mathematics as a weak inverse operation for the Cartesian product. That is, you could get one of the original domains out of a tuple.

19.2 Restriction

A *restriction* operates on a single table to produce a new table by removing rows in the original table. The rule for removing rows is given as a logical predicate. The rule in SQL is that you keep the rows for which the predicate tested TRUE (i.e., discard those that tested FALSE or UNKNOWN).

19.3 Computations

Computations were not part of Codd's original operators, but you need them if you are going to do any real work. You can think of them as the opposite of a projection because they add columns instead of removing them.

In SQL, computations create new columns in the result table using constants, functions, values from other columns, or even values from other tables.

19.3.1 Simple Operators and Expressions

SQL has numeric, string, temporal, bit, and whatever other datatypes a particular implementation supports. The operators on these datatypes can be closed, which means that they produce a result that is of the same datatype as the operands. Operators can also be classified by the number of operands—unary, binary, ternary, or *n*-ary.

19.3.2 Expressions Using Other Tables

The scalar subquery expression is a new concept in SQL-92. They are subqueries that return a single value, and because they return a single value, they can be used anywhere that a scalar expression can be used. Perhaps the best way to think of them is that they are functions whose definition is given with a SELECT statement instead of by procedural code, as they would have been in a traditional programming language.

19.4 Joins

A join takes two tables and creates a result table by using the rows in the original tables to construct new rows with columns from both tables. The simplest form of a join is the CROSS JOIN, or Cartesian product. Each row from one table is attached to a copy of each row from the second table, so that you get all possible combinations in the result table.

In set theory, the Cartesian product was defined as $(A \times B)$, and it produces the set of all ordered pairs (a, b) such that $((a \in A) \land (b \in B))$. This means that $(A \times B)$ is not the same as $(B \times A)$. Since the result of a Cartesian product is a set of ordered pairs, there are no duplicates.

The CROSS JOIN is a little different. The CROSS JOIN produces a table whose rows have no ordering to their columns, so it is a closed operation. This means that A CROSS JOIN B *is* the same as B CROSS JOIN A. Since the result of a CROSS JOIN is a table, there can be duplicate rows.

CROSS JOINs tend to give you large, meaningless result sets. If table A has 100 rows and table B has 100 rows, their CROSS JOIN will have (100 * 100) = 10,000 rows. Unless you were trying to construct all possible combinations of A and B rows, most of these combinations are meaningless.

The reasons for having a CROSS JOIN are completeness, the fact that sometimes you do need to construct all possible combinations of two tables, and the fact that it is useful in defining other joins.

19.4.1 INNER JOIN

The INNER JOIN operator is the most common type of join and breaks down into several subtypes. SQL-92 introduced syntax for the INNER JOINs that is closer to the notation used in Codd's relational algebra than the method used in the SQL-89 standard.

An INNER JOIN can be defined as a CROSS JOIN, followed by a restriction.

A NATURAL JOIN is a special case of the INNER JOIN. It takes the column names that are common betwen the two tables and constructs an equi-join on them. Then only one of the common columns is retained in the result table. Notice that this means if the tables have no common column names, you will get a CROSS JOIN as the result.

19.4.2 OUTER JOIN

The OUTER JOIN operator is new to SQL-92 and has only three subtypes. SQL-92 introduced syntax for the OUTER JOINs that is different from the notation used in many existing SQL implementations. Codd's relational algebra did not define an OUTER JOIN notation.

One (or both) of the two tables in an OUTER JOIN is designated as the preserved table. Each row in the preserved table is joined to the rows in the second table in the usual manner (i.e., we have an INNER JOIN). However, any row in the preserved table(s) that was not matched to a row in the other table is padded out with NULLs in the columns derived from the other table.

LEFT OUTER JOIN

In a LEFT OUTER JOIN, the table on the left side of the operator is preserved.

RIGHT OUTER JOIN

In a RIGHT OUTER JOIN, the table on the right side of the operator is preserved.

FULL OUTER JOIN

In a FULL OUTER JOIN, the tables on both sides of the operator are preserved.

19.4.3 Self-Join

A self-join is any join in which the same table appears more than once. In order to do this, you must give each copy of the table a separate name.

19.4.4 UNION JOIN

The UNION JOIN is a creature that is new to SQL-92 and not widely implemented yet. Actually, I don't know of any product that has it at this writing. It is somewhat like the complement of a FULL OUTER JOIN.

Transactions and Concurrency Control

IN THE OLD days when we lived in caves and used mainframe computers with batch file systems, transaction processing was easy. You batched up the transactions to be made against the master file into a transaction file. The transaction file was sorted, edited, and ready to go when you ran it against the master file from a tape drive. The output of this process became the new master file, and the old master file and the transaction files were logged to magnetic tape in a huge closet in the basement of the company.

When disk drives, multiuser systems, and databases came along, things got complex—and SQL made it more so. But mercifully the user does not have to see the details. Well, here is the first layer of the details.

20.1 Sessions

The concept of a user session involves the user first connecting to the database. This is like dialing a phone number, but with a password, to get to the database. The SQL-92 syntax for this statement is

```
CONNECT TO <connection target>

<connection target> ::=
   <SQL-server name>
     [ AS <connection name> ]
     [ USER <user name> ]
 | DEFAULT
```

but you will find many differences in vendor SQL products and perhaps operating system level logon procedures that have to be followed.

Once the connection is established, users have access to all the parts of the database to which they have been granted privileges. During this session, they can execute zero or more transactions. As a user inserts, updates, and deletes rows in the database, these changes are not made a permanent part of the database until that user issues a COMMIT WORK command for that transaction. However, if the user does not want to make the changes permanent, then he or she can issue a ROLLBACK WORK command, and the database stays as it was before the transaction.

20.2 ACID Properties

There is a handy mnemonic for the four characteristics we want in a transaction: the ACID properties. The initials are short for four properties we have to have in a transaction processing scheme: atomicity, consistency, isolation, and durability.

20.2.1 Atomicity

Atomicity means that the whole transaction becomes persistent in the database or nothing in the transaction becomes persistent. The data becomes persistent in SQL-92 when a COMMIT statement is successfully executed. The transaction is removed by a ROLLBACK statement, and the database restored to its prior (consistent) state before the transaction began.

The COMMIT or ROLLBACK statement can be explicitly executed by the user or by the database engine when it finds an error. Most SQL engines default to a ROLLBACK, unless it is configured to do otherwise.

Atomicity means that if I were to try to insert one million rows into a table and one row of that million violated a referential constraint, then the whole set of one million rows would be rejected, and the database would do an automatic `ROLLBACK WORK`.

Here is the trade-off. If you do one long transaction, then you are in danger of being screwed by just one tiny little error. However, if you do several short transactions in a session, then other users can have access to the database between your transactions, and they might change things—much to your surprise.

The solution has been to implement `SAVEPOINT` or `CHECKPOINT` options, which act much like a bookmarker. A transaction sets savepoints during its execution and lets the transaction perform a local rollback to the checkpoint. In our example, we might have been doing savepoints every 1,000 rows, so that when the 999,999th row inserted has an error that would have caused a `ROLLBACK`, the database engine removes only the work done after the savepoint was set, and the transaction is restored to the state of uncommitted work (i.e., rows 1 through 990,000) that existed before the savepoint.

This method was debated in the ANSI X3H2 Database Standards Committee and ISO. Generally speaking, Americans favored savepoints, while the Europeans did not. The XA transaction model from the X/Open Consortium is probably going to be the ISO standard, but you need to look at each particular product you are actually using.

20.2.2 Consistency

When the transaction starts, the database is in a consistent state, and when it becomes persistent in the database, the database is in a consistent state. The phrase "consistent state" means that all of the data integrity constraints, relational integrity constraints, and any other constraints are true.

However, this does not mean that the database might not go through an inconsistent state during the transaction. The SQL-92 standard has the ability to declare a constraint to be `DEFERRABLE` or `NOT DEFERRABLE` for finer control of a transaction.

Consider the single UPDATE statement to increment the PRIMARY KEY of a table:

```
UPDATE Foobar SET keycol = keycol + 1;
```

where the values of keycol are (1, 2, 3, 4). When any of the first three rows are incremented, we will have two rows with duplicate values, which temporarily violates the PRIMARY KEY constraint. But at the end of the UPDATE, the values are (2, 3, 4, 5), which is consistent with the constraints. The same principle applies when the transaction has multiple statements or fires triggers that affect other tables.

20.2.3 Isolation

One transaction is isolated from all other transactions. Isolation is also called serializability because it means that transactions act as if they were executed in isolation of each other. One way to guarantee isolation is to go back to serial execution like we had in batch systems. In practice, this might not be a good idea, so the system has to decide how to interleave the transactions to get the same effect.

This actually becomes more complicated in practice because one transaction may or may not actually see the data inserted, updated, or deleted by another transaction. This will be dealt with in detail in section 20.3.2.

20.2.4 Durability

The database is stored on a durable media, so that if the database program is destroyed, the database itself persists. Furthermore, the database can be restored to a consistent state when the database system is restored. Log files and backup procedures figure into this property, as well as disk writes done during processing.

This is all well and good if you have just one user accessing the database at a time. But one of the reasons you have a database system is that you also have multiple users who want to access it at the same time in their own sessions. This leads us to concurrency control.

20.3 Concurrency

Concurrency control is the part of transaction handling that deals with how multiple users access the shared database without running into each other—like a traffic light system. One way to avoid any problems is to allow only one user in the database at a time. The only problem with that solution is that the other users are going to get lousy response time. Can you seriously imagine doing that with a bank teller machine system or an airline reservation system where tens of thousands of users are waiting to get into the system at the same time?

20.3.1 The Three Phenomena

If all you do is execute queries against the database, then the ACID properties hold. The trouble occurs when two or more transactions want to change the database at the same time. In the SQL model, there are three ways that one transaction can affect another.

1. P1 ("Dirty read"): Transaction T1 modifies a row. Transaction T2 then reads that row before T1 performs a `COMMIT WORK`. If T1 then performs a `ROLLBACK WORK`, T2 will have read a row that was never committed and that may thus be considered to have never existed.

2. P2 ("Nonrepeatable read"): Transaction T1 reads a row. Transaction T2 then modifies or deletes that row and performs a `COMMIT WORK`. If T1 then attempts to reread the row, it may receive the modified value or discover that the row has been deleted.

3. P3 ("Phantom read"): Transaction T1 reads the set of rows that satisfy some `<search condition>`. Transaction T2 then executes statements that generate one or more rows that satisfy the `<search condition>` used by transaction T1. If transaction T1 then repeats the initial read with the same `<search condition>`, it obtains a different collection of rows.

These phenomena are not always bad things. If the database is being used only for queries, without any changes being made during

the workday, then none of these problems will occur. The database system will run much faster if you do not have to try to protect yourself from them. They are also acceptable when changes are being made under certain circumstances.

Imagine that I have a table of all the cars in the world. I want to execute a query to find the average age of drivers of red sports cars. This query will take some time to run, and during that time, cars will be crashed, bought and sold, new cars will be built, and so forth. But I accept a situation with the three phenomena because the average age will not change that much from the time I start the query to the time it finishes. Changes after the second decimal place really don't matter.

However, you don't want any of these phenomena to occur in a database where the husband makes a deposit to a joint account and his wife makes a withdrawal. This leads us to the transaction isolation levels.

20.3.2 The Four Isolation Levels

In standard SQL, users get to set the isolation level of the transactions in their sessions. The isolation level avoids some of the phenomena we just talked about and gives other information to the database. The syntax for the `SET TRANSACTION` statement is

```
SET TRANSACTION <transaction mode list>

<transaction mode> ::=
   <isolation level>
 | <transaction access mode>
 | <diagnostics size>

<diagnostics size> ::= DIAGNOSTICS SIZE <number of conditions>
<transaction access mode> ::= READ ONLY | READ WRITE
<isolation level> ::= ISOLATION LEVEL <level of isolation>
<level of isolation> ::=
   READ UNCOMMITTED
 | READ COMMITTED
 | REPEATABLE READ
 | SERIALIZABLE
```

The optional <diagnostics size> clause tells the database to set up a list for error messages of a given size. (This is an SQL-92 feature, so you might not have it in your particular product.) The reason is that a single statement can have several errors in it, and the engine is supposed to find them all and report them in the diagnostics area via a GET DIAGNOSTICS statement in the host program.

The <transaction access mode> explains itself. The READ ONLY option means that this is a query and lets the SQL engine know that it can relax a bit. The READ WRITE option lets the SQL engine know that rows might be changed, and that it has to watch out for the three phenomena.

The important clause, which is implemented in most current SQL products, is the <isolation level> clause. The isolation level of a transaction defines the degree to which the operations of one transaction are affected by concurrent transactions. The isolation level of a transaction is SERIALIZABLE by default, but the user can explicitly set it in the SET TRANSACTION statement.

The four isolation levels all guarantee that each transaction will be executed completely or not at all, and that no updates will be lost. A ROLLBACK WORK statement may be initiated by the SQL engine when it detects the inability to guarantee the serializability of two or more concurrent transactions or when it detects unrecoverable errors.

Let's take a look at a table of the isolation levels and the three phenomena. A "yes" means that the phenomenon is possible under that isolation level:

Isolation Levels and the Three Phenomena

Isolation Level	P1	P2	P3
SERIALIZABLE	no	no	no
REPEATABLE READ	no	no	yes
READ COMMITTED	no	yes	yes
READ UNCOMMITTED	yes	yes	yes

The SERIALIZABLE isolation level is guaranteed to produce the same results as the concurrent transactions would have if they had been done in some serial order. A serial execution is one in which

each transaction executes to completion before the next transaction begins. The users act as if they are standing in a line waiting to get complete access to the database.

A REPEATABLE READ isolation level is guaranteed to maintain the same image of the database to the user during the session.

A READ COMMITTED isolation level will let transactions in this session see rows that other transactions commit while this session is running.

A READ UNCOMMITTED isolation level will let transactions in this session see rows that other transactions create without necessarily committing while this session is running.

Regardless of the isolation level of the transaction, phenomena P1, P2, and P3 should not occur during the implied reading of schema definitions performed on behalf of executing a statement, the checking of integrity constraints, and the execution of referential actions associated with referential constraints. We do not want the schema itself changing on users.

The SQL standards do not say *how* you are to achieve these results. However, there are two basic classes of concurrency control methods—optimistic and pessimistic. Within those two classes, vendors will have their own implementation.

20.4 Pessimistic Concurrency Control

Pessimistic concurrency control is based on the idea that transactions are expected to conflict with each other, so we need to design a system to avoid the problems before they start.

All pessimistic concurrency control schemes use locks, which are flags placed in the database that give exclusive access to a schema object to a user. Imagine an airplane toilet door, with its "occupied" sign.

The differences are the level of locking they use; setting those flags on and off costs time and resources. If you lock the whole database, then you have a serial batch processing system since only one transaction at a time is active. In practice, you would do this only for system maintenance work—there are no other transactions that involve the whole database.

If you lock at the table level, then performance can suffer because users must wait for the most common tables to become available. However, there are transactions that do involve the whole table and this will use only one flag.

If you lock the table at the row level, then other users can get to the rest of the table and you will have the best possible shared access. You will also have a huge number of flags to process and performance will suffer. This approach is generally not practical.

Page locking is in between table and row locking. This approach puts a lock on subsets of rows within the table that include the desired values. The name comes from the fact that this is usually implemented with pages of physical disk storage. Performance depends on the statistical distribution of data in physical storage, but it is generally the best compromise.

20.5 Optimistic Concurrency Control

Optimistic concurrency control is based on the idea that transactions are not very likely to conflict with each other, so we need to design a system to handle the problems as exceptions after they actually occur.

Most optimistic concurrency control uses a timestamp to track copies of the data. Imagine that you go to the central records department of a company and ask to see a document stored on microfilm. You do not get the microfilm, but instead they make a timestamped photocopy for you. You take the copy to your desk, mark it up, and return it to the central records department. The records clerk timestamps your updated document and adds it to the end of the roll of microfilm.

But what if user number two also went to the central records department and got a timestamped photocopy of the same document? The records clerk has to look at both timestamps and make a decision. If you attempt to put your updates into the database while the second user is still working on the second copy, then the clerk has to either hold the first copy and wait for the second copy to show up or return the first copy to you. When both copies are in hand, the clerk stacks the copies on top of each other, holds them up to the light, and looks to see if there are any conflicts. If both updates can be made to

the database, the clerk does so. If there are conflicts, the clerk must either have rules for resolving the problems or reject both transactions. This is a kind of row-level locking, done after the fact.

20.6 Logical Concurrency Control

Logical concurrency control is based on the idea that the machine can analyze the predicates in the queue of waiting queries and processes on a purely logical level and then determine which of the statements can be allowed to operate on the database at the same time.

Clearly, all `SELECT` statements can operate at the same time since they do not change the data. After that, it is tricky to determine which statements conflict with each other. For example, one pair of `UPDATE` statements on two separate tables might be allowed only in a certain order because of `PRIMARY KEY` and `FOREIGN KEY` constraints. Another pair of `UPDATE` statements on the same tables might be disallowed because they modify the same rows and leave different final states in them. However, a third pair of `UPDATE` statements on the same tables might be allowed because they modify different rows and have no conflicts with each other.

There is also the problem of statements waiting too long in the queue to be executed. This is a version of livelock, which we discuss in the next section. The usual solution is to assign a priority number to each waiting transaction and then decrement that priority number when they have been waiting for a certain length of time. Eventually, every transaction will arrive at priority one and be able to go ahead of any other transaction.

This approach also allows you to enter transactions at a higher priority than the transactions in the queue. Although it is possible to create a livelock this way, it is not a problem, and it lets you bump less important jobs in favor of more important jobs, such as payroll checks.

20.7 Deadlocks and Livelocks

It is possible for a user to fail to complete a transaction for reasons other than the hardware failing. A *deadlock* is a situation where two or more users hold resources that the others need, and neither party will

surrender the objects to which they have locks. To make this more concrete, imagine user A and user B both need tables X and Y. User A gets a lock on table X, and user B gets a lock on table Y. They both sit and wait for their missing resource to become available; it never happens. The common solution for a deadlock is for the database administrator to kill one or more of the sessions involved and roll back their work.

A *livelock* involves users who are waiting for a resource, but never get it because other users keep grabbing it before they get a chance. None of the other users hold onto the resource permanently as in a deadlock, but as a group they never free it. To make this more concrete, imagine user A needs all of table X. But table X is always being updated by a hundred other users, so that user A cannot find a page without a lock on it in the table. User A sits and waits for all the pages to become available; it never happens.

The database administrator can again kill one or more of the sessions involved and roll back their work. In some systems, the administrator can raise the priority of the livelocked session so that it can seize the resources as they become available.

None of this is trivial, and each database system will have its own version of transaction processing and concurrency control. This should not be of great concern to the applications programmer, since it should be the responsibility of the database administrator. But it is nice to know what happens under the covers.

Functional Dependencies

FUNCTIONAL AND MULTIVALUED dependencies are the basis for data normalization and keys. They express mappings from one attribute to another attribute in the same relation.

A functional dependency (FD) means that if I know the value of one attribute, I can always determine the value of another. The term "functional dependency" comes from the behavior of a mathematical function that accepts a value as a parameter and always returns a single result. The notation used in relational theory is an arrow between the two attributes, for example, $A \rightarrow B$, which can be read as "A determines B" in English. For example, if I know your employee number, I can determine your name; if I know a part number, I can determine the weight and color of the part; and so forth.

It is important to understand that this relationship cannot be a mere coincidence in the current values in the table. You also need to remember that two different left-hand values might determine the same value on the right-hand side (e.g., a train number determines departure time, but different trains can depart at the same time). A functional dependency is a rule that has to hold for all possible

values that could ever be in the table (e.g., to be an employee, you must have an employee number).

The situation where $A \rightarrow B$ and $B \rightarrow A$ can be written as $A \leftrightarrow B$ with a double-headed arrow. In the real world, one example might be two different part numbers, the old and the new, on the same inventory. This notation is not used much, since it is more convenient to have both FDs shown explicitly when doing calculations for normalization.

Likewise, the situation that A does not determine B can be shown with a slashed arrow, $A \not\rightarrow B$, but it is not used much.

21.1 Armstrong's Axioms

Functional dependencies have a defined system of axioms that can be used in normalization problems. These six axioms, known as Armstrong's axioms, are given below:

- Reflexive: $X \rightarrow X$
- Augmentation: if $X \rightarrow Y$
  then $XZ \rightarrow Y$
- Union: if ($X \rightarrow Y$ and $X \rightarrow Z$)
  then $X \rightarrow YZ$
- Decomposition: if $X \rightarrow Y$ and Z a subset of Y
  then $X \rightarrow Z$
- Transitivity: if ($X \rightarrow Y$ and $Y \rightarrow Z$)
  then $X \rightarrow Z$
- Pseudotransitivity: if ($X \rightarrow Y$ and $YZ \rightarrow W$)
  then $XZ \rightarrow W$

They make good sense if you just look at them, which is something we like in a set of axioms. In the real world, the FDs are the business rules we are trying to model.

In the normalization algorithm for a third normal form (3NF) (developed by Bernstein 1976), we use the axioms to get rid of redundant FDs. For example, if we are given

$A \rightarrow B$

$A \rightarrow C$

$B \rightarrow C$

$DB \rightarrow E$

$DAF \rightarrow E$

$A \rightarrow C$ is redundant because it can be derived from $A \rightarrow B$ and $B \rightarrow C$ with transitivity. Also, $DAF \rightarrow E$ is redundant because it can be derived from $DB \rightarrow E$ and $A \rightarrow B$ with transitivity (which gives us $DA \rightarrow E$) and augmentation (which then allows $DAF \rightarrow E$). What we would like to find is the smallest set of FDs from which we can generate all of the given rules. This is called a *nonredundant cover.* For the FDs above, one cover would be

$A \rightarrow B$

$B \rightarrow C$

$DB \rightarrow E$

Once we do this, Bernstein shows that we can just create a table for each of the FDs where A, B, and DB are the respective keys.

21.2 Multivalued Dependencies

The notation for multivalued dependency is a double-headed arrow between two attributes, $A \twoheadrightarrow B$. In English, a multivalued dependency means that "if I know a value of A, I can determine a subset of B values."

This relationship was also axiomized by Beri, Fagin, and Howard (1977). Their axioms are

- Reflexive: $X \twoheadrightarrow X$
- Augmentation: if $X \twoheadrightarrow Y$
then $XZ \twoheadrightarrow Y$
- Union: if $X \twoheadrightarrow Y$ and $X \twoheadrightarrow Z$
then $X \twoheadrightarrow YZ$

- Projection: if $X \twoheadrightarrow Y$ and $X \twoheadrightarrow Z$
  then $X \twoheadrightarrow (Y \cup Z)$
  and $X \twoheadrightarrow (Y - Z)$
- Transitivity: if $X \twoheadrightarrow Y$ and $Y \twoheadrightarrow Z$
  then $X \twoheadrightarrow (Z - Y)$
- Pseudotransitivity: if $X \twoheadrightarrow Y$ and $YW \twoheadrightarrow Z$
  then $XW \twoheadrightarrow (Z - YW)$
- Complement: if $X \twoheadrightarrow Y$ and $Z = (R - XY)$
  then $X \twoheadrightarrow Z$
- Replication: if $X \rightarrow Y$
  then $X \twoheadrightarrow Y$
- Coalescence: if $X \twoheadrightarrow Y$ and $Z \twoheadrightarrow W$
  where $W \subset Y$
  and $Y \cup Z = \emptyset$
  then $X \rightarrow W$

21.3 Mappings

There are several kinds of mappings from one set to another:

1. The determiner set matches to every element of the determined set. This is an “onto” relationship.
2. The determiner set does not cover every element of the determined set. This is an “into” relationship.
3. The determiner set maps one value onto every subset in a partitioning of the determined set.
4. The determiner set maps to some, but not all, of the subsets in a partitioning of the determined set.

Normalization

THE NORMAL FORMS (NF) are an attempt to make sure that you do not destroy true data or create false data in your database. Normalization, in 25 words or less, avoids errors by representing a fact in the database one way, one time, and in one place. If a fact appears more than once, one of the instances of it is likely to be in error—a man with two watches can never be sure what time it is.

Normalization is not mysterious, but it can get complex. You can buy CASE tools to help you do it, but you should know a bit about the theory before you use such a tool.

22.1 Anomalies

In informal terms, normalization seeks to structure the database in such a way that it correctly models reality and avoids anomalies. That is, when I perform a legal action on the database, the database as a whole is a correct model. Because there are three possible actions, there are three basic kinds of anomalies:

1. Insertion anomalies
2. Update anomalies
3. Deletion anomalies

Data anomalies are easier to explain with an example, but first please be patient while I define some terms. A *predicate* is a statement of the form A(X), which means that X has the property A. For example, "John is from Indiana" is a predicate statement; here, "John" is the subject and "is from Indiana" is the predicate. A *relation* is a predicate with two or more subjects. "John and Bob are brothers" is an example of a relation. The common way of visualizing a set of relational statements is as a table where the columns are attributes of the relation and each row is a specific relational statement.

Now consider a table of students, their majors, and their departmental advisors. Let us assume that each student has one department, and each department has one advisor.

student	**advisor**	**department**
'Higgins'	'Celko'	'Comp Sci'
'Jones'	'Celko'	'Comp Sci'
'Wilson'	'Smith'	'English'

1. *Insertion anomalies:* When you try to insert a new student into the English department, you also have to know that Dr. Smith is the departmental advisor or you cannot insert the new row.
2. *Update anomalies:* Higgins decides that Dr. Celko's database course is too hard and switches her major to Sanskrit. Unfortunately, this creates the row ('Higgins', 'Celko', 'Sanskrit'), which contains the false fact that Dr. Celko is the advisor for the Sanskrit department.
3. *Deletion anomalies:* If Dr. Smith gives up his position in the English department, then deleting his row will also destroy the fact that Wilson was an English major. We can assume school policy is not to expel all the students when an advisor leaves.

This table really should be two tables, one for students and one for advisors. The process of normalization is based on a hierarchy of normal forms, which I will now explain. Each normal form is built on the previous normal form and corrects a problem in its predecessor.

22.2 First Normal Form (1NF)

Consider a requirement to maintain data about class schedules. We are required to keep the course, section, department, time, room, professor, student, major, and grade. Suppose that we initially set up a Pascal file with records that look like this:

```
Classes = RECORD
          course: ARRAY [1:7] OF CHAR;
         section: CHAR;
          time: INTEGER;
          room: INTEGER;
        roomsize: INTEGER;
       professor: ARRAY [1:25] OF CHAR;
       Students : ARRAY [1:classsize]
                  OF RECORD
                     student ARRAY [1:25] OF CHAR;
                     major ARRAY [1:10] OF CHAR;
                     grade CHAR;
                     END;
          END;
```

This table is not in the most basic normal form of relational databases. First normal form means that the table has no repeating groups. That is, every column is a scalar (or atomic) value, not an array or a list or anything with its own structure. In SQL, it is impossible not to be in 1NF unless the vendor has added array or other extensions to the language. The Pascal record could be "flattened out" in SQL to look like this:

```
CREATE TABLE Classes (course CHAR(7) NOT NULL,
 section CHAR(1) NOT NULL,
 time INTEGER NOT NULL,
 room INTEGER NOT NULL,
 roomsize INTEGER NOT NULL,
 professor CHAR(25) NOT NULL,
 student CHAR(25) NOT NULL,
 major CHAR(10) NOT NULL,
 grade CHAR(1) NOT NULL);
```

This table is acceptable to SQL. In fact, we can locate a row in the table with a combination of (course, section, student), so we have a key. But what we are doing is hiding the Students record array, which has not changed its nature by being flattened. There are problems.

If Professor Jones of the math department dies, we delete all his rows from the Classes table. This also deletes the information that all his students were taking a math class, and maybe not all of them wanted to drop out of the class just yet. I am deleting more than one fact from the database. This is called a deletion anomaly.

If student Wilson decides to change one of his math classes, formerly taught by Professor Jones, to English, we will show Professor Jones as an instructor in both the math and the English departments. I could not change a simple fact by itself. This creates false information and is called an update anomaly.

If the school decides to start a new department, which has no students yet, we cannot put in the data about the professors we just hired until we have classroom and student data to fill out a row. I cannot insert a simple fact by itself. This is called an insertion anomaly.

There are more problems in this table, but you see the point. Yes, there are some ways to get around these problems without changing the tables. We could permit `NULL`s in the table. We could write routines to check the table for false data. These are tricks that will only get worse as the data and the relationships become more complex. The solution is to break the table up into other tables, each of which represents one relationship or simple fact.

22.2.1 Note on Repeated Groups

The definition of 1NF is that the table has no repeating groups and that all columns are scalar. This means no arrays, linked lists, tables within tables, or record structures, like those you would find in other programming languages. As I have already said, this is very easy to avoid in SQL, since arrays and structured data are simply not supported.

The way you "fake it" in SQL is to use a group of columns where all the members of the group have the same semantic value; that is, they represent the same attribute in the table. Consider the table of an employee and his children:

```
CREATE TABLE Employees
(empno INTEGER NOT NULL,
 empname CHAR(30) NOT NULL,
 . . .
 child1 CHAR(30), birthday1 DATE, sex1 CHAR(1),
 child2 CHAR(30), birthday2 DATE, sex2 CHAR(2),
 child3 CHAR(30), birthday3 DATE, sex3 CHAR(1),
 child4 CHAR(30), birthday4 DATE, sex4 CHAR(1));
```

This looks like the layouts of many existing file system records in Cobol and other 3GL languages. The birthday and sex information for each child is part of a repeated group and therefore violates 1NF. This is faking a four-element array in SQL!

Suppose I have a table with the quantity of a product sold in each month of a particular year and I originally built the table to look like this:

```
CREATE TABLE Abnormal
(product CHAR(10) NOT NULL PRIMARY KEY,
 bin_01 INTEGER,
 bin_02 INTEGER,
 . . .
 bin_12 INTEGER);
```

and I wanted to flatten it out into a more normalized form, like this:

```
CREATE TABLE Normal
(product CHAR(10) NOT NULL,
 bin_nbr INTEGER NOT NULL,
 qty INTEGER NOT NULL,
 PRIMARY KEY (product, bin_nbr));
```

I can use the statement

```
INSERT INTO Normal
SELECT product, 1, bin_01
  FROM Abnormal
 WHERE bin_01 IS NOT NULL
UNION ALL
```

```
SELECT product, 2, bin_02
  FROM Abnormal
 WHERE bin_02 IS NOT NULL

UNION ALL
SELECT product, 12, bin_12
  FROM Abnormal
 WHERE bin_12 IS NOT NULL;
```

While a UNION ALL query is usually slow, this has to be run only once to load the normalized table and then the original table can be dropped.

22.3 Second Normal Form (2NF)

A table is in second normal form if it has no partial key dependencies. That is, if X and Y are columns and X is a key, then for any Z that is a proper subset of X, it cannot be the case that Z → Y. Informally, the table is in 1NF and it has a key that determines all nonkey attributes in the table. In English, the table is in second normal form if any of the following are true:

1. The primary key has only one column.
2. The table has no nonkey columns.
3. Every nonkey attribute is determined by the entire set of primary key attributes (i.e., no partial key dependencies).

In the example, our users tell us that knowing the student and course is sufficient to determine the section (since students cannot sign up for more than one section of the same course) and the grade. This is the same as saying that (student, course) → (section, grade).

After more analysis, we also discover from our users that (student → major)—students have only one major. Since student is part of the (student, course) key, we have a partial key dependency! This leads us to the following decomposition:

```
CREATE TABLE Classes (course, section, room, roomsize, time,
professor, PRIMARY KEY (course, section));
```

```
CREATE TABLE Enrollment (student, course, section, grade, PRIMARY
KEY (student, course));

CREATE TABLE Students (student, major, PRIMARY KEY (student));
```

At this point, we are in 2NF. Every attribute depends on the entire key in its table. Now if a student changes majors, it can be done in one place. Furthermore, a student cannot sign up for different sections of the same class because we have changed the key of Enrollment. Unfortunately, we still have problems.

Notice that while roomsize depends on the entire key of Classes, it also depends on room. If the room is changed for a course and section, we may also have to change the roomsize, and if the room is modified (we knock down a wall), we may have to change roomsize in several rows in Classes for that room.

22.4 Third Normal Form (3NF)

Another normal form can address these problems. A table is in third normal form if for all X → Y, where X and Y are columns of a table, X is a key or Y is part of a candidate key. A candidate key is a unique set of columns that identifies each row in a table; you cannot remove a column from the candidate key without destroying its uniqueness. This implies that the table is in 2NF, since a partial key dependency is a type of transitive dependency. Informally, all the nonkey columns are determined by the key, the whole key, and nothing but the key.

The usual way that 3NF is explained is that there are no transitive dependencies. A transitive dependency is a situation where we have a table with columns (A, B, C) and (A → B) and (B → C), so we know that (A → C). In our case, the situation is that (course, section) → room and room → roomsize. This is not a simple transitive dependency, since only part of a key is involved, but the principle still holds. To get our example into 3NF and fix the problem with the roomsize column, we make the following decomposition:

```
CREATE TABLE Rooms (room, roomsize, PRIMARY KEY (room));

CREATE TABLE Classes (course, section, room, time,
PRIMARY KEY (course, section));
```

```
CREATE TABLE Enrollment (student, course, section, grade,
PRIMARY KEY (student, course));

CREATE TABLE Students (student, major, PRIMARY KEY (student));
```

A common misunderstanding about relational theory is that 3NF has no transitive dependencies. As indicated above, if X → Y, X does not have to be a key if Y is part of a candidate key. We still have a transitive dependency in the example—(room, time) → (course, section)—but since the right side of the dependency is a key, it is technically in 3NF. The unreasonable behavior that this table structure still has is that several courses can be assigned to the same room at the same time.

22.5 Boyce-Codd Normal Form (BCNF)

A table is in BCNF when for all nontrivial FDs (X → A), X is a super key for the whole schema. A *super key* is a unique set of columns that identifies each row in a table, but you can remove some columns from it and it will still be a key. Informally, a super key is carrying extra weight.

BCNF is the normal form that actually removes all transitive dependencies. A table is in BCNF if for all (X → Y), X is a key—period. We can go to this normal form just by adding another key with a `UNIQUE` (room, time) constraint clause to the table Classes. There are some other interesting and useful "higher" normal forms, but they are outside of the scope of this discussion. In our example, we have removed all of the important anomalies with BCNF.

Third normal form was concerned with the relationship between key and nonkey columns. However, a column can often play both roles. Consider a table for computing salespeople's bonus gifts that has for each salesperson their base salary, the number of sales points they have won in a contest, and the bonus gift awarded for that combination of salary range and points. For example, we might give a fountain pen to a beginning salesperson with a base pay rate somewhere between $15,000 and $20,000 and 100 sales points, but give a car to a master salesperson, whose salary is between $30,000 and

$60,000 and who has 200 points. The functional dependencies are, therefore,

(paystep, points) → gift

gift → points

Let's start with a table that has all the data in it and normalize it.

Gifts

salary	points	gift
$15,000	100	pencil
$17,000	100	pen
$30,000	200	car
$31,000	200	car
$32,000	200	car

This schema is in 3NF, but it has problems. You cannot insert a new gift into our offerings and points unless we have a salary to go with it. If you remove any sales points, you lose information about the gifts and salaries (e.g., only people in the $30,000 range can win a car). And, finally, a change in the gifts for a particular point score would have to affect all the rows within the same pay step. This table needs to be broken apart into two tables:

PayGifts

salary	gift
$15,000	pencil
$17,000	pen
$30,000	car
$31,000	car
$32,000	car

GiftsPoints

gift	points
pencil	100
pen	100
car	200

22.6 Fourth Normal Form (4NF)

Fourth normal form makes use of multivalued dependencies (MVDs). The problem it solves is that the table has too many of them. For example, consider a table of departments, their projects, and the parts they stock. The MVDs in the table would be

department $\twoheadrightarrow$ projects

department $\twoheadrightarrow$ parts

Assume that department d1 works on jobs j1 and j2 with parts p1 and p2; that department d2 works on jobs j3, j4, and j5 with parts p2 and p4; and that department d3 works on job j2 only with parts p5 and p6. The table would look like this:

department	job	part
d1	j1	p1
d1	j1	p2
d1	j2	p1
d1	j2	p2
d2	j3	p2
d2	j3	p4
d2	j4	p2
d2	j4	p4
d2	j5	p2
d2	j5	p4
d3	j2	p5
d3	j2	p6

If you want to add a part to a department, you must create more than one new row.

Likewise, to remove a part or a job from a row can destroy information. Updating a part or job name will also require multiple rows to be changed.

The solution is to split this table into two tables, one with (department, projects) in it and one with (department, parts) in it. The definition of 4NF is that we have no more than one MVD in a table. If a table is in 4NF, it is also in BCNF.

22.7 Fifth Normal Form (5NF)

Fifth normal form, also called the join-projection normal form (JPNF) or the projection-join normal form, is based on the idea of a lossless join or the lack of a join-projection anomaly. This problem occurs when you have an *n*-way relationship, where *n* > 2. A quick check for 5NF is to see if the table is in 3NF and all the candidate keys are single columns. As an example of the problems solved by 5NF, consider a table of house notes that records the buyer, the seller, and the lender:

HouseNotes

buyer	seller	lender
Smith	Jones	National Bank
Smith	Wilson	Home Bank
Nelson	Jones	Home Bank

This table is a three-way relationship, but because many CASE tools allow only binary relationships, it might have to be expressed in an ER diagram as three binary relationships, which would generate `CREATE TABLE` statements leading to these tables:

BuyerLender

buyer	lender
Smith	National Bank
Smith	Home Bank
Nelson	Home Bank

SellerLender

seller	lender
Jones	National Bank
Wilson	Home Bank
Jones	Home Bank

BuyerSeller

buyer	seller
Smith	Jones
Smith	Wilson
Nelson	Jones

The trouble is that when you try to assemble the original information by joining pairs of these three tables together, thus:

```
SELECT BS.buyer, SL.seller, BL.lender
  FROM BuyerLender AS BL,
       SellerLender AS SL,
       BuyerSeller AS BS
 WHERE BL.buyer = BS.buyer
   AND BL.lender = SL.lender
   AND SL.seller = BS.seller;
```

you will re-create all the valid rows in the original table, such as ('Smith', 'Jones', 'National Bank'), but there will also be false rows, such as ('Smith', 'Jones', 'Home Bank'), which were not part of the original table. This is called a join-projection anomaly.

There are also strong JPNF and overstrong JPNF, which make use of join dependencies (JD). Unfortunately, there is no systematic way to find a JPNF or 4NF schema because the problem is known to be NP complete.

22.8 Domain-Key Normal Form (DKNF)

Domain-key normal form was proposed by Ron Fagin (1981). The idea is that if all the constraints implied by domain restrictions and by key conditions are true, then the database is in at least 5NF. The interesting part of Fagin's paper is that there is no mention of functional dependencies, multivalued dependencies, or join dependencies.

This is currently considered the stongest normal form possible. The problem is that his paper does not tell you how you can achieve DKNF and shows that in some cases it is impossible.

22.9 Multiple 3NF Schemas

As an example of a schema with more than one 3NF, here is a problem that was used in a demonstration by DBStar Corporation (San Francisco). The company uses it as an example in a demonstration that comes with their CASE tools.

We are given an imaginary, simplified airline that has a database for scheduling flights and pilots. Most of the relationships are obvious things. Flights have only one departure time and one destination. They can get a different pilot and can be assigned to a different gate each day of the week. The functional dependencies for the database are given below:

1. flight → destination
2. flight → hour
3. (day, flight) → gate
4. (day, flight) → pilot
5. (day, hour, pilot) → gate
6. (day, hour, pilot) → flight
7. (day, hour, pilot) → destination
8. (day, hour, gate) → pilot
9. (day, hour, gate) → flight
10. (day, hour, gate) → destination

Your problem is to find 3NF database schemas in these FDs. You have to be careful! You have to have all of the columns, obviously, but your answer could be in 3NF and still ignore some of the FDs. For example, this will not work:

```
CREATE TABLE PlannedSchedule
(flight, destination, hour, PRIMARY KEY (flight));

CREATE TABLE ActualSchedule
(day, flight, gate, pilot, PRIMARY KEY (day, flight));
```

If we apply the union axiom to some of the FDs, we get

(day, hour, gate) → (destination, flight, pilot)
(day, hour, pilot) → (destination, flight, gate)

This says that the user has required that if we are given a day, an hour, and a gate, we should be able to determine a unique flight for that day, hour, and gate. We should also be able to determine a unique flight given a day, hour, and pilot.

Given the PlannedSchedule and ActualSchedule tables, you cannot produce views where either of the two constraints we just mentioned are enforced. If the query "What flight does pilot X have on day Y and hour Z?" gives you more than one answer, it violates the FDs. Here is an example of a schema that is allowable in this proposed schema but is undesirable given our constraints:

TABLE PlannedSchedule

flight	hour	destination
118	17:00	Dallas
123	13:00	Omaha
155	17:00	Los Angeles
171	13:00	New York
666	13:00	Dis

TABLE ActualSchedule

day	flight	pilot	gate
Wed	118	Tom	12A
Wed	155	Tom	13B
Wed	171	Tom	12A
Thu	123	John	12A
Thu	155	John	12A
Thu	171	John	13B

The constraints mean that we should be able to find a unique answer to each of the following questions and not lose any information when inserting and deleting data:

1. Which flight is leaving from gate 12A on Thursdays at 13:00 Hrs? This looks fine until you realize that you don't know about flight 666, which was not required to have anything about its day or pilot in the ActualSchedule table. And likewise, I can add a flight to the ActualSchedule table that has no information in the PlannedSchedule table.
2. Which pilot is assigned to the flight that leaves gate 12A on Thursdays at 13:00 Hrs? This has the same problem as before.
3. What is the destination of the flight in queries 1 and 2? This has the same problem as before.
4. What gate is John leaving from on Thursdays at 13:00 Hrs?
5. Where is Tom flying to on Wednesdays at 17:00 Hrs?
6. What flight is assigned to Tom on Wednesdays at 17:00 Hrs?

It might help if we gave an example of how one of the FDs in the problem can be derived using the axioms of FD calculus, just like you would do a geometry proof:

Given:

1. (day, hour, gate) → pilot
2. (day, hour, pilot) → flight

Prove: (day, hour, gate) → flight

3. (day, hour) → (day, hour); reflexive
4. (day, hour, gate) → (day, hour); augmentation (3)
5. (day, hour, gate) → (day, hour, pilot); union (1, 4)
6. (day, hour, gate) → flight; transitive (2, 5)

Q.E.D.

The answer is to start by attempting to derive each of the functional dependencies from the rest of the set. What we get is several short proofs, each requiring different "given" functional dependencies in order to get to the derived FD.

Here is a list of each of the proofs used to derive the 10 fragmented FDs in the problem. With each derivation we include every derivation step and the legal FD calculus operation that allows me to make that step. An additional operation that we include here that was not included in the axioms we listed earlier is left reduction. Left reduction says that if XX → Y then X → Y. It was not included because it is actually a theorem and not one of the basic axioms. (Side problem: can you derive left reduction?)

Prove: (day, hour, pilot) → gate

a.	day → day;	reflexive
b.	(day, hour, pilot) → day;	augmentation (a)
c.	(day, hour, pilot) → (day, flight);	union (6, b)
d.	(day, hour, pilot) → gate;	transitive (c, 3)

Q.E.D.

Prove: (day, hour, gate) → pilot

a.	day → day;	reflexive
b.	day, hour, gate → day;	augmentation (a)
c.	day, hour, gate → (day, flight);	union (9, b)
d.	day, hour, gate → pilot;	transitive (c, 4)

Q.E.D.

Prove: (day, flight) → gate

a.	(day, flight, pilot) → gate;	pseudotransitivity (2, 5)
b.	(day, flight, day, flight) → gate;	pseudotransitivity (a, 4)
c.	(day, flight) → gate;	left reduction (b)

Q.E.D.

Prove: (day, flight) → pilot

a.	(day, flight, gate) → pilot;	pseudotransitivity (2, 8)
b.	(day, flight, day, flight) → pilot;	pseudotransitivity (a, 3)
c.	(day, flight) → pilot;	left reduction (b)

Q.E.D.

Prove: (day, hour, gate) → flight

a.	(day, hour) → (day, hour);	reflexivity
b.	(day, hour, gate) → (day, hour);	augmentation (a)
c.	(day, hour, gate) → (day, hour, pilot);	union (b, 8)
d.	(day, hour, gate) → flight;	transitivity (c, 6)

Q.E.D.

Prove: (day, hour, pilot) → flight

a.	(day, hour) → (day, hour);	reflexivity
b.	(day, hour, pilot) → (day, hour);	augmentation (a)
c.	(day, hour, pilot) → day, hour, gate;	union (b, 5)
d.	(day, hour, pilot) → flight;	transitivity (c, 9)

Q.E.D.

Prove: (day, hour, gate) → destination

a.	(day, hour, gate) → destination;	transitivity (9, 1)

Q.E.D.

Prove: (day, hour, pilot) → destination

a.	(day, hour, pilot) → destination;	transitivity (6, 1)

Q.E.D.

Now that we've shown you how to derive 8 of the 10 FDs from other FDs, you can try mixing and matching the FDs into sets so that each set meets the following criteria:

1. Each attribute must be represented on either the left or right side of at least one FD in the set.
2. If a given FD is included in the set, then all the FDs needed to derive it cannot also be included.
3. If a given FD is excluded from the set, then the FDs used to derive it must be included.

This produces a set of "nonredundant covers," which can be found with trial and error and common sense. For example, if we excluded (day, hour, gate) → flight, we must then include (day, hour, gate) → pilot and vice versa because each is used in the other's derivation. If you want to be sure your search was exhaustive, however, you may want to apply a more mechanical method, which is what the CASE tools do for you.

The algorithm for accomplishing this task is basically to generate all the combinations of sets of the FDs. (flight → destination) and (flight → hour) are excluded in the combination generation because they cannot be derived. This gives us 2^8, or 256, combinations of FDs. Each combination is then tested against the criteria.

Fortunately, a simple spreadsheet does all the tedious work. In this problem criterion 1 eliminates only 15 sets, criterion 2 eliminates 152 sets, and criterion 3 drops another 67. This leaves us with 22 possible covers, 5 of which are the answers we are looking for (we will explain the other 17 later). These five nonredundant covers are

Set I:
flight → (destination, hour)
(day, flight) → pilot
(day, hour, gate) → pilot
(day, hour, pilot) → gate

Set II:
flight → (destination, hour)
(day, flight) → gate
(day, hour, pilot) → flight
(day, hour, pilot) → flight

Set III:
flight → (destination, hour)
(day, flight) → gate
(day, flight) → pilot
(day, hour, gate) → flight
(day, hour, pilot) → flight

Set IV:
flight → (destination, hour)
(day, flight) → pilot
(day, flight) → gate
(day, hour, gate) → flight
(day, hour, pilot) → flight

Set V:
flight → (destination, hour)
(day, flight) → pilot
(day, hour, gate) → pilot
(day, hour, pilot) → gate
(day, hour, pilot) → flight

At this point we perform unions on FDs with the same left-hand side and make tables for each grouping with the left-hand side as a key. We can also eliminate symmetrical FDs (defined as X → Y and Y → X, and written with a two-headed arrow, X ↔ Y) by collapsing them into the same table.

These five nonredundant covers convert into the following five sets of 3NF relational schemas. They are given in a shorthand SQL DDL (data declaration language) without datatype declarations.

Solution 1:
```
CREATE TABLE R1 (flight, destination, hour,
  PRIMARY KEY (flight));
CREATE TABLE R2 (day, hour, gate, flight, pilot,
  PRIMARY KEY (day, hour, gate));
```

Solution 2:
```
CREATE TABLE R1 (flight, destination, hour,
  PRIMARY KEY (flight));
CREATE TABLE R2 (day, hour, gate, flight, pilot,
  PRIMARY KEY (day, hour, pilot));
```

Solution 3:

```
CREATE TABLE R1 (flight, destination, hour, PRIMARY KEY (flight));
CREATE TABLE R2 (day, flight, gate, pilot,
  PRIMARY KEY (day, flight));
CREATE TABLE R3 (day, hour, gate, flight,
  PRIMARY KEY (day, hour, gate));
CREATE TABLE R4 (day, hour, pilot, flight,
  PRIMARY KEY (day, hour, pilot));
```

Solution 4:

```
CREATE TABLE R1 (flight, destination, hour,
  PRIMARY KEY (flight));
CREATE TABLE R2 (day, flight, gate, PRIMARY KEY (day, flight));
CREATE TABLE R3 (day, hour, gate, pilot,
  PRIMARY KEY (day, hour, gate));
CREATE TABLE R4 (day, hour, pilot, flight,
  PRIMARY KEY (day, hour, pilot));
```

Solution 5:

```
CREATE TABLE R1 (flight, destination, hour,
  PRIMARY KEY (flight));
CREATE TABLE R2 (day, flight, pilot, PRIMARY KEY (day, flight));
CREATE TABLE R3 (day, hour, gate, flight,
  PRIMARY KEY (day, hour, gate));
CREATE TABLE R4 (day, hour, pilot, gate,
  PRIMARY KEY (day, hour, pilot));
```

Once you match up these solutions with the minimal covers that generated them, you will probably notice that the first two solutions have transitive dependencies. But they are still 3NF! This is a point not well understood by most analysts. A relation is in 3NF if for each FD $X \rightarrow Y$, then X is a super key OR Y is part of a candidate key. The first two solutions meet this criterion.

You may also notice that there are no additional candidate keys defined in any of the tables. This would make sense in the first two solutions, but was not done (this is why they are in 3NF and not BCNF). You will find this algorithm used in CASE tool software because SQL-89 only allowed you to define PRIMARY KEY constraints.

SQL-92 allows you to define a UNIQUE constraint on one or more columns in addition. Most implementations of SQL also allow the user to define unique indexes on a subset of the columns.

All of the five solutions are 3NF, but since the first two solutions leave out two FDs, it appears that solutions without all the constraints are considered valid by this particular automated normalizer. These tables could have defined the required candidate keys with UNIQUE constraints, however. The normalizer used to get these solutions may leave out some of the constraints, but still generate 3NF schemas. Watch out! It is assuming that you can handle this outside the schema or are willing to convert the FDs to some sort of constraints.

If we are allowed to drop FDs (as this particular normalizer does), then there are actually 22 solutions (most of which are not generated by this normalizer). These solutions can be found by dropping attributes or whole tables from the solutions above (note that each attribute must still be represented in at least one table). Some of the other 17 solutions can be generated by

1. dropping either or both of the last two tables in the last three solutions
2. dropping combinations of gate, flight, and pilot where they are not keys (remember to keep at least one nonkey in each table, and make sure if an attribute is dropped from one table, it is still represented somewhere else)
3. adding UNIQUE constraints or indexes to the first two solutions

Did you notice that even the last three of the five given solutions to the problem still allow some anomalous states? Consider this: In solution 3 the last two tables could have day and flight combinations that are not part of the valid day and flight list as defined in the second table. The other solutions also have integrity problems.

There is a normal form that fixes this for us: DKNF, defined by Ronald Fagin in 1981. There is not yet a general algorithm that will always generate the DKNF solution given a set of constraints. We can, however, determine DKNF in many special cases. Here is our DKNF solution to the problem:

Solution 6:

```
CREATE TABLE R1 (flight, hour, destination,
  UNIQUE (flight, hour),
  UNIQUE (flight));

CREATE TABLE R2 (day, flight, hour, gate, pilot,
  UNIQUE (day, hour, gate),
  UNIQUE (day, hour, pilot),
  FOREIGN KEY (flight, hour) REFERENCES R1(flight, hour));
```

Notice that this is a case of normalization by dropping a table and adding UNIQUE constraints. The candidate key (flight, hour) may not seem necessary with flight also defined as a candidate key in R1. This is done so that the foreign key in R2 carries the (flight, hour) combination and not just flight. This way, the second relation cannot contain an invalid (flight, hour) combination.

Once we add in the foreign keys to solutions 3, 4, and 5, are all of the anomalies removed? No, not entirely. The only solution that removes all anomalies is still the DKNF solution. The best way to enforce these constraints is to collapse all but the first table into one. This way inconsistent gate, pilot, day, hour, flight combinations cannot exist because, with only one table to hold such a combination, we cannot have the problem of two such tables with many overlapping attributes disagreeing. This is what the DKNF solution accomplishes.

22.10 Practical Hints for Normalization

CASE tools implement formal methods for doing normalization. In particular, ER diagrams are very useful for this. However, a few informal hints can help speed up the process and give you a good start.

Broadly speaking, tables represent either entities or relationships, which is why ER diagrams work so well as a design tool. The tables that represent entities should have a simple, immediate name suggested by their contents—a table named Students has student data in it, not student data and bowling scores. It is also a good idea to use plural or collective nouns as the names of such tables to remind you that a table is a set of entities; the rows are the single instances of them.

Tables representing many-to-many relationships should be named by their contents and should be as minimal as possible. For example, Students are related to Classes by a third (relationship) table for their attendance. These tables might represent a pure relationship, or they might contain attributes that exist within the relationship, such as a grade for the class attended. Since the only way to get a grade is to attend the class, the relationship will have a column for it and will be named ReportCards or Grades.

Avoid NULLs whenever possible. If a table has too many NULLable columns, it is probably not normalized properly. Try to use a NULL only for a value that is missing now, but that will be resolved later. Even better, put missing values into the encoding schemes for that column, as discussed in chapter 14.

A normalized database will tend to have a lot of tables with a small number of columns per table. Don't panic when you see that happen. People who first worked with file systems (particularly on computers that used magnetic tape) tend to design one monster file for an application and do all the work against those records. This made sense in the old days, since there was no reasonable way to join a number of small files together without having the computer operator mount and dismount lots of different tapes. The habit of designing this way carried over to disk systems, since the procedural programming languages were still the same.

The same nonkey attribute in more than one table is probably a normalization problem. This is not a certainty, just a guideline. The key that determines that attribute should be in only one table, and therefore the attribute should be with it.

As a practical matter, you are apt to see the same attribute under different names and need to make the names uniform in the entire database. The columns date_of_birth, birthdate, birthday, and dob are very likely the same attribute of an employee.

22.10.1 CASE Tools for Normalization

Third normal form is very popular with CASE tools, and most of them can generate a schema where all of the tables are in 3NF. They obtain the FDs from an ER diagram or from a statistical analysis of the existing data, then put them together into tables and check for nor-

mal forms. It is often possible to derive more than one 3NF schema from a set of FDs. A good CASE tool will find more than one of them, and ideally will find the highest possible normal form schemas too. Yes, there are still more normal forms we have not mentioned yet. Nobody said this would be easy. Some people will argue that it is all right to "denormalize" a schema for reasons of efficiency. For example, to get a list of all the students and their majors in a given class, we must join Enrollment and Students. The case for leaving the solution normalized is based on reducing the programming requirement. If we denormalize, either we are not enforcing some of the user-required constraints, or we have to write additional code to enforce the constraints.

Not enforcing all the rules is obviously bad. If we choose to write additional code, we have to be sure to duplicate it in all of the programs that work with the DBMS. Normalization reduces programming.

Denormalization

DENORMALIZATION IS THE process of taking a database in some normal form and reducing it to a database in a weaker normal form. This is done deliberately, and we will shortly discuss the goals of such a process. Don't confuse this with failure to design the database in a stronger normal form; that is called "bad design," and it is not a process so much as an error.

There are many database experts, particularly the more academic ones, who feel that any talk of denormalizing a database is like race car driving—a great way to mangle or kill yourself even if you know what you are doing. However, always prone to play the devil's advocate, I will defend the practice and give you some high-speed driving tips.

23.1 Criteria for Denormalization

There is only one reason for denormalizing a database and that is performance. But there are several criteria for making this decision.

First, it is not always clear that you need to denormalize a database just because the current schema has bad performance. You might need to redesign the schema because your data model is

wrong, and the bad performance is due to trying to make it do tasks for which it was not designed.

As an aside, one of the advantages of the NIAM and ORM family of database design methods is that they can produce several different candidate schemas that meet the specifications and are normalized. The database designer is then free to pick the best candidate. On the other hand, ER diagraming tools tend to lock on one and only one schema early in the database design process.

Remember that even after you denormalize, the performance problem you were trying to solve might still be there. Or it might have just moved to another part of the system. My experience is that the second situation is more likely in practice. Mr. X will have a problem with a query in his report or display screen. The DBA then denormalizes the database schema to favor Mr. X's query. Although this is good for Mr. X, the other queries might need to be rewritten or `VIEW`s need to be created that will hide the schema changes from the old queries. Suddenly, the other queries start running like molasses under the new schema and the total system performance is worse. If total query performance is not hurt, then updating, insertion, and deletion can suffer because referential integrity and `CHECK()` constraints have to do the work that normalization did.

That last sentence needs to be explained. You have to maintain data integrity in the database after denormalization. If you have to depend on an application to maintain data or referential integrity in the database, you should not denormalize the schema. Someday, a programmer will write a new application that will not have all the integrity rules in it, and that application will trash your database. This means that data and referential integrity has to be maintained in procedural code within the database (stored procedures and triggers) or in constraints (`CHECK()` and `DEFAULT` clauses) on the denormalized tables. I will discuss this later.

In summary, consider denormalization when

1. No simple normalized schema will help you.
2. Denormalization will not harm *total* system performance.
3. Denormalization will not harm database integrity.

If you can meet only one or two of the three criteria, you should not denormalize the schema.

23.2 Types of Denormalization

There are two approaches to denormalization. You can replace the existing, normalized tables with the denormalized ones, giving you a new schema.

Alternatively, you can retain the normalized schema and add denormalized tables to the schema. These new tables are then built from the denormalized tables before they are needed. Please note that VIEWs will not work for this purpose. A VIEW is either copied as in-line text in the parse tree of the query that invokes it, or it is materialized as a temporary table each time a query or a session references it. VIEWs are shorthand for a query and have no performance advantage over a query.

Although an in-line VIEW expansion might be able to use the indexing on the base tables from which it was constructed, you cannot create new indexes on a VIEW.

The following taxonomy of reasons for denormalization is due to Craig Mullens (1996) and seems to cover the topic quite well. I added overloaded datatypes to his list.

23.2.1 Prejoined Tables

If the same set of two or more tables is joined over and over again in many queries and the cost of this join is high, then you can consider building a base table that represents this join. If the join is repeated many times, but the cost is low, then you should consider using a VIEW instead.

As an example, you are given a database with the following two tables. The Personnel table has thousands of people in it, and the Projects table has hundreds of projects to which they are assigned. All of your queries involve joining Personnel and Projects.

```
CREATE TABLE Personnel
(emp_id BIT (5000) NOT NULL PRIMARY KEY,
 emp_name CHAR (30) NOT NULL,
```

```
 skill_code CHAR (5) NOT NULL,
 . . .);

CREATE TABLE Projects
(project_id INTEGER NOT NULL PRIMARY KEY,
 project_name CHAR (30) NOT NULL,
 emp_id BIT (5000) NOT NULL REFERENCES Personnel (emp_id),
 . . .);
```

While I agree that using an identifier of type `BIT (5000)` is a bit contrived for the example, it is not illegal or impossible. Perhaps we are storing fingerprints as blobs in the database for positive identification. My example could have used multicolumn keys with weird join criteria just as well. The point is that the cost of doing a `JOIN` on `BIT (5000)` columns is going to be quite high.

These two tables could be used to construct the denormalized table:

```
CREATE TABLE ProjectPersonnel
(project_id INTEGER NOT NULL,
 project_name CHAR (30) NOT NULL,
 emp_id BIT (5000) NOT NULL,
 emp_name CHAR (30) NOT NULL,
 skill_code CHAR (5) NOT NULL,
 . . . ,
);
```

In this example, you could also add the constraint `PRIMARY KEY (project_id, emp_id)`, if you know that an employee will not appear on the same project twice. However, if the ProjectPersonnel table was constructed from the original Personnel and Projects tables, you inherit the integrity you need.

23.2.2 Reports

A report table is harder to define exactly because it usually involves many of the other denormalization techniques discussed later. Its purpose is to provide the data for a report in a single table instead of a more complex query.

Obviously, the table will have one column for each column in the report. However, it can mix formatting information in the data. This is a violation of data integrity.

For example, I have a school registration table, and I want to get a simple control break report with a detail line for each student and summary lines with the number of students per course and per section within a course. Assume we have the following:

```
CREATE TABLE Registration
(student INTEGER PRIMARY KEY,
 course CHAR(5) NOT NULL,
 section INTEGER NOT NULL);
```

The trick is to use `UNION` operations to put unlike tables together. We are lucky that `COUNT(*)` will return an `INTEGER` result, so we can `UNION` the total and subtotal results to the same column as student.

```
INSERT INTO RegisterReport
          (controlbreak, course, section, student)
 SELECT 'detail', course, section, student
   FROM Registration
  UNION ALL
 SELECT 'subtotal', course, section, COUNT(*)
   FROM Registration
  GROUP BY course, section
  UNION ALL
 SELECT 'total', course, NULL, COUNT(*)
   FROM Registration
  GROUP BY course;
```

Technically, you should use an `ORDER BY course, controlbreak, section, student` clause when you print out the report in this table to get it in the right order in the hardcopy. But in the real world, you might not have to do that `ORDER BY` clause and a possible extra sort. While the report table does not have to be in any particular order according to the ANSI/ISO standards, most SQL implementations use an internal sort to do a `UNION`. The `UNION` operator has to remove duplicate rows, and a modified sort is a good way to do this. But you

might have to arrange the columns in the table in the somewhat unnatural order of (course, controlbreak, section, student) if the internal sort works from left to right.

The next gimmick is that NULL values always sort either high or low, regardless of the sort order specified on the column. This is implementation defined in the SQL standard. In this case, we do not have to worry about the NULL constant in the final SELECT messing up the sort because there is only one total record per course and that is the lowest column of the ORDER BY clause.

The actual report is probably better done in the host language, but could be done in SQL by using CASE expressions that test the control-break value to determine what formatting actions to take.

23.2.3 Mirrored Tables

A mirrored table is a copy of another table. It can be an exact or a partial copy, but the goal is to duplicate the data in one table into a second table. This is now a respectable technique used to capture data for decision support systems (DSSs). The usual situation is that the original table is being used for transactions during regular operations. Since DSS questions tend to be aggregates over one or more tables, if you allowed DSS queries in regular working hours, they would lock up the database and destroy performance.

23.2.4 Table Splitting

Table splitting consists of breaking a normalized table into two or more tables. A table can be split horizontally (i.e., by a subset of the rows) or vertically (i.e., by a subset of the columns). When the original table is retained, this is probably a special case of a mirrored table.

The usual goal is to get the table into smaller tables that can be handled easier or faster. There is also the implication that the smaller tables will be reassembled in a query to give some aggregate data. The splitting criteria can be based on almost anything, but the more common ones are

- *Physical:* One table for each telephone sales terminal, instead of one table for the entire order department. When this is used for the split, there is usually a hardware advantage.

- *Spatial:* One table for each state, instead of one table for the country.
- *Temporal:* One table for each month, instead of one table for the year.
- *Procedural:* One table for each step in a task, instead of one table for the entire project.
- *Administrative:* One table for each department, instead of one table for the company.

The horizontally split tables are recombined with a UNION ALL. The great danger when the horizontally split tables are recombined is that they will have more rows than existed in the original, unsplit table.

The vertically split tables are recombined with an INNER JOIN on the key columns. Again, the great danger when the vertically split tables are recombined is that they will have more rows than existed in the original, unsplit table.

This usually means duplicated keys that will create duplicated or even false rows. For example, consider this table:

```
CREATE TABLE TableA
(keycol INTEGER NOT NULL PRIMARY KEY,
 col1 CHAR(1) NOT NULL,
 col2 CHAR(1) NOT NULL);

INSERT INTO TableA
VALUES (1, 'a', 'x'),
       (2, 'b', 'y'),
       (3, 'c', 'z');
```

A possible horizontal split could be to create TableA-H1 and TableA-H2 with the same structure and load them with a split of data from TableA.

```
INSERT INTO TableA-H1 VALUES (1, 'a', 'x');
INSERT INTO TableA-H2 VALUES (2, 'b', 'y');
INSERT INTO TableA-H2 VALUES (3, 'c', 'z');
```

Since we have no connection between the two tables, you add another row to TableA-H1:

```
INSERT INTO TableA-H1 VALUES (1, 'd', 'w');
```

Oops! When you UNION ALL the two tables back together, you have a conflict with (keycol = 1), since it is supposed to be unique.

Likewise, we could create two vertical splits:

```
CREATE TABLE TableA_V1
(keycol INTEGER NOT NULL PRIMARY KEY,
 col1 CHAR(1) NOT NULL,
 col2 CHAR(1) NOT NULL);

INSERT INTO TableA_V1
VALUES (1, 'a'),
       (2, 'b'),
       (3, 'c');

CREATE TABLE TableA_V2
(keycol INTEGER NOT NULL PRIMARY KEY,
 col2 CHAR(1) NOT NULL);

INSERT INTO TableA_V2
VALUES (1, 'x'),
       (2, 'y'),
       (3, 'z');
```

Since we have no connection between the two tables, you add another row to TableA-V1:

```
INSERT INTO TableA-V1 VALUES (4, 'd');
```

Oops! When you try to do an INNER JOIN on the two tables, (keycol = 4) is missing in TableA-V2 and you lose that information.

You can prevent this with elaborate CHECK() clauses in SQL-92 that would reference all the split tables, but the overhead will probably be worse than the cost of a single large table.

23.2.5 Combined Tables

A combined table is a special case of a prejoined table. The difference is that the relationship between the two tables involved is one-to-one. One of the tables is usually much smaller than the other, and they are combined for convenience.

For example, consider an employee at a company with a health plan. We could have two tables like this:

```
CREATE TABLE Personnel
(emp_id INTEGER NOT NULL PRIMARY KEY,
 emp_name CHAR (30) NOT NULL,
 . . .);

CREATE TABLE ParkingSpaces
(space_nbr INTEGER NOT NULL,
 emp_id INTEGER NOT NULL);
```

which could be combined into one table that would have complete employee data along with their parking space number. One problem with a combined table is that you are often forced to use NULLs. In this example, some employees might ride the bus to work and not use a parking space, so we use a NULL to represent this missing data. Another problem is that the relationship might not stay one-to-one forever. The president of the company decides that he wants to park three cars at the office, or he gets a car that takes up three parking spaces, and the whole thing falls apart.

23.2.6 Redundant Data

If you tend to use a set of columns in a table together when joining to a second table, then consider denormalizing the second table by including the whole set instead of just one column. For example, suppose we are given

```
CREATE TABLE Personnel
(emp_id INTEGER NOT NULL PRIMARY KEY,
 emp_name CHAR (30) NOT NULL,
 dept_id INTEGER NOT NULL REFERENCES Departments (dept_id),
 . . .);
```

```
CREATE TABLE Departments
(dept_id INTEGER NOT NULL PRIMARY KEY,
 dept_name CHAR (30) NOT NULL,
 . . .);
```

If we know that all reports use both the department ID number and name, we could move the departmental name into the Personnel table:

```
CREATE TABLE Personnel
(emp_id INTEGER NOT NULL PRIMARY KEY,
 emp_name CHAR (30) NOT NULL,
 dept_id INTEGER NOT NULL REFERENCES Departments (dept_id),
 dept_name CHAR (30) NOT NULL,
 . . .);
```

To guarantee that the assumed assertion that (Personnel.dept_name = Departments.dept_name) holds true for all time, you will have to code a procedure or trigger that will update the two values together. The rules of thumb for this denormalization are

1. Only make a few columns redundant.
2. Only make columns that are stable over time redundant.
3. Write code to keep them redundant or they will become different.

23.2.7 Repeating Groups

A repeating group is a set of columns that are part of a group or data structure instead of individual atomic attributes. The classic example is a billing table that holds the total billings for each customer by category:

```
CREATE TABLE Billings
(customer_id INTEGER NOT NULL,
 customer_name CHAR (30) NOT NULL,
 category CHAR(10) NOT NULL,
 amount DECIMAL (12,2) NOT NULL,
 . . . ,
 PRIMARY KEY (customer_id, category));
```

Getting reports out of this table is difficult and involves using the GROUP BY clause and aggregate functions. Instead, you can construct a denormalized table that changes the category from a value into an attribute:

```
(customer_id INTEGER NOT NULL PRIMARY KEY,
 customer_name CHAR (30) NOT NULL,
 cat1_amount DECIMAL (12,2),
 cat2_amount DECIMAL (12,2),
 cat3_amount DECIMAL (12,2),
 cat4_amount DECIMAL (12,2),
 cat5_amount DECIMAL (12,2));
```

Although printing certain reports is now much easier and some updating is also faster, there are trade-offs. The rules of thumb for this denormalization are

1. The number of columns in the repeated group is stable. You cannot add a new column easily. This example table now requires using an ALTER TABLE statement instead of a new category code. This will mess up every SELECT* clause in your system when you recompile your queries.

2. The group is relatively small. If there are a large number of columns in the group, the denormalized table becomes huge. Can you imagine our example table in a system with a thousand categories?

3. The group is accessed collectively instead of individually. That is to say, the group is really a group and not a random collection of values converted into attributes.

4. You have to be willing to use NULLs when a value is missing or unknown. Insertion, updating, and deletion are not always easy in this type of table.

5. You do not want to aggregate the group across the row. You have to consider all possible places where a NULL could occur, and it gets very messy.

23.2.8 Derivable Data

Many values you want in a query result can be derived from other values in the same row, same table, or same schema. Most of the time, the computer can recalculate these derived values faster than it can read a disk drive, so it is better to put a formula in a `VIEW` or a query than to store the results of the calculation in the table.

However, there are situations where the calculation is both repeated and complex enough to justify storing the results. The problem is that you must update the derived columns whenever one of their parameters changes. If you fail to do this, then the data is invalid and all your reports based on it are wrong.

It is a good idea to create a table with the parameters as columns and one column for the result, then to use this table to look up the calculations.

As an example, technically speaking, a customer's credit rating could be recalculated every time we do a query. It merely requires 15 minutes per row in the customer table and a fairly complicated procedure to dial the national credit bureau for today's report and combine it with the local data we have.

23.2.9 Hierarchy Tables

There are several ways to define a hierarchy or tree structure. Formally, it is a graph with no cycles, or it is a graph where all nodes except the root have indegree 1 and the root has indegree 0. (Indegree is the number of edges coming into a node, and outdegree is the number of edges leaving the node.) Another defining property is that a path can be found from the root to any other node in the tree by following the edges in their natural direction.

Informally, we draw trees as charts made up of boxes and arrows, and we use them to represent parts explosions and company organizational charts. In the United States, we like to put the root at the top and grow the tree downward; Europeans will often put the root at the bottom and grow the tree upward, or grow the tree from left to right across the page. Genealogists like this second presentation because it makes it easy to fill in the names of the family members horizontally.

It should be no surprise that hierarchies were very easy to represent in hierarchical databases, where the structure of the data and the structure of the database were the same. In fact, one reason that hierarchical databases were created was to accommodate the existing hierarchical data structures.

When programmers first tried to represent trees in SQL, they translated the boxes and arrows into what is called an *adjacency matrix* and put it in a table. This is just a matter of copying the picture into the most obvious data representation.

Let's use a simple organizational chart as an example. The nodes of the original graph are the employees, and the edges are the chain of command (i.e., "X is the boss of Y") in the organization. The table now records the node (emp) and its parent (boss) along with any other information on the employee; we will use salary.

```
CREATE TABLE Personnel
(emp CHAR(20) PRIMARY KEY,
 boss CHAR(20),
 salary DECIMAL(6,2) NOT NULL);
```

Personnel

emp	boss	salary
'Albert'	NULL	1000.00
'Bert'	'Albert'	900.00
'Chuck'	'Albert'	900.00
'Donna'	'Chuck'	800.00
'Eddie'	'Chuck'	700.00
'Fred'	'Chuck'	600.00

The one good feature of this representation is that it is very easy to INSERT a new employee because you only need to know the employee's immediate boss. If 'Fred' gets an assistant named 'George', we simply add the new row ('Fred', 'George', $200.00) and we are finished.

It is also supported by vendor extensions in Oracle and XDB, which will give you procedural tree traversals in SQL. But if your

product does not have these extensions, this representation can be used with a CURSOR, and you can print out the hierarchy with indentations showing the nesting levels.

But look at the problems with this approach:

1. 'Chuck' decides to change his name to 'Charles', so you have to update *both* the emp and boss columns because the same fact appears in four different locations in the table. This redundancy is a major denormalization.

2. 'Chuck' gets fired. If we simply remove his row based on the emp column value, ('Chuck', 'Albert', 900.00), we would still leave his three subordinates, ('Donna', 'Eddie', 'Fred'), reporting to him. We need to decide if we want to promote one of them or make his entire department report directly to 'Albert' instead. Either way, this table needs three UPDATEs along with the DELETE FROM statement.

3. It is very difficult to aggregate over the hierarchy. You would have to write procedural code to calculate the total salary of each employee along with their subordinates to get a budget.

4. There is a great danger that you will write a cycle in the table. That is, a subordinate employee will be the superior of one of his or her own superiors. When this happens, programs, cursors, and queries tend to hang in endless loops.

I have several chapters on representing trees in SQL in my book *SQL for Smarties* (Celko 1995), so I will not dwell on how to avoid this type of denormalization. The technique involves using a nested-sets model of a tree instead of an adjacency pair list as shown here.

23.2.10 Overloaded Datatypes

This sort of denormalization usually occurs in translation tables. A translation or lookup table is a table for converting encodings into something a human being or a query can use. The usual schema for these tables is

```
CREATE TABLE Translations
(encode_1 <datatype> NOT NULL UNIQUE,
 encode_2 <datatype> NOT NULL UNIQUE,
    . . .
 encode_n <datatype> NOT NULL UNIQUE,
 meaning <datatype> NOT NULL UNIQUE,
 PRIMARY KEY (encode_1, encode_2, . . . , encode_n));
```

They are tables in which one or more encodings lead to a unique meaning, though technically, I suppose, an ambiguous encoding is possible. An example of such a schema when $n = 1$ would be a lookup table for ZIP codes and the corresponding city and state (zipcode, city-state); this is probably the most common class of translation table. For $n = 2$, we could use (longitude, latitude, city-state).

Notice that these tables are all keys, and this implies that the table is in fifth normal form, which means that you can decompose this table with projections and not have anomalies. Now, let us consider a novel approach to handling translation tables. Instead of keeping just the encodings and the meaning in the table, add an extra column that identifies the code. This lets us put all the encodings in one table, instead of many small tables, each holding one encoding and translation.

```
CREATE TABLE Translations
(encode_type CHAR(n) NOT NULL,
 encoding VARCHAR(n) NOT NULL,
 meaning VARCHAR(m) NOT NULL,
 PRIMARY KEY (encode_type, encoding));
```

The reason for doing this is that having all encodings in one table lets you write a single front-end program to maintain all the encodings. I do not write front-end programs myself, but I was told that this is a common trick among front-end programmers.

I hope not. This method has several disadvantages:

1. *Storage size:* The total storage required for the "monster table approach" is greater than the storage required for the "one encoding, one table" approach because of the redundant encoding type column.

2. *Datatypes:* All encodings are forced into one datatype, which has to be a string of the largest length that any encoding uses in the system. But VARCHAR(n) is not always the best way to represent data. CHAR(n) data often has advantages for access and storage in many SQL products. Numeric encodings can take advantage of arithmetic operators for ranges, check digits, and so forth with CHECK clauses. Dates can be used as codes that are translated into holidays and other events. Datatypes are not a "one size fits all" affair.

3. *Validation:* The only way to write a CHECK() clause on the monster table is with a huge CASE expression of the form

```
CREATE TABLE Translations
(encode_type CHAR(n) NOT NULL
   CHECK (encode_type IN (<type 1>, . . . , <type n>)),
 encoding VARCHAR(n) NOT NULL
       CHECK (CASE WHEN encode_type = <type 1>
                        AND <validation rule 1>
                   THEN 1 = 1
                     . . .
                   WHEN encode_type = <type n>
                        AND <validation rule n>
                   THEN 1 = 1
                   ELSE 1 = 2 END),
 meaning VARCHAR(m) NOT NULL,
 PRIMARY KEY (encode_type, encoding));
```

This means that validation is going to take a long time because every change will have to be considered by all the WHEN clauses in this oversized CASE expression until the SQL engine finds one that tests TRUE. You also need to add a CHECK() clause to the encode_type column to be sure that the user does not create an invalid encoding name.

4. *Flexibility:* The monster table is created with one column for the encoding, so it cannot be used for n-valued encodings where $n > 1$.

5. *Security:* To avoid exposing rows in one encoding scheme to unauthorized users, the monster table has to have VIEWs defined on it that restrict users to the encode_types that they are allowed to update. At this point, some of the rationale for the single table is gone because the front end must now handle VIEWs in almost the same way that it would handle multiple tables. These VIEWs also must have the WITH CHECK OPTION clause, so that users do not make a valid change that is outside the scope of their permissions.

6. *Normalization:* The real reason that this approach does not work is that it is an attempt to violate 1NF. Yes, I can see that these tables have a primary key and that all the columns in an SQL database have to be scalar and of one datatype.

But I will still argue that it is not a 1NF table. I realize that people use the term "datatype" to mean different things, so let me clarify my terms. I mean those primitive, built-in things that come with the computer. I then use datatypes to build domains. The domains then represent the values of attributes.

As an example, I might decide that I need to have a column for Dewey decimal codes in a table that represents library books. I can then pick DECIMAL(6,3), NUMERIC(6,3), REAL, FLOAT, or a pair of INTEGERs as the datatype to hold the "three digits, decimal point, three digits" format of the Dewey decimal code domain.

The fact that two domains use the same datatype does not make them the same attribute. The extra encode_type column changes the domain of the other columns and thus violates 1NF.

Before the more experienced SQL programmer asks, the INDICATOR that is passed with an SQL variable to a host program in embedded SQL to indicate the presence of a NULL is not like this. It is not changing the domain of the SQL variable.

A "Fireside" Chat

The relational model's inventor comments on SQL, relational extensions, abstract data types, and modern RDBMS products.

In the last *DBMS* interview with Dr. Edgar F. Codd (*DBMS,* December 1990), former Editor in Chief Kevin Strehlo drew an analogy between Codd and Einstein, pointing out that Einstein's work led to the nuclear age, while Codd's work led to the relational age. One could debate the relative importance of relational theory and the theory of relativity, but Strehlo's point is well-taken. In his 1970 paper that defined relational theory and in subsequent writings, Codd swept away years of ad hoc and proprietary data-management approaches by identifying the basic requirements for the structure, integrity, and manipulation of data. To satisfy these requirements, he devised the relational model, a general approach to data management based on set theory and first-order predicate logic. Today, while often misunderstood, misapplied, and misstated, relational theory—like relativity—remains relatively unscathed.

In retrospect, Strehlo may have stretched the Codd-Einstein analogy too far. He noted that Einstein resisted new research in quantum theory, and that Codd also resists new approaches. By analogy, Strehlo implied that Codd erred in dismissing the new approaches and, as a kind of proof, suggested that "users and vendors are succumbing to the heady performance improvements offered by nonrelational (or imperfectly relational) alternatives." On the contrary, since that interview three years ago, users and vendors have adopted relational technology (perfect or imperfect) in greater numbers than ever before, and no theory has yet emerged to compete with relational theory. When critics claim that relational databases don't work effectively with the complex data found in applications such as CASE and CAD, and they propose nonrelational solutions, Codd correctly points out that it is the implementation of the relational model, not the underlying theory, that is lacking.

In this month's interview [December 1993], *DBMS* contributor Matthew Rapaport touches on a variety of issues, ranging from prerelational systems, to SQL shortcomings, to relational extensions. Rapaport, who earlier had interviewed Codd for *Database Programming & Design,* writes "When I first interviewed Dr. Codd in 1988, I thought that one day I should like to visit him at his home, sit with him by the fire (perhaps sipping brandy), and listen to him tell his tales of IBM. When he graciously agreed to do this interview, I did get the opportunity to visit his home. We didn't sit by a fire, and there was no brandy, but he managed, nevertheless, to deliver some good quips while answering my questions."

The following is an edited transcript of the conversation.

DBMS: Have the potential applications for the relational model grown since the 1970s?

CODD: Acceptance started growing rapidly, but only after the early products were released. The early products were much slower coming out than I expected. It was 1982–1983 when IBM produced its first relational product.

IBM's delay was unnecessary. Every report I produced was available internally before it was published internally. Very early in my work on the relational model I discovered a solid wall against it, due to IBM's declaration that IMS was the only DBMS product they would support. In one way, I understand that. Programmers keep building upon small differences as new products emerge. If you let that go on endlessly, corporate direction can become diffused. Yet there wasn't enough attention paid to drastic new development. This didn't apply only to DBMS.

DBMS: What were the applications you had in mind

when you developed the relational model? Weren't these the more classical data-processing business applications, such as accounting, inventory, and bill of materials?

CODD: I don't think the relational model was ever that constrained. I looked at existing systems, databases, and DBMS. I asked people why they made the kinds of design choices they did. Typically, individual applications constrained all the design choices, usually for performance. When application number two and number three came along, different constraints imposed all manner of artificial extensions on the original design. Today you need multiple application programs and interactivity between the programs, users, and data. Anyone, from his or her own desk, should be able to query a database in a manner suited to their needs, subject to proper authorization.

One of the bad things about prerelational systems was that highly specialized technical people were needed to use the database, let alone maintain it. No executive could obtain information from a database directly. Executives would have to go through the "wizards"—the programmers.

DBMS: But, even now, senior executives are reluctant to formulate queries. They know what views of the data they are likely to want, and they rely on programmers to build them a push-button entry screen to such a view.

CODD: That's understandable. People don't like to adjust to change though it is the one certainty of life. Even today, some users are programming relational DBMS as if it were an access method. It's painful because they're not getting nearly the use or power from the system that they could.

DBMS: Every application I've ever built needed some record-by-record management at some point.

CODD: That doesn't mean you always need to pull records one at a time from the database. An example occurs in a Bill of Materials (BOM) problem where you might want to determine the time and expense of producing some ordered amount of product. Computation goes on as the system runs through the product structure relations. I see that happening not a record at a time, but by having some system that enables one to specify, for each branch of the product graph or web, a package of code containing no loops. As the system makes the connection between a part and a product, it applies the appropriate functions to the part and product. The relational model addresses a classic BOM problem: Most products cannot be represented as trees (exactly what IMS was designed to do) because there is usually a many-to-many relationship between products and parts. The tree is only one possible kind of relationship in the relational model.

DBMS: Are there niches today, such as CAD, that require searches through large quantities of unstructured data that fit the relational model but have not yet made proper use of it?

CODD: Certain extensions are needed to the relational model to apply it effectively to what I call nonrelational data, such as data from images, radio signals, voice patterns, diagrams, and so on.

DBMS: Have you been making those extensions?

CODD: I've been thinking about it, but have not yet recorded it in a sufficiently precise way. I have developed what I consider to be its most fundamental part. Nonrelational data differs from relational data in that the position of the data becomes much more important. For example, on a map, distance alone will not specify the relationship between point A and point B. You must also know direction.

There can be more complexities. If you're making a long trip, you want your database to describe a great circle using three-dimensional geometry. To connect such information to a relational DBMS, you need special predicates that apply to the kind of data you're dealing with. With maps, you want a direction type of predicate. Then, given the coordinates of two points, you can get truth values from them, represented in this case as the direction between your points. These truth values can form part of a relational request that states what data to extract and the constraints to which the process should be subject.

Excerpt from *DBMS* interview with Edgar F. Codd, "A Fireside Chat." *DBMS,* Dec. 1993, pgs. 54–56. Reprinted with permission from *Intelligent Enterprise Magazine.* This and related articles can be found on *www.intelligententerprise.com.*

Metadata

METADATA IS OFTEN described as "data about your data," and that is not a bad way to sum up the concept in 25 words or less. It is not enough to simply give me a value for a data element in a database. I have to know what it means in context, the units of measurement, its constraints, and a dozen other things before I can use it. When I store this information in a formal system, I have metadata.

There is a Metadata Council, which is trying to set up standards for the interchange of metadata. IEEE is developing a data dictionary standard as the result of a request from the Council of Standards Organizations (CSO). Also, NCITS L8 is a committee devoted to this topic.

24.1 Data

ISO formally defines *data* as "A representation of facts, concepts, or instructions in a formalized manner suitable for communication, interpretation, or processing by humans or by automatic means," which matches the common usage fairly well. However, you need to break this concept into three categories of data: data assets, data engineering assets, and data management assets.

24.1.1 Data Assets

Data assets are not just the data elements, but also include the things needed to use them, such as business rules, files and databases, data warehouses, reports, computer screen displays, and so forth. Basically, this is anything having to do with using the data elements.

24.1.2 Data Engineering Assets

Data engineering assets are one level higher conceptually and include information about data element definitions, data models, database designs, data dictionaries, repositories, and so forth. These things are at the design level of the model, and there are tools to support them.

24.1.3 Data Management Assets

Data management assets deal with the control of the data and the intent of the enterprise. They include information about goals, policies, standards, plans, budgets, metrics, and so forth. They are used to guide, create, and maintain the data management infrastructure of the enterprise and are outside the scope of a computerized system because they reside in human beings.

It is worth mentioning that people are now discussing setting up business rules servers that would not be part of the database system per se, but would use a nonprocedural language to state business rules and goals, then compile them into procedures and constraints on the database.

24.1.4 Core Data

Core data is the subset of data elements that are common to all parts of the enterprise. The term is a little loose in that it can refer to data without regard to its representation and sometimes can mean the representation of these common elements.

For example, data about customers (name, address, account number, etc.) that every part of the enterprise has to have to function might be called core data, even though some parts of the enterprise do not use all of the data directly.

Another meaning of core data is a standardized format for a data element. This might include using only the ISO 8601 date and time formats, using a set of ethnicity codes, and so forth. These are elements that could appear in almost all of the tables in the database.

24.2 Metadata Management

The concept of metadata is a better way to handle data than simply managing the instances of data elements. What happens is that you find an error and correct it, but the next time the values are inserted or updated, the errors reappear. Trying to keep a clean database this way is simply not effective.

For example, if I have a standard format for an address, say, the ones used by the U.S. Postal Service for bulk mailings, I can scrub all of the data in my database and put the data into the proper format. But the next time I insert data, I can violate my rules again.

A better approach is to record the rules for address formatting as metadata about the address elements and then see if I can enforce those rules in some automatic way.

A number of data management tools can help handle metadata management: DBMSs, data dictionaries, data directories, data encyclopedias, data registries, and repositories. Commercial products usually do several different jobs in a single package, but let's discuss them individually so we can see the purpose of each tool.

24.2.1 Database Management Systems

The basic purpose of a DBMS is to organize, store, and provide access to data elements. However, you will find that they are able to hold business rules in the form of constraints, stored procedures, and triggers.

Although not designed for metadata, the DBMS is probably the most common tool to actually implement these concepts.

24.2.2 Data Dictionary

A data dictionary is a software tool that documents data element syntax and some of the semantics. The weakest form of semantics is just

the name and definition of the element, but you would really like to have more information.

The gimmick is that this information is independent of the data store in which the values of the data element are stored. This means that if an item only appears on a paper form and never gets put into the database, it should still be in the data dictionary. This also implies that the data dictionary should be independent of the DBMS system.

24.2.3 Data Directory

A data directory is a software tool that tells you where you used a data element, independent of the data stores in which their instance values are stored. A data directory may be a stand-alone tool (such as Easy View) or a component of a DBMS.

When the data directory is part of a database, it is usually limited to that database and might even give physical addresses as well as logical locations (i.e., tables, views, stored procedures, etc.) of the data elements. Stand-alone tools can go across databases and show all databases that contain a particular data element. These tools usually give only the logical locations of data elements, since physical locations are pretty useless.

24.2.4 Data Encyclopedia

A data encyclopedia is a software tool that has a data dictionary and additional contextual information about the data elements, such as data element classification structures, thesaurus or glossary capabilities, mappings of data elements to data models and the data models themselves, and so forth.

The data encyclopedia is a tool for a particular system(s) or applications and not the enterprise as a whole. A data encyclopedia may be a stand-alone tool, or (more typically) a component of a CASE tool, such as ADW, Bachman, or IEF tools. A data encyclopedia is more of a modeling and database development tool.

24.2.5 Data Element Registry

A data element registry is a combination of data dictionary, logical data directory, and data encyclopedia for the purpose of facilitating enterprisewide standardization and reuse of data elements, as well as the interchange of data elements among enterprise information trading partners. In short, it goes across systems.

The data element registry is a relatively new concept developed by an ISO/IEC JTC1 standards body and formalized in the ISO 11179 standard ("Specification and Standardization of Data Elements"). This standard provides metadata requirements for documenting data elements and for progressing specific data elements as enterprise standard or preferred data elements.

No commercially available data element registries exist, but you can find registries inside such organizations as Bellcore, the Environmental Protection Agency, and the U.S. Census Bureau.

A general consensus is developing in the NCITS L8 (formerly ANSI X3L8) Committee, Data Representation (which held editorship for five of the six parts of ISO 11179), that ISO 11179 concepts of the data element registry need to be extended to that of a data registry. The data registry is intended to document and register not only data elements but their reusable components as well, and provide structured access to the semantic content of the registry. Such reusable components include data element concepts and data element value domains and also classes, property classes, and generic property domains. The extension of data element registry concepts is proceeding within the overall framework of the X3L8 Metamodel for Management of Sharable Data, ANSI X3.285-1997, which explains and defines terms.

24.2.6 Repository

A repository is a software tool specifically designed to document and maintain all informational representations of the enterprise and its activities; that is, data-oriented representations, software representations, systems representations, hardware representations, and so forth. Repositories typically include the functionality of data dictionaries, data directories, and data encyclopedias, but also add documentation of the enterprise's existing and planned applications, systems, process models, hardware environment, organizational structure, strategic plans, implementation plans, and all other IT and business representations of the informational aspects of the enterprise. Commercially available repositories include Rhochade, MSP, Platinum, and Transtar offerings.

24.3 Data Dictionary Environments

There are three distinct "levels" of data dictionaries: application systems' data dictionaries, functional area data dictionaries, and the ITS data dictionary.

24.3.1 Application Data Dictionaries

Each application systems level data dictionary is devoted to one application system. Usually these data dictionaries contain only data elements used in achieving the functions of that system. Very often, they are part of the DBMS software platform upon which the application's database is built and cannot refer to outside data.

24.3.2 Functional Area Data Dictionaries

Functional area data dictionaries go across several systems that work together in a related functional area. Examples of these data dictionaries include the Traffic Management Data Dictionary and Advanced Public Transportation Systems Data Dictionary. These dictionaries contain data element information relevant to the functional area, from all or most of the application systems supporting the functions in the functional area. Data interchange among the application systems is a major goal.

24.3.3 The ITS Data Dictionary/Registry

The ITS data dictionary goes across functional areas and tries to capture the whole enterprise under one roof.

24.4 NCITS L8 Standards

The 11179 standard is broken down into six sections:

- 11179-1: Framework for the Specification and Standardization of Data Elements Definitions

- 11179-2: Classification for Data Elements
- 11179-3: Basic Attributes of Data Elements
- 11179-4: Rules and Guidelines for the Formulation of Data
- 11179-5: Naming and Identification Principles for Data
- 11179-6: Registration of Data Elements

Since I cannot reprint the standard, let me remark on the highlights of some of these sections.

24.4.1 Naming Data Elements

Section 11179-4 has a good simple set of rules for defining a data element. A data definition shall

1. be unique (within any data dictionary in which it appears)
2. be stated in the singular
3. state what the concept is, not only what it is not
4. be stated as a descriptive phrase or sentence(s)
5. contain only commonly understood abbreviations
6. be expressed without embedding definitions of other data elements or underlying concepts

The document then goes on to explain how to apply these rules with illustrations. There are three kinds of rules that form a complete naming convention:

- Semantic rules based on the components of data elements
- Syntax rules for arranging the components within a name
- Lexical rules for the language-related aspects of names

While the following naming convention is oriented to the development of application-level names, the rule set may be adapted to the development of names at any level. Annex A of ISO 11179-5 gives an example of all three of these rules.

Levels of rules progress from the most general (conceptual) and become more and more specific (physical). The objects at each level are called "data element components" and are assembled, in part or whole, into names. The idea is that the final names will be both as discrete and complete as possible.

Although this formalism is nice in theory, names are subject to constraints imposed by software limitations in the real world. Another problem is that one data element may have many names depending on the context in which it is used. It might be called something in a report and something else in an EDI file. Provision for identification of synonymous names is made through sets of name-context pairs in the element description. Since many names may be associated with a single data element, it is important to also use a unique identifier, usually in the form of a number, to distinguish each data element from any other. ISO 11179-5 discusses assigning this identifier at the international registry level. Both the identifier and at least one name are considered necessary to comply with ISO 11179-5. Each organization should decide the form of identifier best suited to its individual requirements.

Levels of Abstraction

Name development begins at the conceptual level. An object class represents an idea, abstraction, or thing in the real world, such as tree or country. A property is something that describes all objects in the class, such as height or identifier. This lets us form terms such as "tree height" or "country identifier" from the combination of the class and the property.

The level in the process is the logical level. A complete logical data element must include a form of representation for the values in its data value domain (the set of possible valid values of a data element). The representation term describes the data element's representation class. The representation class is equivalent to the class word of the prime/class naming convention many data administrators are familiar with. This gets us to "tree height measure," "country identifier name," and "country identifier code" as possible data elements.

There is a subtle difference between "identifier name" and "identifier code," and it might be so subtle that we do not want to model it. But we would need a rule to drop the property term in this case. The property would still exist as part of the inheritance structure of the data element, but it would not be part of the data element name.

Some logical data elements can be considered generic elements if they are well defined and are shared across organizations. Country names and country codes are well defined in ISO Standard 3166 ("Codes for the Representation of Names of Countries"), and you might simply reference this document.

Note that this is the highest level at which true data elements, by the definition of ISO 11179, appear: they have an object class, a property, and a representation.

The next is the application level. This is usually done with a quantifier that applies to the particular application. The quantifier will either subset the data value domain or add more restrictions to the definition so that we work with only those values needed in the application.

For example, assume that we are using ISO 3166 country codes, but we are only interested in Europe. This would be a simple subset of the standard, but it will not change over time. However, the subset of countries with more than 20 cm of rain this year will vary greatly over time.

Changes in the name to reflect this will be accomplished by the addition of qualifier terms to the logical name. For example, if an application of "country name" were to list all the countries a certain organization had trading agreements with, the application data element would be called "trading partner country name." The data value domain would consist of a subset of countries listed in ISO 3166. Note that the qualifier term "trading partner" is itself an object class. This relationship could be expressed in a hierarchical relationship in the data model.

The physical name is the lowest level. These are the names that actually appear in the database table column headers, file descriptions, EDI transaction file layouts, and so forth. They may be abbreviations or use a limited character set because of software restrictions.

However, they might also add information about their origin or format.

In a registry, each of the data element names and name components will always be paired with its context so that we know the source or usage of the name or name component. The goal is to be able to trace each data element from its source to wherever it is used, regardless of the name it appears under.

24.4.2 Registering Standards

Section 11179-6 is an attempt to build a list of universal data elements and specify their meaning and format. It includes codes for sex, currency, country names, and many other things.

REFERENCES

Baxley, J., and E. K. Hayashi. 1978. "A Note on Indeterminate Forms." *American Mathematical Monthly.* 85:484–86.

Beech, David. 1989. "New Life for SQL." *Datamation.* (February 1).

Beri, C., Ron Fagin, and J. H. Howard. 1977. "Complete Axiomatization for Functional and Multivalued Dependencies." *Proceedings, 1977 ACM SIGMOD International Conference on Management of Data.* Toronto.

Bernstein, P. A. 1976. "Synthesizing Third Normal Form Relations from Functional Dependencies." *ACM Transactions on Database Systems.* 1(4):277–98.

Bernstein, P. A., V. Hadzilacos, and N. Goodman. 1987. *Concurrency Control and Recovery in Database Systems.* Addison-Wesley Publishing. ISBN 0-201-10715-5.

Bojadziev, George and Maria. 1995. *Fuzzy Sets, Fuzzy Logic, Applications.* World Scientific Publishers. ISBN 981-02-2388-9.

Briggs, John. 1992. *Fractals: The Patterns of Chaos: A New Aesthetic of Art, Science, and Nature.* Touchstone Books. ISBN 0-671-74217-5.

Briggs, John, and F. David Peat. 1989. *Turbulent Mirror.* Harper & Row. ISBN 0-060-91696-6.

Burch, John G., Jr., and Felix R. Strater, Jr. 1974. *Information Systems: Theory and Practice.* John Wiley & Sons. ISBN 0-471-53803-5.

Celko, Joe. 1981. "Father Time Software Secrets Allows Updating of Dates." *Information Systems News.* (February 9).

Celko, Joe. 1992. "SQL Explorer: Voting Systems." *DBMS.* (November).

Celko, Joe. 1994. "The Great Key Debate." *DBMS.* (September).

Celko, Joe. 1995. *SQL for Smarties.* Morgan Kaufmann. ISBN 1-55860-323-9.

Celko, Joe. 1997. *SQL Puzzles and Answers*. Morgan Kaufmann. ISBN 1-55860-453-7.

Cichelli, R. J. 1980. "Minimal Perfect Hash Functions Made Simple." *Communications of the ACM*. 23(1).

Codd, E. F. 1970. "A Relational Model of Data for Large Shared Data Banks." *Communications of the ACM*. 13(6):377–87. Association for Computing Machinery.

Codd, E. F. 1990. *The Relational Model for Database Management, Version 2*. Addison-Wesley Publishing. ISBN 0-201-14192-2.

Crossen, Cynthia. 1996. *Tainted Truth: The Manipulation of Facts in America*. Touchstone Press. ISBN 0-684-81556-7.

Damerau, F. J. A. 1964. "A Technique for Computer Detection and Correction of Spelling Errors." *Communications of the ACM*. 7(3):171–76.

Date, C. J. 1986. *Relational Database: Selected Writings*. Addison-Wesley Publishing. ISBN 0-201-14196-5.

Date, C. J. 1990. *Relational Database Writings, 1985–1989*. Addison-Wesley Publishing. ISBN 0-201-50881-8.

Date, C. J. 1993a. "According to Date: Empty Bags and Identity Crises." *Database Programming & Design*. (April).

Date, C. J. 1993b. "A Matter of Integrity, Part III." *DBMS*. (December).

Date, C. J. 1993c. "Relational Optimizers, Part II." *Database Programming & Design*. 6(7):21–22.

Date, C. J. 1993d. "The Power of the Keys." *Database Programming & Design*. 6(5):21–22.

Date, C. J. 1994. "Toil and Trouble." *Database Programming & Design*. 7(1):15–18.

Date, C. J. 1995. "Say No to Composite Columns." *Database Programming & Design*. (May).

Date, C. J., and Hugh Darwen. 1992. *Relational Database Writings, 1989–1991*. Addison-Wesley Publishing. ISBN 0-201-54303-6.

Date, C. J., and Hugh Darwen. 1997. *A Guide to the SQL Standard, 4th Edition*. Addison-Wesley Publishing. ISBN 0-201-96426-0.

Date, C. J., and David McGoveran. 1994a. "Updating UNION, INTERSECT, and EXCEPT Views." *Database Programming & Design*. (June).

Date, C. J., and David McGoveran. 1994b. "Updating Joins and Other Views." *Database Programming & Design*. (August).

Elmagarmid, Ahmed K. (ed.). 1992. *Database Transaction Models for Advanced Applications*. Morgan Kaufmann. ISBN 1-55860-214-3.

Eppinger, Jeffrey L. 1991. *Camelot and Avalon: A Distributed Transaction Facility*. Morgan Kaufmann. ISBN 1-55860-185-6.

Fagin, Ron. 1981. "A Normal Form for Relational Databases That Is Based on Domains and Keys." *ACM TODS*. 6(3).

Gardner, Martin. 1983. *Wheels, Life, and Other Mathematical Amusements*. W. H. Freeman Company. ISBN 0-7167-1588-0.

Gleason, Norma. 1981. *Cryptograms and Spygrams*. Dover Books. ISBN 0-486-24036-3.

Goodman, Nathan. 1990. "VIEW Update Is Practical." *INFODB*. 5(2).

Gordon, Carl E., and Neil Hindman. 1975. *Elementary Set Theory: Proof Techniques*. Hafner Press. ISBN 0-02-845350-1.

Graham, Ronald, Don Knuth, and Oren Patashnik. 1994. *Concrete Mathematics*. Addison-Wesley Publishing. ISBN 0-201-55802-5.

Gray, Jim (ed.). 1991, 1993. *The Benchmark Handbook for Database and Transaction Processing Systems*. Morgan Kaufmann. ISBN 1-55860-292-5.

Gray, Jim, and Andreas Reuter. 1993. *Transaction Processing: Concepts and Techniques*. Morgan Kaufmann. ISBN 1-55860-190-2.

Halpin, Terry. 1995. *Conceptual Schema and Relational Database Design*. Prentice Hall. ISBN 0-13-355702-2.

Henstell, Bruce. 1994. *Los Angeles Times*. (June 9): Food section.

Hitchens, Randall L. 1991. "Viewpoint." *Computerworld*. (January 28).

Hively, Will. 1996. "Math against Tyranny." *Discover Magazine*. (November).

Jean, Georges. 1992. *Writing: The Story of Alphabets and Scripts*. English translation is part of the *Discoveries* series by Harry N. Abrams. ISBN 0-8109-2893-0.

Kaufmann, Arnold, and Madan Gupta. 1985. *Introduction to Fuzzy Arithmetic: Theory and Applications*. Van Nostrand Reinhold. ISBN 0-442-23007-9.

Kay, Roger L. 1994. "What's the Meaning?" *Computerworld*. (October 17).

Knuth, D. E. 1992. "Two Notes on Notation." *American Mathematical Monthly*. 99(5):403–22.

Lagarias, Jeffrey C. 1985. "The $3 * n + 1$ Problem and Its Generalizations." *American Mathematical Monthly*. (Volume 92).

Lum, V., et al. 1984. "Designing DBMS Support for the Temporal Dimension." *Proceedings of ACM SIGMOD 84.* (June):115–30.

Lynch, Nancy, Michael Merritt, William Weihl, and Alan Fekete. 1994. *Atomic Transactions.* Morgan Kaufmann. ISBN 1-55860-104-X.

MacLeod, P. 1991. "A Temporal Data Model Based on Accounting Principles." University of Calgary, Ph.D. Thesis.

Mandelbrot, Benoit B. 1977. *Fractals: Form, Chance and Dimension.* W. H. Freeman. ISBN 0-7167-0473-0.

McKenzie, L. E., et al. 1991. "Evaluation of Relational Algebras Incorporating the Time Dimension in Databases." *ACM Computing Surveys.* 23:501–43.

Melton, Jim. 1998. *Understanding SQL's Stored Procedures.* Morgan Kaufmann. ISBN 1-55860-461-8.

Melton, Jim, and Alan Simon. 1993. *Understanding the New SQL.* Morgan Kaufmann. ISBN 1-55860-245-3.

Mullens, Craig. 1996. *DB2 Developer's Guide.* Sams Publishing. ISBN 0-672-30512-7.

Murakami, Y. 1968. *Logic and Social Choice* (Monographs in Modern Logic Series, G. B. Keene, ed.). Dover Books. ISBN 0-7100-2981-0.

Paige, L. J. 1954. "A Note on Indeterminate Forms." *American Mathematical Monthly.* 61:189–90. Reprinted in Mathematical Association of America, *Selected Papers on Calculus.* 1969. 210–11.

Paulos, John Allen. 1990. *Innumeracy: Mathematical Illiteracy and Its Consequences.* Vintage Books. ISBN 0-679-72601-2.

Paulos, John Allen. 1991. *Beyond Numeracy.* Knopf. ISBN 0-394-58640-9.

Pickover, Clifford (ed.). 1996. *Fractal Horizons.* St. Martin's Press. ISBN 0-312-12599-2.

Roman, Susan. 1987. "Code Overload Plagues NYC Welfare System." *Information Systems Week.* (November).

Rotando, Louis M., and Henry Korn. 1977. "The Indeterminate Form 0^0." *Mathematics Magazine.* 50(1):41–42.

Roth, Mark A., Henry Korth, and Abraham Silberschatz. 1998. "Extended Relational Algebra and Relational Calculus for Nested Relational Databases." *ACM Transactions on Database Systems.* 13(4).

Sager, Thomas J. 1985. "A Polynomial Time Generator for Minimal Perfect Hash Functions." *Communications of the ACM*. 28(5).

Snodgrass, Richard T. (ed.). 1995. *The TSQL2 Temporal Query Language (Kluwer International Series in Engineering and Computer Science No. 330)*. Kluwer Academic Publishers. ISBN 0-7923-9614-6.

Snodgrass, Richard T. 1998a. "Modifying Valid-Time State Tables." *Database Programming & Design*. 11(8):72–77.

Snodgrass, Richard T. 1998b. "Of Duplicates and Septuplets." *Database Programming & Design*. 11(6):46–49.

Snodgrass, Richard T. 1998c. "Querying Valid-Time State Tables." *Database Programming & Design*. 11(7):60–65.

Snodgrass, Richard T. 1998d. "Temporal Support in Standard SQL." *Database Programming & Design*. 11(10):44–48.

Snodgrass, Richard T. 1998e. "Transaction-Time State Tables." *Database Programming & Design*. 11(9):46–50.

Stevens, S. S. 1957. "On the Psychophysical Law." *Psychological Review*. (64):153–81.

Stewart, Jill. 1994. "Has Los Angeles Lost Its Census?" *Buzz*. (May).

Swarthmore University. Dr. Math archives: Why are operations of zero so strange? Why do we say 1/0 is undefined? Can't you call 1/0 infinity and –1/0 negative infinity? What is 0 * (1/0)? What is the quantity 0^0?

Taylor, Alan D. 1995. *Mathematics and Politics: Strategy, Voting Power and Proofs*. Springer-Verlag. ISBN 0-387-94391-9.

Umeshar, Dayal, and P. A. Bernstein. 1982. "On the Correct Translation of Update Operations on Relational VIEWs." *ACM Transactions on Database Systems*. 7(3).

Vaughan, H. E. 1970. "The Expression 0^0." *Mathematics Teacher*. 63:111–12.

Verhoeff, J. 1969. "Error Detecting Decimal Codes." *Mathematical Centre Tract #29*. The Mathematical Centre (Amsterdam).

Xenakis, John. 1995. "The Millennium Bug, The Fin de Siecle Computer Virus." *CFO*. (July).

Yozallinas, J. R. 1981. *Tech Specialist*. (May): Letters column.

Zerubavel, Eviatar. 1985. *The Seven Day Circle: The History and Meaning of the Week*. The Free Press. ISBN 0-02-934680-0.

For ANSI and ISO standards:

American National Standards Institute
1430 Broadway
New York, NY 10018
Phone: (212) 354-3300

Director of Publications
American National Standards Institute
11 West 42nd Street
New York, NY 10036
Phone: (212) 642-4900

Copies of the documents can be purchased from
Global Engineering Documents Inc.
2805 McGaw Avenue
Irvine, CA 92714
Phone: (800) 854-7179

INDEX

D

E

J

O